THE CHINESE ARMED FORCES IN THE 21st CENTURY

Edited by
Larry M. Wortzel

University Press of the Pacific
Honolulu, Hawaii

The Chinese Armed Forces in the 21st Century

Edited by
Larry M. Wortzel

ISBN: 1-4102-1775-2

Copyright © 2004 by University Press of the Pacific

Reprinted from the 1999 edition

University Press of the Pacific
Honolulu, Hawaii
http://www.universitypressofthepacific.com

All rights reserved, including the right to reproduce this book, or portions thereof, in any form.

*****

The views expressed in this report are those of the authors and do not necessarily reflect the official policy or position of the Department of the Army, the Department of Defense, or the U.S. Government. This report is cleared for public release; distribution is unlimited.

*****

CONTENTS

Introduction
    James R. Lilley v

1. Geographic Ruminations
    Michael McDevitt 1

2. The Chinese Military and the Peripheral States in the 21st Century: A Security *Tour d'Horizon*
    Eric A. McVadon 7

3. PLA Capabilities in the 21st Century: How Does China Assess Its Future Security Needs?
    Michael Pillsbury 89

4. Advanced Military Technology and the PLA: Priorities and Capabilities for the 21st Century
    Bernard D. Cole
    Paul H.B. Godwin 159

5. U.S.-Chinese Military Relations in the 21st Century
    Larry M. Wortzel 217

6. Taiwan's Military in the 21st Century: Redefinition and Reorganization
    Arthur Shu-fan Ding
    Alexander Chieh-cheng Huang 253

7. Taiwan's Military: A View from Afar
    June Teufel Dreyer 289

8. Concluding Comment: The Political Angle—New Phenomena in Party-Army Relations
    Ellis Joffe 321

About the Authors 329

Index 333

INTRODUCTION

James R. Lilley

The debate about China and Taiwan is re-emerging in the United States. The accidental bombing of the Chinese Embassy in Belgrade, of course, put on the front burner the way that nationalistic fervor has grown in China, at least some of it as a result of manipulation by the Communist Party. President Lee Teng-hui's comments about state-to-state relations between Taiwan and the mainland raised the temperature of relations across the strait and among the three concerned parties (China, the United States, and Taiwan). China threatened, China postured, and China ran political campaigns against the United States and Lee. But the questions of military capability, security policy, and intent are rarely treated seriously. This book is a serious look at the armed forces of China and how they will evolve.

The chapters in this volume were developed from papers prepared for the eighth in a series of conferences on the People's Liberation Army (PLA). The people at the conferences were recognized experts on armed forces and security matters in China and drawn from academe, government, the military, and policy think tanks. Each chapter's author was challenged to analyze some aspect of the Chinese armed forces as they moved into the next century. The goal was to contribute a realistic view of how domestic and international pressures would shape both Beijing's and Taipei's security environment. Over a 2-day period at Wye Plantation, Maryland, each paper was discussed and criticized by a wider body of participants and then revised for publication. Not surprisingly, when a body of experts of such high caliber is assembled and dialogue flows freely, comments by participants at the conference led to the development of two more papers. The first, addressing strategic geography from Michael McDevitt, appears as Chapter 1. The second from Ellis Joffe, summarizing changes in party-army relations in China, appears as Chapter 8. The result is a highly readable and relevant publication applicable to today's politico-military environment.

One of the participants in this series of annual conferences on the PLA refers to the event as an "azimuth check of trends and ideas in the community of China watchers." To anyone who has had to navigate the land, sea, or air by compass, the meaning of this analogy will be instantly clear. It is difficult to move through uncharted areas, where conditions change often and in unpredictable ways, attempting to reach a common goal or objective with others. This goal is even more difficult to reach because we all travel on different intellectual paths. Therefore, from time to time it is useful and necessary to confirm one's course. This set of conferences served that purpose. In the context of the PLA conferences held over the years, the common objective is a realistic appreciation of the policies, power, and operational dimensions and limitations of the PLA. The majority of the participants in this effort came from the United States, but all of them come from democracies with important security interests in China and Asia. Thus, the other common goal shared by the participants is a strong desire to ensure that the security of their own nation is not adversely affected by events in China.

Readers of this volume should understand that "checking one's azimuth" does not mean conforming one's ideas to match those of others. The authors of the chapters contained herein, and their interlocutors at the conference, whose comments and critiques sharpened the chapters, are independent thinkers. Still, the "azimuth" analogy holds, since one must check from time to time whether one has been blown or veered off course by an unperceived change in external events. This book, therefore, is not simply an exercise in recording "group think." Each chapter differs in tone and assessment, but the work is unified by a commitment to a realistic assessment of what the PLA and China's security policies will look like in the coming years.

The need to arrive at some kind of common understanding of what is happening in China is critical today. The Congress, in the Committee Report on the Fiscal Year 2000 Defense Authorization Act, has expressed serious concerns about the types of military-to-military exchanges conducted between the United States and China—Chapter 5 addresses that issue. In addition, in the same legislation, the Secretary of Defense has been directed by Congress to produce a report on the current and future strategy of the People's Republic of China (PRC), including the probable future course of military-technological developments, the subject of Chapter 4 of this book. Thus, the publishers and authors are able to provide some thoughts early that will stimulate further thinking on these vital issues.

As noted earlier, Chapter 1 developed out of a comment at the conference. Michael McDevitt reminds us in that chapter that there is a permanent, predictable feature in Asia's security landscape—geography. As he states it, "China's central position on the Asian mainland allows it to command internal lines of communication on the continent." Combined with other factors, this makes China "the dominant military power on the continent of Asia." The central question posed in McDevitt's reminder about the influence of geography is whether China will choose to expand its military reach beyond the continent in ways that would destabilize the rest of Asia. McDevitt cautions security analysts to distinguish between "token Chinese military capabilities intended to show the flag . . . and an attempt to create a truly dominant projection force." He concludes that with the "proper mix of United States forces in the region, rimland and maritime Asia will always have the ability to 'trump' Chinese projection attempts."

In Chapter 2, Eric McVadon examines the security contacts and relationship forged or developing between China's military and the states on its periphery. He opens with an analysis of China's two White Papers on national defense, issued by the State Council, concluding that Beijing has strong interest "in the security aspects of its relations with neighboring countries." Reinforcing the "geographic ruminations" of Michael McDevitt in Chapter 1, McVadon also notes that China's 1998 National Defense White Paper reminds the reader that China is a country with enduring interests and a central position in the Asia-Pacific. McVadon raises another issue that will echo in the other chapters of this book—the centrality of economic factors, including oil, for China's future development and military power. He reminds us that for Beijing, economics is the "most important component of China's comprehensive national power."

Michael Pillsbury, in Chapter 3, critiques methodologies to make assessments of the PLA and provides a framework for a more objective "net assessment" of China's military forces. He also makes a major contribution to our understanding of how the PLA evaluates itself with an extensive review of internal writings on security and defense from the Chinese armed forces. Following up on his earlier work in other books, Pillsbury makes accessible to those who cannot read Chinese critical military-strategic writings from institutes of higher learning in the PLA. Pillsbury's earlier works are seminal contributions to our understanding of how the PLA evaluates itself and thinks about its future, again particularly for those who do not read Chinese. In this chapter, he synthesizes that work and cautions the reader that a number of analysts of Chinese military capabilities inside and outside of government, for a variety of reasons, make the dangerous mistake of systematically minimizing the war-fighting abilities and the military-production capabilities of China. Pillsbury warns us of the danger of such an approach, pointing out that many Chinese military thinkers see strengths in the same characteristics that Western analysts characterize as weaknesses. Therefore, Pillsbury concludes, underestimating the PLA or China's defense industrial capacity may be a fatal mistake for the United States.

Bernard Cole and Paul Godwin, in Chapter 4, apply a unique methodology to an assessment of the PLA's advanced technology acquisition and development priorities for the future. Cole and Godwin first assess the national military strategy of China, and then they apply that assessment to a broader overview of the ability of China's high-technology and defense-industrial complex to develop and produce what the PLA needs. The yardstick used by these two authors to determine what is critical for future high-technology-based warfare is the *Militarily Critical Technologies List* developed by the U.S. Department of Defense in concert with other agencies and departments of the U.S. Government. Cole and Godwin conclude that the shock of the allied (particularly the U.S.) defeat of Iraqi forces in Operation DESERT STORM showed the PLA just how far it had fallen behind when compared with the capabilities of the world's advanced industrial powers. The ambitions of the PLA in technology acquisition, according to Cole and Godwin, are outlined clearly, and these ambitions clearly parallel the military doctrinal thinking discussed by Michael Pillsbury in Chapter 3. However, Cole and Godwin do not anticipate any rapid, across-the-board "great leap forward" in China's military-technical revolution. Instead, they expect Beijing to stumble through what might be an "erratic expansion" of the capabilities of China's military-industrial complex.

Chapter 5, by Larry Wortzel, focuses on military-to-military relations between the United States and China. Like Michael McDevitt, Wortzel first focuses on geography and the relationship between geography and strategy, concluding that Beijing sees itself as the central power in Asia, which *must* be considered in any geo-political and military equation. But Larry Wortzel is not sanguine about the future U.S.-China military relations. He predicts competition, tension, and conflict, and this prediction was made well before the accidental bombing of the Chinese

Embassy in Belgrade and the statements by Taiwan President Lee Teng-hui about "state-to-state" relations between China and Taiwan. Wortzel believes that the PLA is working very hard to prepare itself to "fight against American tactics and equipment, whether employed by Taiwan, any other nation, or the United States." That said, according to Wortzel, China's preparations do not necessarily mean that there must be a war. He also examines shared interests between the United States and China, such as participation in the United Nations and other international organizations, trade, and a desire for regional stability and economic growth. Mistrust between the two countries contributes to this climate of tension and strategic competition, and only some form of continued contact can alleviate mistrust. But in Wortzel's view, this military-to-military contact should not do anything to improve China's ability to project force against its neighbors or Taiwan, especially since China will not renounce the use of force to reunite a democratic Taiwan with the mainland.

This is a book about China's armed forces, not only the military forces of the PRC. Chapters 6 and 7, therefore, focus on military and national security reform in Taiwan. In Chapter 6, Arthur Shu-fan Ding and Alexander Chieh-cheng Huang provide an in-depth analysis of the transformation that is taking place in Taiwan's armed forces. First, the Taiwan military has abandoned its Bolshevik-inspired ideology, converting itself from an army loyal to a single political party into the defender of a democratic state with a popularly elected government. Second, there is a serious structural reform taking place in the military, with a view to creating a more effective joint armed force. Meanwhile, constitutional reform is converting civil-military relations in Taiwan. These pressures challenge Taiwan's military modernization plans. Thus, as Ding and Huang tell us, the future of Taiwan's civilian-controlled military rests "less on the acquisition of new hardware and more on such 'software' issues as strategies, missions, doctrine, education, and training." June Teufel Dreyer continues the discussion of the transformation of Taiwan's military in Chapter 7. She notes that challenges stemming from a combination of procurement scandals, recruiting shortfalls, and a vulnerability to missile attack have created serious problems for the Taiwan armed forces. The major challenge, however, according to Dreyer, is the ability to counteract pressures from Beijing, especially pressure on the United States to cut off arms sales to Taiwan under the auspices of the Taiwan Relations Act.

In the concluding comments of the book, Ellis Joffe, in Chapter 8, discusses party-army relations in the PRC. In Joffe's view, the PLA is a pivotal player in Chinese leadership politics because of the internal role in the military of Jiang Zemin. By encouraging military professionalism and getting the military out of business activities, Jiang distanced military chiefs from the political arena. His posts as general secretary of the Communist Party, chairman of its Central Military Commission, and President give him power and keep him in the public eye. The result is a mutually beneficial arrangement between military and civilian leaders that probably can only be changed by military intervention in politics, according to Joffe.

In the 1997 book from that year's conference, *Crisis in the Taiwan Strait*, I said that the events of March 1996, when the United States sent two aircraft carrier battle groups to the region, might repeat themselves. In 1999, the events almost did exactly that. In this volume, the authors have taken a serious look at the future. They have written a book designed to wrestle with questions of what sort of military force might be fielded by Taiwan and China and what security policy and structures these two armed forces might operate under. There is no "group think" involved here. The reader should know that there was serious, spirited debate about these chapters when they were drafted, and the authors continue to debate the issues today. Indeed, the goal of the publishers is to stimulate wider debate. *Our Congress has recognized the need to further explore Chinese grand strategy, security strategy, military strategy, and operational concepts for the next 20 years, and this book is offered as a means to do so.*

CHAPTER 1
GEOGRAPHIC RUMINATIONS

Michael McDevitt

Because it is so well understood among China experts and East Asian strategists, discussions regarding China and the future of the People's Liberation Army (PLA) in the 21st century often neglect the most predictable feature of Asia's security landscape. I am referring, of course, to geography.

In Roosevelt Hall, home of the National War College in Washington, DC, an enormous map of the world hangs in the main stairwell. Below this map is a plaque with a cautionary reminder for potential strategists. It reads, "Everything changes but geography." Applying that wisdom to Asia, it is important to visualize and then reflect upon Asia's distinctive geography. For me, the three most striking features of that geography are (1) the vast distances involved, (2) the number of significant states that are totally, or very nearly, surrounded by water (Japan, Taiwan, the Philippine Islands, Indonesia, Singapore, Malaysia—connected to the continent only by the slender Isthmus of Kra—Australia, Papua New Guinea, and New Zealand), and (3) the geographic centrality and physical enormity of China. These three features, really geographic facts, interrelate in ways that both facilitate and limit the strategic choices, in fact, the strategic circumstances, facing China.

What are those circumstances? Starting with the last point made, the centrality and enormity of China, I will briefly comment on China's strategic geography. This discussion is based primarily on capabilities and is in no way intended to suggest China's intentions. The purpose is to illuminate an often overlooked feature of security planning and dialogue and to add a geographic context to these discussions. China's central position on the Asian mainland allows it to command internal lines of communication throughout the continent. This central fact, plus the military protection afforded by the Himalayas and the deserts of western China, the improving militarily useful infrastructure (roads, airports, communications media), a large modernizing army, the demonstrated ability to absorb punishment and keep on fighting in the guerrilla or People's War tradition, an enormous population, and a strong sense of national identity, leads one to the conclusion that China is the **dominant military power on the continent of Asia**.

When one considers the nations with which China shares a common land frontier and mentally calculates the "comprehensive national power" of North Korea, Vietnam, Laos, Burma, Bhutan, Nepal, India, Pakistan, Tajikistan, Kyrgyzstan, Kazakhstan, Mongolia, and Russia, it is clear that China need not worry unduly about the threat of invasion from a neighboring state. Today there are no serious continental military threats—save for nuclear weapons which China deters with her own nuclear weapons—to China's continental predominance. Being secure against invasion is only part of the continental dominance equation. Being able to intimidate continental neighbors with the capability to invade is the other side of the dominance coin.

This capability exists, but with some important caveats. Although Vietnam gave China a bloody nose in 1979, the operational capabilities of the People's Army of Vietnam (PAVN) and PLA have gone in opposite directions since that time. The PAVN is a shadow of its former self while the PLA has continued to gradually improve. If China chose to invade Vietnam and to pay a heavy price, Vietnam would lose. It is hard to imagine how India and China could find enough suitable terrain to get at one another in a militarily decisive way. They can punish but not conquer one another.

To a degree, the same situation exists between China and Russia. But if we consider just the Russian Far East, the balance tips decisively in favor of China. The Chinese could seize much of the Russian Far East and hold it for a very long time. The threat of nuclear war obviously makes this a fanciful proposition in terms of intentions—but the capability is there. An important exception to being able to intimidate militarily its continental neighbors might be a united Korea. It is possible to imagine a united Republic of Korea (ROK) Army dug in along the Yalu and Tumen, with the United States alongside, holding off a Chinese attack.

With this possible exception, this brief analysis appears to confirm the truth of the observation that China is the dominant power on the continent of Asia. While this power is real, it is also limited by the other realities of the geography of Asia. The vastness of the East Asian region is a major limiter, as is the fact that many of the most important countries of Asia, in terms of wealth, resources, technology, and military capability, do not abut China. They are on the rimland of the Asian continent or are island and archipelagic states. They are beyond the direct grasp of China's single most important military capability: its huge army.

Geography limits the ability of China to be militarily preeminent in all of Asia because the PLA is woefully *unbalanced* in terms of military capability. Its ability to project militarily decisive force beyond China's immediate neighbors is almost non-existent. The sort of military capability required to accomplish a projection mission, principally naval and air forces, is in most cases either rudimentary, obsolete, small, or nonexistent. Forces to control the sea and airspace around and over a non-contiguous objective, to lift large numbers of troops by sea or air, to conduct surveillance around "maritime Asia," and to conduct sustained long-range bombardment from the air are not in the PLA inventory. (The PLA's conventional ballistic missile force is an obvious strength and exception to this litany.)

There are good and sensible, as well as uniquely Chinese, reasons why the PLA developed as it has. The threat, Japanese or Nationalist, was in China; manpower was abundant, but technology and modern equipment were not; the very nature of a revolution means that the decisive military action takes place on the ground; and the fact that in Chinese military history, at least until the 19th and 20th centuries, threats have come from the north.

Military historians and geo-strategists can also discern some more universal factors at work when they compare China and traditional European "continental" powers. Certainly Germany, Russia, and, for much of its modern military history, France have also neglected maritime and force-projection capabilities and lavished resources and prestige on ground forces. Like China, these historically army-dominated military cultures developed because of the geographic circumstances of the respective nations. But, unlike China, none of them had the luxury of militarily dominating their continent except for fleeting periods under Napoleon, Hitler, and Stalin.

Throughout modern history the successful domination of Europe by a single power has been seen as *very destabilizing* and worth fighting unlimited wars to prevent, while China's implicit domination of Asia today is greeted with near equanimity—certainly in the United States. (The closer geographically to China, the less equanimous, particularly if a territorial dispute is involved.) The fact that China is the dominant military power on the Asian continent is not considered destabilizing and has not triggered an arms race. Continental neighbors, following the withering of Communist solidarity, have not sought collective security regimes to balance China's dominance, although one can make the case that Vietnam's eagerness to join the Association of Southeast Asian Nations (ASEAN) was as much driven by strategic interests as by economic considerations. Vietnam is an exception to the rule precisely because China has been militarily assertive about competing claims in the Tonkin Gulf and South China Sea.

Another reason for equanimity in the face of continental dominance is because so many of Asia's most important nations lie beyond China's military reach on the continental rimland or are separated from the continent by expanses of open ocean. Because of geography and the U.S. military presence, Asia is considered stable today, despite the very real concerns over conflict in Korea or between China and Taiwan. Beyond these two pieces of unfinished Cold War business, one other action could destabilize Asia. That would be an attempt by China to grow from a continental to a region-wide "suzerain."

Geography and China's economic development now present China with a strategic dilemma. Should it take advantage of its continental dominance and the absence of a serious neighboring threat to reallocate defense resources in a fundamental way toward redressing the projection shortfalls it has? Or, does it accept the fact that important countries of Asia will remain beyond its ability to influence through military intimidation? Certainly, were China to make a choice to become truly serious about developing a region-wide projection capability, those countries currently beyond China's reach would attempt to restabilize the situation through the development of counter-projection military capabilities, e.g., submarines, surveillance, air defense, and local air superiority, or through alliance with the United States, or both.

We see hedging by rimland and maritime Asian nations in this direction today. But realistically, it is important to appreciate that it would take decades for China to develop such a capability. Security analysts must be able to differentiate between token Chinese military capabilities intended for prestige and showing-the-flag, for example a single medium-size aircraft carrier, which has no real strategic weight, and an attempt to create a truly dominant projection force. The most immediate example that comes to mind of the latter would be Wilhelmine Germany's attempt to outbuild the British Royal Navy. China has apparently decided not to take this destabilizing road. Hopefully this is because it has no desire to seek such a military predominance, but also presumably because it can appreciate that, with the proper mix of U.S. forces in the region, rimland and maritime Asia will always have the ability to "trump" Chinese projection attempts.

CHAPTER 2
THE CHINESE MILITARY
AND THE PERIPHERAL STATES[1]
IN THE 21st CENTURY:
A SECURITY *TOUR D'HORIZON*

Eric A. McVadon

> Mankind is about to enter the 21st century.... At the turn of the century, an important historical period, China is devoting itself to its modernization drive. China needs and cherishes dearly an environment of long-term international peace, **especially a favorable peripheral environment**.[2] [Emphasis added.]

Thus begins the White Paper on China's National Defense, issued by the State Council in July 1998. In contrast, the November 1995 Chinese White Paper included these words sprinkled through its foreword:

> China needs a peaceful environment in order to be able to devote itself completely to its socialist modernization program. It resolutely . . . seeks to actively develop good relations with neighboring nations . . . China does not seek world or regional hegemony.[3]

What conclusions might we draw from this conspicuous emphasis given to the peripheral environment in the most recent White Paper? Care should be exercised, of course, in assigning great import to the difference in wording between 1995 and 1998, especially as the 1995 paper was primarily focused on arms control matters. However, it might be safely noted that the drafters and senior approvers of the July 1998 White Paper, cognizant of the wording of the earlier seminal paper, included prominent reference to the peripheral environment in the fourth sentence of the English version of the document. Beijing's interest in the security aspects of its relations with neighboring countries is certainly not waning. That fact is clear from the words of this and other official documents and statements and also from China's actions, as this chapter will examine.

The 1998 White Paper on China's National Defense contains many direct and indirect references to China's regional security policy. The document is a propitiously opened window through which we may scrutinize Beijing's view of prospects for security relations with peripheral states in the 21st century—or at the very least the view that Beijing wishes us to see. It includes the following broad official statement of Beijing's regional security policy:

> As a country in the Asia-Pacific region, China places great importance on the region's security, stability, peace and development. China's Asia-Pacific security strategy has three objectives, i.e., China's own stability and prosperity, peace and stability in its surrounding regions, and conducting dialogue and cooperation with all countries in the Asia-Pacific region.[4]

The statement above begins with what might seem a gratuitous "geography lesson," as if it were necessary to remind others that China is a country in the Asia-Pacific region. The drafters may, appropriately in their view, have directed those words toward the American audience, an audience that Beijing believes often forgets that China has more enduring and profound interests in Asia than does the United States. Of course, that opening phrase is also a reminder to its neighbors that China is a major (and arguably *the* major) country of the region—and that it will always be such. The implied message for China's neighbors is that the United States (and almost all others) does not have anything approaching that status, and that Americans, despite their current interests and military presence, should not be looked to and trusted over the long term for support. There is the further suggestion that Asian matters should properly be handled by Asian nations, by nations that understand "Asian values" and Asian methods. This statement starts, therefore, with the point that China wants to be recognized as a major player in regional security.

Although the English syntax in the translation is labored, this meaning is made clear in other words from the same chapter:

> The countries in the Asia-Pacific region rely more and more on each other economically, and, to solve their disputes by peaceful means, to stress the search for the meeting points of their common interests and to strengthen cooperation and coordination are becoming the main current of the relations among the countries of the region.[5]

The 1998 White Paper emphasizes Chinese advocacy of regional security dialogue and cooperation at various levels and in different ways, implying that the methods China advocates are superior to those employed by others, especially outsiders to Asia. As might be expected, phrases like "participation on an equal footing," "reaching unanimity through consultation," and "seeking common ground while reserving differences" are included. China's active participation in official and "Track II" forums is touted. Beijing uses the White Paper to argue forcefully, if not persuasively to all, that China is a responsible and reasonable force in regional security.[6] In apparent recognition that many will doubt or question this assertion, there is the unspoken suggestion that those who previously saw China in another light should alter their opinions.

Pre-eminence of Economic Concerns.

It is noteworthy, but certainly not surprising, that economic factors are featured very prominently in this thoroughly internally coordinated 1998 statement concerning security relationships with regional countries. Although the 1995 White Paper's words on regional security were very near the end of that long document, there was only slightly less prominence given to regional economic matters.[7] Economic considerations with respect to regional security might be conveniently divided into two categories: (1) the relative national priorities assigned to the development of national economic power and to the development of military power and (2) economic security and economic interdependence as key factors in security relations with neighboring countries.

With respect to the first category, both White Papers, and particularly the more recent document, clearly demonstrate Beijing's view of the relative importance assigned to economic development compared to defense modernization. First, there is the obvious fact that China over recent decades has achieved far greater success in its national economic development than in its military modernization. One of the reasons for this is that both Chinese policy pronouncements and practical emphasis have been directed to the pre-eminence of national economic development. The foreword of the 1998 White Paper essentially repeats the wording of the 1995 document in stating:

> China unswervingly ... keeps national defense construction in a position subordinate to and in the service of the nation's economic construction. . . .

Whether or not such statements are accepted by outside observers, they appear in the 1998 White Paper altogether too many times to ignore. One may argue, for example, that economic success is the most important factor in fueling modernization of the People's Liberation Army (PLA). On the other hand, it is obvious that the PLA does not get all that it wants and that economic (budget) considerations are a major factor in procurement decisions. A well-connected and well-informed PLAN officer has stated bluntly, "If there were enough money, the PLAN would have a carrier now."[8]

Although some may quibble about the practical application of this oft-stated priority of economic development over building the military, it is clear that this category of economic consideration is a primary factor in

China's regional security. The PLA has been constrained both by direct budget limitations and by its inability to acquire and assimilate technology rapidly—in significant part a function of inadequate funding for research and development. Consequently, Beijing necessarily views its rise to the status of a regional (and prospective global) power more in terms of economic development than military capabilities. An excerpt from Chapter I of the 1998 White Paper supports the point, albeit in a slightly oblique Chinese way (by referring to others when meaning itself):

> The political security situation in the Asia-Pacific region is relatively stable. The development of the trend toward multipolarity in this region is being quickened. . . . Despite the emergence of a financial crisis in Asia, the Asia-Pacific region remains one of the areas with the greatest economic development vitality in the world, and developing the economy is the most important task for each country.[9]

Although the partially modernized PLA is without question a formidable *regional* military force, it is not as modern, as large, or as threatening as it might have been had Beijing given high priority to developing a more powerful force. The regional security situation would have been markedly different if China had devoted greater attention and resources to the PLA and if the PLA had been able to absorb the systems and technologies it might have received (a very big "if").

The second category of economic consideration encompasses both economic security and economic interdependence. When Beijing views its regional security relations, it sees them more and more through an economic lens. China, in an increasingly sophisticated way that has been further intensified by the Asian economic crisis, looks beyond the stark outlines of military confrontations and threats when it contemplates its neighbors, as illustrated by this excerpt, also from the first chapter in the White Paper entitled "The International Security Situation."

> Economic security is becoming daily more important for state security. In international relations, geopolitical, military security and ideological factors still play a role that cannot be ignored, but the role of economic factors is becoming more outstanding, along with growing economic contacts among nations. The competition to excel in overall national strength, focused on economy and science and technology, is being further intensified; globewide struggles centered on markets, natural resources and other economic rights and interests are daily becoming sharper; and the quickening of economic globalization and intensification of the formation of regional blocs render the economic development of a country more vulnerable to outside influences and impacts. Therefore, more and more countries regard economic security as an important aspect of state security. The financial crisis in Asia has made the issue of economic security more prominent, and has set a new task for governments of all countries to strengthen coordination and face challenges together in the course of economic globalization.[10]

In other words, China's regional security relationships cannot be framed in traditional military security terms. Economic considerations, even if not seen as replacing military means, are given priority over military development considerations. Moreover, economic factors are seen as more important than conventional threat analysis and force comparisons or balances. Economic security has top priority, and economic interdependence is seen as a primary tool in managing regional security. This is not because China has become benevolent or ignores the utility of military forces in the region, although those forces have been assigned a clearly subordinate, albeit still significant, status. It means at least that the PLA cannot do all that China might wish of it, and that other means—economic and political—must be relied upon, at least in the short term. This further suggests that these may be seen by Beijing as the preferable means for the long term as well. China cannot compete with Japan or even a weakened Russia, for example, and excel in a specifically military sense, especially with U.S. forces present in the region, but it can lean much more heavily on the economic aspects of overall national power. It can make the most of its economic ties and work to minimize economic tensions with its neighbors, all the while pursuing modernization of the PLA at a pace that places minimal drag on the national economy and is not unduly upsetting to other nations.

Over the longer term, China could eventually become a much more formidable military power, especially regionally. There could be temptation to re-emphasize military means in regional security relations. Further, it is hardly certain that the leadership in Beijing will recognize fully the implications and opportunities of China as an economic giant—and the implications of squandering those opportunities and potential in a military adventure. Despite appearances, it may not be understood or appreciated fully in Beijing that greater economic clout concomitantly implies that economic security is the overwhelmingly important consideration in China's strategic relations with peripheral states and the world at large. Beijing's rhetoric still emphasizes force; so it is not a foregone conclusion that Beijing will continue indefinitely down its present path. If Beijing were to continue into the next century to rely primarily on economic considerations, it would be because of a fuller appreciation by the Chinese leadership that China's true national power lies primarily in its national economic development and regional economic relations rather than in its military modernization and defense "construction." Already Beijing seems to have accepted that the penchant to resort to hostilities is effectively deterred when regional countries appreciate that the increasingly important economic ties with neighboring countries would be severely jeopardized or even severed were military forces to be employed.

For now and for the future, the manner in which Beijing incorporates this sort of thinking into its strategic calculus will reveal the degree to which Chinese leaders truly recognize that China's interests are better served by avoiding or resolving conflicts through economic power and political maneuver rather than employment of military force. In the final analysis however, China is doubtless seeking to gain what it sees as an appropriate mix of economic, political, and military power. Of interest is whether the relative priorities assigned these three kinds of power will remain as they appear now, with economic considerations having the greatest importance. This would offer a welcome measure of assurance that Beijing means what it says about a strong preference for relations based on peaceful cooperation and friendship and that, as seems to be the case, Chinese strategic thinking is profoundly and permanently influenced in a favorable direction by the economic considerations described.

Taiwan, of course, is a somewhat different matter—but possibly less so than it might appear at first glance. There is no question that Beijing gives full emphasis to its ability to cope with the military forces of Taiwan and to deter, discourage, and intimidate the government and populace. However, even in this seemingly irreconcilable situation, the enormous economic factors at play in cross-strait relations raise at least the faint hope that as economic links continue to gain importance, more traditional military considerations will tend to wane even with respect to Taiwan.

New Affection for Multilateral Contacts, Even Confidence-Building Measures (CBMs); Abhorrence of Alliances.

Chinese attitudes are changing in other areas. Beijing's favorable view of global multipolarity, as opposed to a bipolar or unipolar world, is neither new nor surprising. The 1998 White Paper states:

> The sustained development of the multipolarity tendency and economic globalization has further deepened their [developing countries'] mutual reliance and mutual condition and helped toward world peace, stability and prosperity.[11]

However, this Chinese fondness for what is termed "the multipolarity tendency" has been accompanied by a surprising abrogation of the traditional Chinese abhorrence of multi *lateral* means to handle problems. Beijing had, until recently, fostered a reputation for pursuing bilateral undertakings to the virtual exclusion of multilateral efforts, feeling, according to most analysts, that China could best utilize its size and weight to achieve its goals through one-on-one methods. Further, CBMs and transparency were seen by Beijing as means devised by outsiders to probe China's secrets and to reveal the PLA's backwardness and shortcomings. Recently, changes in these attitudes have been seen. Later in the first chapter of the 1998 White Paper are these somewhat unexpected words:

> Various forms of regional and sub-regional multilateral cooperation are constantly being developed, and security dialogues and cooperation are being carried out at many levels and through many channels.[12]

Chinese officials, including many influential PLA officers, have reached at least tentative conclusions that China's interests are in some cases served by the implementation of CBMs and that there is merit to gaining trust from neighboring capitals through a significant degree of transparency in military affairs. The White Paper goes so far as to describe CBMs with neighboring countries as "a new kind of security concept *vigorously advocated* by China . . . [emphasis added]."[13]

Many are not yet ready to accept these Chinese assertions at face value. The issue of CBMs is illustrative. The paper asserts that the agreements that China has reached with neighboring countries on CBMs "embody some principles and spirit of universal significance for Asian-Pacific security dialogues and cooperation."[14] Considerable attention is given in the White Paper to China's co-sponsorship with the Philippines of the Conference on Confidence-Building Measures held in Beijing in 1996. It is noted that during the conference foreign representatives were invited to visit PLA units and observe exercises. However, according to personal reports that came to the attention of the author, many participants of the conference thought they were shown very little of real interest during the visits.

It is further asserted in the White Paper that China has offered "constructive suggestions" in support of the Association of Southeast Asian Nations (ASEAN) Regional Forum (ARF) exploration of confidence-building measures. However, the areas of potential CBMs listed (e.g., "military medicine," the "science of military law," high-level visits, and port calls) fall well short of the type of substantive CBMs that others envision.[15] This seems to leave open the question of whether China is serious about proceeding with worthwhile CBMs or whether its actions actually are stalling tactics to put off indefinitely consideration of meaningful measures. At least it can be said that the expression "CBMs" no longer causes PLA senior officers and Chinese officials automatically to recoil.

There is yet something else important at work here. A major component of China's attitude toward regional security is intensified opposition to military alliances, primarily the U.S. alliance structure, which it sees as pointed at China. Beijing in the White Paper alludes to these bilateral alliances, without directly mentioning that the United States is a party, as pacts that create confrontations, and Beijing also condemns arrangements "infringing upon the security interests of any other nation."[16] There is the further suggestion that in place of such arrangements, there should be a new form of mutual understanding and trust. The White Paper describes it as follows:

> Hence China devotes its efforts to promoting equal treatment and friendly cooperation with other countries, and attaches importance to developing healthy and stable relations with all countries and all major forces in the region; actively participates in regional economic cooperation and promotes an open type of regionalism; insists on handling and settling disputes among

countries through peaceful means; and takes an active part in the dialogue and cooperation process aimed at regional security.[17]

Further, Beijing recalls that China has sought to resolve by nonmilitary means many of the enduring disputes that have plagued it. Although many may justifiably view Beijing's somewhat pompous proclamations with a measure of cynicism, the following are the words of the White Paper in this regard:

> On the basis of equal consultation, mutual understanding and mutual accommodation, China has solved in an appropriate manner border issues with most of its neighbors. As for remaining disputes on territorial and marine rights and interests between China and neighboring countries, China maintains that they are to be solved through consultation by putting the interests of the whole above everything else, so that the disputes will not hamper the normal development of state relations or the stability of the region. China has clearly stated that relevant disputes should be properly solved through peaceful negotiation and consultation, in accordance with commonly accepted international laws and modern maritime laws, including the basic principles and legal systems as prescribed in the United Nations Convention on the Law of the Sea.[18]

Whether or not Beijing's assertions and commitments concerning the proper manner for resolution of regional disputes are accepted as presented here, the use of this language affords others an opportunity to test Chinese resolve to use peaceful means and international law, as opposed to military means, especially as regards the disputed claims in the South China Sea. More broadly, the tendency of Chinese leaders to conform to international norms and to comply with international law offers a very different prospect for China's relations with peripheral states compared to the relations with those states only a few years ago.

Military-to-Military Contacts with Regional States.

The White Paper asserts near the beginning of the chapter on International Security Cooperation:

> China has placed the development of military contacts with adjacent countries in a prominent position..., especially contacts on the senior level. In 1996 and 1997 alone, China sent more than 100 military delegations to most of its adjacent countries, and hosted over 130 military delegations from such countries.[19]

Beijing considers these contacts, which it terms military diplomacy, as an important component of China's overall diplomacy. It is noteworthy that, in addition to the highly publicized visits by PLAN combatant ships to North and South America in the spring of 1997, similar PLAN visits were made at the same time to the Philippines, Malaysia, and Thailand. Beijing asserts that its military contacts have fostered "mutual understanding and trust between the PLA and other armed forces" and have contributed to keeping regional peace.[20]

Summarizing Beijing's Proclamations on Regional Security.

Beijing's stated overall approach to regional security relations as the new century begins might be summarized as follows:

- Increased attention to its peripheral environment, primarily because China needs regional stability to continue national economic development.

- More effective, but gentler, assertion of China's role as a pre-eminent power in the Asia-Pacific region and as the appropriate permanent pillar of regional stability.

- Pursuit of the conviction that China's national power is primarily a function of economic development rather than military capabilities.

- A new acceptance of, even a budding preference for, use of multilateral means and international law to settle disputes—but a hardening of opposition to alliances.

This is the picture painted by Beijing's own brush strokes, some meant to be seen by the world as new and others as a consequence of China's style. It is a picture at variance with Beijing's traditional bullying and blustering behavior toward its neighbors, and it is very different from what many might anticipate as China's approach to security relations with the peripheral states in the coming years. It is, of course, not possible to forecast with confidence how Beijing will proceed. Nevertheless, it is possible to apply this purported approach to an examination of China's relations with its various neighboring states, test how Beijing is now proceeding by looking at current events, and thereby speculate in a more informed way about what the next century will bring with respect to the Chinese military and the peripheral states.

A cautionary note is in order at this juncture, however. Neither the 1998 White Paper nor other Chinese statements and actions, official or otherwise, suggest that the "Taiwan problem" can be pursued along the lines suggested above for handling regional security relationships and resolving disputes with neighboring countries. Taiwan is painted as an internal, not a regional, issue. Similarly, Beijing would not consider that matters of contention concerning Tibet, Xinjiang, or Inner Mongolia would fall within the rubric of disputes "between China and neighboring countries." Beijing sees all these as internal matters, about which its attitudes have changed not at all and for which significant change is not now foreseen.

The View into "West Turkestan."

When thinking of China's peripheral states, Westerners often tend to think last about the countries of the former Soviet Union that lie to the northwest of China, the newly independent nations of Central Asia bordering China's restive Xinjiang Uighur Autonomous Region.[21] This area across China's far northwestern border, composed of Kazakhstan, Kyrgyzstan, and Tajikistan, is certainly not overlooked by Beijing. Historically, it was known as West Turkestan. The adjacent area within China that is now Xinjiang (meaning "New Territories") was formerly known as East Turkestan and is populated largely by the Turkic-speaking Uighur Muslim minority. The Uighurs are far from content with their economic and political status and receive sympathetic support from fellow Uighurs in the Central Asian Republics, especially Kazakhstan. There is a small, but active, cross-border Islamic independence movement. Border disputes between China and the Central Asian states, carried over from the Soviet period, have been an additional complicating factor.

Xinjiang has been and remains a hotbed of anti-Beijing unrest, especially in recent years. This Muslim dissent is fueled by exacerbating factors such as the conspicuous transition to independence of the Turkic Central Asian nations, the rise in the region of Islamic fundamentalism,[22] and unhappiness with Beijing's domestic policies for the "autonomous" region—one of five such regions in China. In addition to the very large and aggravating influx of ethnic Chinese,[23] for which Beijing is sharply criticized, Uighurs feel that other Chinese policies or failures to act are keeping them in poverty. The Hans are perceived as reaping most of the benefits of exploitation of Xinjiang's considerable natural resources and profiting from the growing economic links with the neighboring countries. Beijing's poverty eradication measures are viewed with disdain and considered a meager, token effort. Not surprisingly, some of the same complaints about Beijing's policies are heard from Tibet.

Bombings, rioting, and assassinations by separatists have been met by Beijing with police raids, very large-scale arrests, and numerous executions of Uighurs—all in an attempt to curb terrorist actions and crush the independence movement. Some of the Uighur terrorist incidents and killings were provocatively timed to coincide with the funeral in February 1997 of former paramount leader Deng Xiaoping and the visit to China in June and July 1998 by U.S. President William J. Clinton. Reports of the frequent killing by separatists of police in cities near the borders continue, with eight such deaths alleged in August 1998.[24] Harsh action in Xinjiang by Beijing may have included use of armored PLA units in addition to the People's Armed Police (PAP). Stringent security measures have been instituted to prevent further unrest and have even spread to western Beijing where thousands of Uighurs live. Although the number of actual separatists in Xinjiang appears to be relatively small, resentment among the minority population is widespread. The Uighur population as a whole bridles under the restrictions and opposes Beijing's actions. The many highly resented Han Chinese in Xinjiang remain fearful for their personal safety.

Neighboring countries' support for the dissidents is significant. Kazakh activists have accused Beijing of persistent human rights violations in Xinjiang and of repressing their fellow Uighurs. A pro-separatist organization in Kazakhstan[25] named the United National Revolutionary Front calls for the removal of Han Chinese from Xinjiang and the establishment of an independent Islamic Republic of East Turkestan. Beijing feels that moral support, sanctuary, and arms have been provided by sympathizers in the bordering Central Asian countries. Separatists supported in this way are seen by Chinese leaders as menacingly, and increasingly, well-armed and financed.

Despite its heavy-handed security and military actions within Xinjiang, China has met the threat from Kazakhstan and its Central Asian neighbors with a diplomatic and economic offensive. In April 1996 in Shanghai, President Jiang Zemin signed an agreement with Russia, Kazakhstan, Kyrgyzstan, and Tajikistan on security and confidence-building measures on their borders. The (significantly) multilateral agreement is designed to reduce border tensions although no clashes had occurred in some years, but it also serves to make clear to Washington the nature and range of Beijing's options and influence. The three Central Asian states signed the agreement despite protests by the Uighur minorities in their countries. These opponents argue that China is trying to obliterate or neutralize Uighurs in Xinjiang. The specific provisions of the treaty require the parties to inform each other about military exercises within 100 kilometers of the borders, ban military exercises directed toward another party, and state that military forces of the five states will not attack one another.[26] The treaty, it should be noted, also serves to establish solid links between Beijing and the Central Asian capitals for cooperation in quelling cross-border Uighur dissent.

A year after that agreement, in April 1997, following serious unrest in Xinjiang in February 1997, the presidents of these five countries concluded another treaty, this one signed in Moscow. It provides for troop reductions on China's borders with these countries of the former Soviet Union. In an especially noteworthy step toward transparency and confidence-building, the pact limits forces within 100 kilometers of the borders and provides for mutual inspection. The agreement was also pointedly described as a lasting model for regional security arrangements, pointing up China's verbal campaign against alliances. Former Foreign Minister Qian said:

> We have tried alliance, and we have tried confrontation. Both did not work, and now we must find something else. Our relations are not confrontational, but they are not an alliance as well.[27]

Several months later, as unrest in Xinjiang simmered, China and Kazakhstan signed a $9.5 billion oil and pipeline deal.[28] The arrangement was evaluated by Western specialists as economically infeasible.[29] Beijing, however, was undeterred by this projection. China's purpose went beyond development of oil fields and pipelines; the Chinese economic offensive also had as its target fostering Kazakh cooperation in curbing Uighur separatist efforts and other Muslim dissent.

More recently in July 1998, the "group of five," as the gathering of the five countries was called informally, met in Almaty (still the commercial center of Kazakhstan, with the new capital being Astana) and agreed to collaborate on fighting organized crime and *political separatism*. On the margins of that meeting, Chinese President Jiang and Kazakh President Nazarbayev signed an agreement settling border disputes, described as the *final document* concerning borders between the two countries. The resolution reportedly slightly favored the smaller country, with Kazakhstan gaining undisputed possession of 53 percent of the disputed areas. Of greater consequence was agreement between Jiang and Nazarbayev to develop a 15-year economic program, including a proposed automobile plant in Kazakhstan, electrical transmission arrangements, Chinese investment in the country, and construction work by China in the new capital.[30] Also of significance was further confirmation by the two leaders of the September 1997 oil production and transport deal, although Western executives continued to express doubts about the viability of the proposal.[31]

These diplomatic and economic undertakings by Beijing suggest that in this pesky situation China is far more ready to employ military force *within* its borders than without. This seems to be the case although the small countries involved would not likely be able to repel a PLA force dispatched to "assist" in crushing the Uighur movement in Kazakhstan, for example. Certainly, there are many good reasons for Beijing to refrain from the use of force in such situations with a neighbor. However, its readiness to employ force in 1962 against India, in 1979 in Vietnam, and on other occasions against Vietnam in the South China Sea cannot be ignored in contemplating which options Beijing is prone to select. It appears there was not even the threat, direct or implied, of the use of the PLA in the difficulties, which spanned a number of years, which were designed to undermine Chinese sovereignty in Xinjiang, and which included efforts to embarrass Beijing on the world scene.

Instead, Beijing has cast its lot in the direction of cooperative arrangements with these comparatively tiny neighbors. In its effort to cement bonds with the Central Asian states, Beijing took full advantage of the good will engendered by settling border disputes and then went so far as to hold out the promise of sweeping economic ties. Consequently, it seems the most likely role at the beginning of the next century for the PLA in this troublesome region for China will be to safeguard pipeline construction as much as to back up the PAP and the Public Security Bureau forces in their activities within Xinjiang.

Looking Northward to Russia: Strategic Partner or Potential Threat?

In April 1996, erstwhile antagonists China and Russia unveiled what they termed a *strategic partnership* for the future. On that occasion in Shanghai, President Jiang said, "China is not posing, and will not pose in the future, any threat to Russia." President Boris Yeltsin, with customary unbridled enthusiasm, said, "I view the Sino-Russian partnership . . . as a model for relations between two countries. . . . I can't name a single question on which we would have different opinions."[32] Near the end of 1997, both Moscow and Beijing reportedly described the Sino-Russian relationship more fully as "constructive cooperation aimed at strategic partnership in the twenty-first century."[33] Over the more than 2 years since the term "strategic partnership" was introduced, various versions of the description have been employed. It has been called a "strategic *cooperation* partnership" and a "strategic *coordination* partnership," the latter expression thought by some to be favored by the Chinese. An April 1997 Sino-Russian joint statement that might be seen as a definitive definition of the concept used the words "strategic partnership of equality and mutual trust," omitting the much-discussed adjectives.[34]

Regardless of the precise wording of the description of the bilateral arrangement, its mere existence and other pertinent factors reveal at the very least a desire in Beijing and Moscow to demonstrate to Washington and others considerable confidence that the bilateral relationship is on a firm footing for the future. First and foremost, there is the repeated attention to extolling the virtues of the purportedly new form of relationship. Other relevant factors are that Presidents Jiang and Yeltsin (despite the Russian's bad health) have conducted six summit meetings in recent years and that there have been numerous bilateral and multilateral security undertakings and bilateral economic undertakings. This apparent mutual confidence in a stable, positive relationship is not something to be taken for granted. Recent history (certainly on the Chinese time scale) has witnessed abrupt swings in relations between Moscow and Beijing.

Obvious to all was the very close Sino-Soviet cooperation in the 1950s, which gave way to animosity and distrust in the early 1960s, with good relations resumed in the 1980s. Less obvious is that at the end of the 1980s, when then-President Mikhail Gorbachev visited a China on the brink of the Tiananmen Square debacle, the Soviet Union was coasting economically, and the Soviet Communist Party seemed to have found a way to achieve reform and remain viable. Now, the situation is quite different. With Russia's political and economic reform in peril, unresolved by the recent International Monetary Fund (IMF) bailout, China can gloat over the status of its economy and a Communist Party that has stayed in power through flexibility and adjustment during a time of great change in Chinese society. China smoothly effected the transition of national presidents, with Jiang Zemin consolidating his own power as he replaced Yang Shangkun, and of premiers, with Zhu replacing Li. In contrast, the Russian transition from President Gorbachev to President Yeltsin was tumultuous. With respect to prime ministers, Russia has also experienced turbulence, shifting from Viktor Chernomyrdin to Sergei Kiriyenko and then to temporary limbo, all in a matter of 5 months. It is now the lot of Russian leaders to be envious; yet neither that emotion nor Chinese crowing has been evident as an irritant in the relationship.

The Economic Victors and Vanquished. Another pertinent aspect of these events not lost on Chinese leaders is that national economic developments, not comparative military prowess, have been instrumental in the reversal of roles between China and Russia. The change in the military condition has been an indirect consequence of economic and political developments in both countries. Significantly, as the foreign ministers of China and Russia met in Beijing in July 1998 specifically to discuss security issues and prepare for another meeting between their presidents, they ignored the IMF flurry and deteriorating political environment in Moscow and talked of ways that their countries could cooperate to achieve a breakthrough in the Asian financial crisis. This makes it clear that the regional security tools that are most appealing to China and Russia are economic and not military. Foreign Minister Yevgeny Primakov reinforced that instinct among Chinese leaders when he effusively praised China's economic successes.[35] The contrast between the countries could hardly be more stark: Russia's economic crisis deepens, and China, even with weakening economic growth prospects, seems to be weathering the Asian crisis better by far than almost all its neighbors. China has achieved a secure relationship, even something that can be termed a *strategic partnership*, almost completely through its national economic progress. All the while, the bested partner, Russia, is benignly cooperating with China in challenging the U.S. role in the region. Many in Beijing must feel that they have succeeded in subduing the bear and that China can be much more secure when it looks northward.

America Bashing. Challenging the United States is another important aspect of the solidarity between Beijing and Moscow that has enhanced the partnership. The bilateral bonds have been strengthened by the perception of having a common adversary on an important matter. Both capitals have taken great satisfaction in directing barbs at Washington. In December 1996, Premier Li Peng and President Yeltsin candidly vowed to forge closer military and economic ties to counter the influence of the United States in the post-Cold War world.[36] Washington is characterized by these partners as coveting its superpower status in a unipolar world, clinging to Cold War thinking, and pursuing confrontation in its relations with China, while Beijing and Moscow show the world a new model for peaceful relationships. The April 1997 China-Russia joint statement on the bilateral arrangement expresses grandly that the purpose of the partnership is "to promote the multipolarization of the world and the establishment of a new world order." With evident reference to the United States, it explains,

> The establishment of a just and equitable new international political and economic order based on peace and stability has become the pressing need of the times and the inevitable necessity of history. . . . No country should seek hegemony, practice power politics, or monopolize international affairs.

Of course, international economic disparities are not overlooked. On this issue the joint statement reads:

> It is imperative to eliminate discriminatory policies and practices in economic relations and to strengthen and expand on the basis of equality and mutual benefit exchanges and cooperation in the economic, trade, scientific, technological fields with a view to promoting common development and prosperity.[37]

With respect to political aspects of the partnership, Beijing supported Moscow's early opposition to the eastward expansion of the North Atlantic Treaty Organization (NATO). The April 1997 statement said:

> Both sides stand for the establishment of a new and universally applicable security concept, believing that the "Cold War mentality" must be abandoned and bloc politics opposed.
>
> The differences or disputes between states must be settled through peaceful means without resorting to the use or threat of force. Dialogue and consultation should be pursued to promote mutual understanding and build confidence, and peace and security should be sought through coordination and cooperation at bilateral or multilateral levels. . . .[38]

Returning the political favor, Moscow offered its confirmation that both Tibet and Taiwan are inseparable parts of China. Russian Defense Minister Rodionov reportedly went so far in an April 1997 speech in Beijing at the Academy of Military Science (AMS) as to express readiness to support China in an armed conflict on the Korean Peninsula. He blamed the potential for conflict there on alliance arrangements and said, "Russia will not be able to remain aloof."[39]

Maligning Alliances. Amidst all this blatant rhetorical bashing of Americans, one detects a good measure of smug passion for this aspect of the collaboration. Moreover, there is in all this a campaign to discredit alliances, especially alliances involving the United States, as alluded to by Rodionov in his speech at the PLA's AMS. The 1997 Sino-Russian joint statement contains these words:

> It constitutes an important practice toward the establishment of a new international order for the two countries . . . to forge a partnership that is characterized by good neighborliness and friendship, equality and trust, mutually beneficial cooperation and common development, in strict compliance with the principles of international law and formulation of a new type of long-term state-to-state relationship not directed against any third country.[40]

The Roots of Partnership. China has cultivated in Russia an excellent partner for the future: partly Asian, until recently communist, residually authoritarian, presently nonthreatening, and ready to criticize and even challenge

Washington. The question is whether this marriage is one of convenience or whether there are qualities in the relationship that will endure into the next century. Already, the amount of attention given by Beijing and Moscow to touting the partnership seems to have waned significantly.

The Role of Arms and Technology Transfers. There is, however, one area of unquestioned substance and apparent durability in Sino-Russian relations: arms sales and military technology transfer, which pre-dates the formation of the partnership. Three months before the partnership was announced, Russian Deputy Foreign Minister Aleksandr Panov said that connections with the PLA and cooperation on armaments manufacture "are being developed and will be developed." He noted the importance of China as a market for the deteriorating Russian arms industry. Russia's goal under the 5-year military cooperation agreement it signed with China in 1993, Panov said, was to promote the sale of Russian military equipment without upsetting the military balance in the region.[41]

Taking a jab at Washington, the Russian minister said, "We do not see anybody objecting to such cooperation between Russia and China or fearing it," noting pointedly that "it was deemed normal for Taiwan to get hundreds of aircraft." Actually, the initial Su-27 deliveries occurred before the decisions by Washington and Paris to sell Taiwan F-16s and *Mirage* 2000-5s. Panov asserted that Washington had been consulted and would not be concerned if the scope of the cooperation was not great and remained within "definite limits."[42] Washington acknowledged the conversation but said that U.S. officials were informed, rather than consulted, about the sale of additional Russian Su-27 fighter aircraft to China. An unnamed State Department representative said, "[Panov] neither sought nor did we convey to him any approval."[43]

Although arms sales and military technology transfer seem clearly to be the most active and conspicuous aspect of the strategic partnership, problems remain in that area.

Since the mid-1990s, Moscow has pressed Beijing hard for payment in hard currency rather than largely in barter—as had been the case prior to about 1994. Reportedly, in 1994 Beijing and Moscow signed an agreement to transition to payments in hard currency, but the degree of success of that arrangement is not yet clear to outsiders. Price, form of payment, and financing methods between the two countries remain troublesome.

In March 1998, unofficial but well-connected sources believed that contract arrangements had not yet been concluded for the licensed production in China of 200 Su-27 fighter aircraft, despite reports concerning provisions for assembly in Northeast China.[44] Thus, 2 years after the licensing arrangement had been revealed and a total of more than 6 years since Beijing had begun pressing Moscow to allow Su-27s to be assembled in China, payment methods were still under discussion. A very reliable Chinese official, with whom this author spoke, said that negotiations on payment and financing of the *Sovremenny* destroyers were still in progress. That was well over a year from the time that the deal was made public. The PLAN also wants more than the four *Kilo*-class diesel submarines that China has purchased. It needs to buy more comprehensive training from the Russian Navy for the crews of the delivered submarines. However, the PLAN's hopes for more submarines and more extensive training have foundered because of the refusal of the Chinese government to provide the needed hard currency. Looking across the board at arms transfers, it is pertinent that only a fraction of the innumerable expensive items mentioned by news reports and by observers in the West has actually been delivered from Russia to China. There are numerous explanations, but prominent among them is the inability or unwillingness of Beijing to pay for this equipment and technology in ways acceptable to Moscow.

Russia's deepening financial crisis is an additional complicating factor. China, in coming years, will be no less inclined to seek favorable terms, but Russian officials are not likely to become any more generous, and they may well make greater demands for payments in hard currency and for "normal" financing terms. On the other hand, Russian arms industries will likely become more desperate for markets abroad. Russian research scientists, technicians, and others with specialized knowledge of value to the PLA and China's defense industries will be more inclined to accept paying work in China, temporarily or permanently. Regional neighbors and others, including the United States, will have heightened concerns; however, because Moscow and Beijing are now more linked to their neighbors, both will take those neighbors' concerns into account in decisions about arms sales and technology transfers.

All these factors will introduce strains into the Sino-Russian military cooperative arrangements. In light of these factors, one cannot help but wonder how Beijing views the military supply relationship. Does Russia appear reliable in the eyes of the PLA leadership as a supplier of technology, training, and weapons? The PLA has sound grounds for at least some measure of concern. It was badly burned by the dissolution of the arms and technology transfer relationship with the Soviets around 1960. The PLA was emphatically reminded of that peril again in 1989 by the imposition of sanctions by the United States after its Tiananmen Square intervention—rupturing a budding military supply and technology transfer relationship of great value to the PLA. From a broader perspective, it simply cannot be assumed that the flow of arms from Russia to China will remain a major feature of their bilateral relationship. It is highly likely, but hardly assured.

Other Ties That Bind. Some less conspicuous aspects of the strategic partnership appear to be quite solid. Long-standing border disputes have been resolved through multilateral agreements. Many of the disputes over specific border areas were extremely difficult to resolve with considerable strong feelings on all sides, especially between the Russians and the Chinese. On one occasion, President Yeltsin, just before a visit to Beijing, had to intervene angrily to squelch objections by Yevgeny Nazdratenko,[45] governor of the far eastern Primorsky region. Nevertheless, both capitals had the will to resolve the contentious border problems. There have been regular biannual meetings of a high-level defense commission. By September 1996, there had been 20 rounds of talks on reduction of military forces in border areas, with successful results. The first secure telecommunications hotline between Beijing and a foreign capital was established with Moscow in May 1998. These seem to add up to a significant bank of goodwill that can be drawn on in the future.

What does all this portend for security relations in the 21st century between the world's largest nation and the world's most populous nation? Regardless of whether their strategic partnership truly takes on the mantle of a "universal security concept that would promote world peace," as Xinhua termed it last year, the most pertinent aspect is what this partnership means for Sino-Russian bilateral relations and the effects that has on regional security. In the early 1990s, one could not go very long in discussion with Chinese security specialists without hearing about the potential threat from a reawakening Russian bear. Now, in place of fears of Russian unpredictability, much is heard about equality and trust in the relationship. Admittedly, the tone and frequency of such pronouncements give reason to wonder whether this is whistling in the dark. Does Beijing truly see Moscow as a regional security partner in Asia? Or is Russia perceived as seeking to protect from the Chinese hordes its troubled expanses of Siberia and the Russian Far East? Or is Moscow simply a convenient partner used by Beijing to challenge Washington and its alliances at a time in history when China's other neighbors are not inclined to do so? There are no ready answers to these questions, but this is one of those situations where knowing the questions is of considerable value.

Eastward to Japan: Squinting into the Rising Sun.

The Reciprocal Context. Despite a quarter century of normalized relations, the security intercourse between China and Japan remains complex and uncertain. Each fears the economic and military rise of the other, yet does not wish the other to falter or fail. Before trying to piece together the puzzle from the Chinese perspective, it is helpful first to recollect the security context in which Japan contemplates China. There are, of course, all the very well-known major concerns including military modernization, to be covered later, but there are also other concerns and irritants that privately trouble Japanese analysts.

A Cataclysmic China? Some Japanese fear that China, by virtue of its size and relative backwardness, could become an Asian nightmare in ways beyond the current anxiety about China's devaluing its currency and thereby exacerbating the Asian financial crisis. A fractured China rocked by social and political disorder would have major repercussions for Japan and others in the region. China's huge population, under conditions of domestic chaos or ferment, could boil over its borders and encroach upon its neighbors, even reaching Japan. If its scattering population did not engulf neighboring countries, then its spreading uncontrolled pollutants, corruption, and other contagion might. In another scenario, a swelling China might become the scourge of Asia as it encounters some desperate agricultural or energy crisis. It is very difficult to determine how many Japanese still seriously harbor such concern about the consequences of an overpopulated and underdeveloped China, but the sentiment lingers.

The Chinese Attitude. Whatever the nature of other latent feelings, the Chinese do unabashedly hark back to World War II with a firm dislike and distrust for Japan. These feelings have apparently lessened little, if any, even in the generations born after 1945. The Chinese feelings about the Japanese have been maintained through continued reference to the horrific events from 1931 to 1945 and by Japanese reticence over the decades to acknowledge full culpability. When Americans witness demonstrations of this profound animosity, there is the temptation to consider the strong statements from China as displays exaggerated by emotions or possibly even staged to make some point. One might, for example, attribute the frequent voicing of hateful anti-Japanese rhetoric to an attempt to disparage the close American links with Japan (and the relationship of that to the Taiwan issue), suggesting that Washington is being duped by the cunning Japanese. However, the depth of feeling displayed by many otherwise measured Chinese scholars, officials, and military officers seems to contradict that possibility. Chinese antagonistic attitudes toward the Japanese seem to be deeply rooted, passed from generation to generation, and certain to remain a persistent feature of the bilateral relationship well into the next century.

These strong feelings do not keep China from accepting Japanese investment, financial aid, and loans of various sorts, but this investment has not erased Chinese dislike and distrust. In many cases, the Japanese commercial and financial presence is accepted grudgingly or even with loathing. Some Chinese resentfully call it "economic imperialism." Chinese do business with the Japanese because they feel they have no choice. The billions of Japanese yen lavished on China are not buying Chinese forgiveness for past transgressions.

Mutual Military Concerns. Tokyo watches carefully the direction that Beijing takes in modernization of the PLA. There is general concern about incipient Chinese aspirations to regional hegemony. China's potential role with respect to the Korean Peninsula is an abiding concern. Enhancements to the PLAN and the Strategic Rocket Force are specifically troublesome and viewed as potentially threatening or challenging by Japan. The Chinese, however, turn this issue on its head and pose the question: How can Japan justify fear of some future specter of Chinese military power? Japan, they remind, is the demonstrated colonizer and aggressor of Asia and could succumb to the temptation once more. China, Beijing argues, is neither expansionist nor threatening and has no reason to become so. Nevertheless, Chinese concerns about potential resurgence of Japanese militarism are mirrored by Japanese concerns about Chinese development of a power-projection capability.

Like the persistent Chinese enmity for Japan, the Chinese nourish the conviction that Japan is truly a potential military threat to its Asian neighbors. Even on decorous occasions, pointed reminders can be expected. In 1996, when then Japanese Prime Minister Ryutaro Hashimoto was taking office, the People's Republic of China (PRC) Foreign Ministry spokesman offered congratulations but quickly added that Japanese wartime actions must not be glossed over. The spokesman said, "Mr. Hashimoto ... is an old friend with whom we have had contact for many years." But noting Hashimoto's reputation for nationalist leanings, he remarked, "We hope Japanese politicians can have real foresight and sagacity," and that Japanese politicians should "lead the Japanese people to treat history correctly, learn the lessons that should be learned, and continue to walk the path of peaceful development."[46]

A good measure of China's penetrating gaze toward Japan consequently dwells on the constraints on, and actions of, the Japanese Self-Defense Force (JSDF). There are no stronger advocates than the Chinese for strict Japanese compliance with Article 9 of its national constitution, the article that prohibits both Japanese participation in wars and the establishment of armed forces. Of course, Beijing would not like to see that article permissively revised, as some have suggested might occur. Beijing sounds the alarm each time it sees the roles of the JSDF apparently expanded to any extent whatsoever. The dispatch of JSDF forces for peace operations in Cambodia and Mozambique and the deployment of Maritime Self-Defense Force (MSDF) minesweeping ships to the Persian Gulf gave rise to great concern. With respect to the

Cambodia and Mozambique operations, Japan took pains to have its troops transported part way on Russian Air Force transport aircraft. Nevertheless, these minor troop movements outside of Japan were very unsettling for Beijing.[47]

Japanese Pacifism Doubted. Most Chinese do not believe that post-World War II pacifism is deeply ingrained among Japan's citizenry. Many are convinced that the often-mentioned social and constitutional constraints on Japan's building a full-fledged set of armed forces might be quickly overwhelmed or eliminated by militarists, who, the Chinese would stress, already show their true jingoistic colors in such adventures as the recurrent spats over the Senkaku Islands (Diaoyutai in Chinese).[48] There are, however, diverse views in China about the seriousness of the threat of resurgent Japanese militarism. Some consider it unrealistic that any Japanese government could override international and domestic forces and restraints and develop the political will, the military forces, and the defense industrial base necessary for a military that would seriously threaten a steadily strengthening China.

New Defense Guidelines—and Unintended Consequences? Others analyze the prospects for a remilitarized Japan from a different perspective. They fear the unintentional effect on Japanese militarism of the recent tinkering with the U.S.-Japan security arrangements. These Chinese strategists consider that the primary concern China should have about this enhanced U.S.-Japanese security cooperation is the potential it fosters for more capable Japanese forces with expanded roles—rather than a more direct concern about Japanese support of U.S. forces in a conflict involving China. There have been intense exchanges since 1996 among China, Japan, and the United States as new defense guidelines were being considered for the U.S.-Japanese security alliance. As part of this debate, Liu Jiangyong, the director of Northeast Asian Studies at the Chinese Institute of Contemporary International Relations, said in 1997 that

U.S. pressure for Japan to shoulder more responsibility could lead to Japan's bursting its constitutional shackles and developing essentially unrestrained military strength. He suggested that expanded guidelines for security cooperation would serve as justification for the expansion of Japan's military strength in Asia and asserted such a move created more uncertainty concerning regional security.[49]

The Ineluctable Taiwan Factor. There is, of course, a much more obvious aspect of Chinese concern about the first revision since 1978 of the so-called defense guidelines for the U.S.-Japanese security alliance: the issue of the applicability of the treaty to a conflict in the Taiwan Strait. This process of revising the guidelines began with the reaffirmation of the alliance by President Clinton and Prime Minister Hashimoto in April of 1996,[50] the month following China's second round of launching ballistic missiles to intimidate Taiwan after President Lee Teng-hui visited the United States. Although the timing of the U.S.-Japanese declaration on alliance affirmation was largely coincidental and despite visits by U.S. officials to Beijing in advance to explain the guidelines, the impact on Beijing was undiluted. The Clinton-Hashimoto meeting followed several difficult years in U.S.-Japanese trade relations and the eruption of significant concerns in Okinawa about the presence of U.S. forces there. Beijing might have hoped, under these circumstances, for tepid results from a U.S.-Japanese summit at that time. Instead, the meeting provided renewed momentum for ideas dating back to 1994 about changes and clarifications that might be appropriate for the defense guidelines.[51] The Chinese reaction was prompt and pointed, the first serious concern expressed about the U.S.-Japanese alliance since the end of the Cold War. The day after the Clinton-Hashimoto reaffirmation statement, PRC Foreign Ministry spokesman Shen Guofang said:

> The Japan-U.S. treaty on the guarantee of security is a bilateral arrangement left over from history. And such an

arrangement should not go beyond its bilateral dimension, otherwise it would complicate the situation in the region.[52]

China then had a year and a half to chafe and protest as the revised guidelines were discussed, drafted, and finally presented in September 1997. As mentioned, there were concerns expressed by the Chinese about the revised guidelines providing license for the JSDF to become a threatening military force. However, the most intense exchanges concerned the geographic scope of the security arrangements. The United States said that there had been no change and that the alliance was not aimed at any country. The Japanese prime minister and a senior spokesman created consternation in Beijing by suggesting that the alliance could be considered applicable not only to the Taiwan Strait and vicinity, but also all the way to the South China Sea.[53] During a visit to China, Prime Minister Hashimoto masterfully employed ambiguity on this issue. He assured then-Chinese Prime Minister Li Peng that Japan would continue to be constrained by its constitution, that it would be transparent about revisions to the security pact with the United States, and that the alliance was not aimed at specific countries but rather at threatening situations.[54] Hashimoto told Li that the review underway of U.S.-Japanese military arrangements was not based on geography but on "the nature of the situation."[55] He dismissed questions about Taiwan as "totally hypothetical."[56]

The Japanese leader admitted at the end of the visit that he had failed to dispel Chinese concerns about the alliance and Taiwan.[57] Nevertheless, the Chinese leaders, interestingly, did not press the matter inordinately, choosing not to create a rift in the relationship.[58] Maybe it is, as some analysts suggest, that China expects Japanese support of U.S. forces in a Taiwan intervention action. After all, in March 1996, the U.S. battlegroups sent to the Taiwan Strait were, in part, based in Japan. Many Chinese leaders also expect that the support might extend to the use of the Japanese MSDF in some role, large or small. Depending on the interpretation one prefers, Hashimoto had either made it clearer that Japan would act in concert with the United States over Taiwan or added another little piece of strategic ambiguity for Li Peng and Jiang Zemin to contemplate as the Japanese-U.S. security alliance nears its 40th anniversary and moves into the 21st century.

Alliance Bashing. The day after President Clinton and Prime Minister Hashimoto issued the "Japan-U.S. Joint Declaration on Security—Alliance for the 21st Century" in Tokyo in April 1996,[59] Clinton presented his view of the future in the first speech to the Japanese Parliament by a U.S. President since the one given by Ronald Reagan in 1983:

> As the world's two largest economies, and two of its strongest democracies, Japan and the United States must forge an alliance for the 21st century.[60]

Beijing was listening, as would be expected. However, Chinese leaders must have anticipated this message. On precisely that day, April 18, 1996, Beijing, preparing for the visit of Russian President Boris Yeltsin, announced its new form of model bilateral relationship meant to supersede alliances. Foreign Ministry spokesman Shen Guofang said:

> We have established a new type of good neighborly relations between China and Russia which are not based on confrontation or alliance. [The relationship would] serve the interests of the people of the two countries and contribute at the same time to peace and stability in the region.[61]

China marshaled its assault on alliances and by a year later had developed a broader attack. In the spring of 1997, Zhao Jieqi, research fellow and former deputy director of the Japanese Studies Institute of the Chinese Academy of Social Sciences (CASS), said:

> The short-term goal of the [strengthened U.S.-Japan and U.S.-Australia] alliances is to deal with the "instability" in the Taiwan Strait, the South China Sea, and on the Korean

Peninsula. The long-term goal is to deal with the imaginary "troubles" made by an economically and militarily stronger China.[62]

Liu Jiangyong, director of the Department of Northeast Asian Studies of the China Institute of Contemporary International Relations (CICIR), amplified the concept:

> The structure [of U.S. alliances] is said to aim to maintain the peace of this region. But it sowed seeds of friction and instability.... It is sure to create tension among Asian countries.[63]

What Beijing Wants Now and What It Dreams Of for the Future. China, no doubt, is unhappy as a general matter with U.S. alliances in Asia and enamored of its touted new concept of security without confrontation and absent alliances. Nevertheless, a distinction should be made between Chinese aspirations and efforts to achieve a distant goal on the one hand and the more pressing combination of realistic expectations and short-term concerns on the other. Does China really want Japan "loosed on Asia," as those who fear Japan the most might put it? And there are more pointed questions that an increasingly realistic and worldly Chinese leadership must have begun to ponder: Is an American-Japanese-South Korean-Australian *entente*, or some permutation thereof, against China realistic under any scenario short of the most abominable actions by China against its neighbors? Do not Chinese leaders understand, even if they cannot say so, that none of these alliances would act against China unless Beijing essentially forced them to do so? Furthermore, there have been private reports that the current Chinese leadership gives at least some credence to the assertion that the U.S. military presence in the region has been beneficial, if not instrumental, both to regional stability and economic development, including that of China.

Americans in Asia Forever? Beijing is not pressing Washington to beat a hasty retreat from East Asia. Looking at the long term, Beijing is less tolerant of a seemingly interminable U.S. military presence, but it expects that U.S. forces would be reduced or withdrawn deliberately, so as not to precipitate a crisis or foster regional instability—such as a dramatic increase in Japanese military capability or confrontation on the Korean Peninsula. Chinese leaders recognize that achieving severe reductions or complete withdrawal of U.S. forces, while avoiding these pitfalls, would be a tricky proposition. This is reflected in the manner in which Beijing in 1996 and 1997 simultaneously handled its proposal (in concert with Moscow) that new security relations should eschew alliances and yet did not call for the dismantlement of the U.S.-Japanese alliance. Beijing wishes to milk alliances for their merit for Chinese interests in the short term but work deliberately toward a time when China, not the United States, is seen as the pillar of East Asian security. That vision of the 21st century, as Beijing sees it, does not feature security alliances.

Some in China who have confidence in China's ability to become a relatively stronger economic and military power in Asia think it might be preferable in the next century to have Japanese forces alone to confront in the region, rather than a combined and well-coordinated U.S. and Japanese force. "Who's afraid of the big, bad Japanese?" these more optimistic analysts seem to say. The view is also offered that the U.S. presence in Japan will increasingly be seen by all parties, including the American public and Congress, as an anachronism. Moreover, some suggest, Japan will subordinate itself to the United States for only so long. In other words, China need only be patient, and the Americans will either leave of their own volition, be asked to leave, or be ejected. These offerings might be seen as efforts by some Chinese strategists to cover all the bases, end up on the "right side of history," or just as wishful thinking about an Asia for Asians, with commensurate elevation of Beijing's position; but they offer insights into the Chinese view of the future.

China's Future Place in Asian Security. The matter to be considered for the future is that China wants what it perceives as its rightful place in the framework of Northeast Asian security. That central place for China in the architecture is something Beijing can seemingly never have as long as the U.S.-Japanese alliance retains its status as the keystone of regional security; and there is the implication that one of the roles of the alliance is to keep China in line—or knock it back in line if it strays. China wants its enhanced status in the region, its improved international posture, and its potential for far greater power to be accepted and to be prime considerations with respect to regional security in the 21st century. Put another way, the obverse of alliance bashing in this context is China "dignification."

The Ballistic Missile–Theater Ballistic Missile Defense Imbroglio. There is a far cruder, but very specific, way in which China is attempting to ensure its relevance in regional security. The PLA excels in very few warfare areas, but one of them is its arsenal of short- and medium-range ballistic missiles—primarily (but not necessarily) tipped with conventional warheads. By some definitions, this is one of the asymmetric means that China can bring to bear to overcome U.S. and Japanese technological advantages. Chinese leaders expect that these missiles would have a deterrent effect on any Japanese proclivity to get involved with the United States in a Taiwan intervention. Beijing does not want Tokyo (and certainly not Taipei!) to attain the capability to neutralize the threat of that force—either alone or in concert with the United States. China has offered almost every conceivable argument against the development and deployment of theater ballistic missile defense (TBMD). Beijing is also allegedly working in more sophisticated ways behind the scenes to undermine support of the program with the Japanese public, legislature, and government to reinforce existing opposition.[64] Japanese Defense Agency (JDA) Director General Kyuma said in early 1997 to a committee of the Diet: "We won't be able to go ahead with the program without taking into account the costs, the benefits and the accuracy [of the missile system]."

Other Japanese officials said their participation in a regional missile defense system could be interpreted by nations such as China as upsetting the regional military balance of power.[65] Beijing does not wish to enter into a confrontation wherein it would launch missiles against Japan or U.S. bases in Japan, with all that might imply for the future of China and coveted Chinese economic growth, but it wants the concern about that threat to remain undiminished in the coming years. Beijing wants Tokyo, Washington, and Taipei to worry.

One of the earlier Chinese lines of reasoning against TBMD, used sparingly recently, has been called the "shield and sword" argument: Japan, behind the shield of ballistic missile defense, could develop in a very short time the sword of nuclear weapons and the missiles to deliver them. Although the shield and sword argument may be heard less now, Beijing is no less determined than in the past to preclude Japanese development of nuclear weapons. China calls attention to Japan's technological prowess in the nuclear field and notes that its more than 50 nuclear power plants, producing over a third of the country's electrical power, are also a supplier of plutonium that can be used in weapons. Japan has rejected suggestions that it reconsider its ambitious nuclear energy program, heightening Beijing's anxiety. The issues of the potential deployment of theater missile defense and the development of nuclear weapons will remain crucial, and possibly explosive, matters in China's perspective of its security relationship with Japan and the bearing that relationship has on regional security in the coming years.

Military Relations. Tokyo has recently made overtures to Beijing for better military-to-military relations between the two former adversaries. There have been noteworthy exchanges in recent years, including the April 1997 visit to Japan of Chinese Defense Minister General Chi Haotian, the first such visit in 13 years. Chi proposed that the director general of the Japanese Defense Agency visit China. Before that could occur, Prime Minister Hashimoto went to China in September 1997 to mark 25 years of normalized bilateral relations and attempt to ease Chinese concerns about the revised U.S.-Japanese defense guidelines that were about to be presented. While there, he complained that the military contacts between Japan and China were "insufficient" compared to the burgeoning economic, political, and cultural ties. It seems his concern was listened to politely.[66]

When JDA Director General Kyuma, acting on Minister of Defense Chi's earlier invitation, went to China in May 1998, his visit to PLAN facilities there was made memorable by the simultaneous sailing of a Chinese marine research ship into waters off the Senkaku Islands claimed by Japan as well as by China. The Chinese ship defied warnings by the Japanese coast guard.[67] It was not clear whether this untimely rekindling of the Senkakus spat was coincidental, but personal conversations by the author with Japanese defense specialists clearly conveyed the impression that Japan's overtures for military-to-military contacts were being rebuffed. When the matter was raised by the author with a knowledgeable PLA officer specializing in politico-military affairs, the officer said unequivocally that the PLA does not want to proceed with such contacts. He explained that there were questions about how much China might gain from such contacts, but the more important reason, according to this officer, was that hatred of the Japanese military persisted to such a degree in China that most PLA officers did not want to participate in such discussions. There was ample reason for Japan to be mistrusted—a lesson that had apparently been wasted on Americans, he added, warming to his subject.

Trilateral Track II Talks. China has rejected proposals for official trilateral (PRC, United States, Japan) security talks based, in part, on insurmountable dislike and distrust of the Japanese. No doubt, Beijing was also loath to face two treaty allies. However, Beijing did accept a proposal early in 1998 for Track II talks among civilian scholars. The first session was held in the summer of 1998. Chinese participants did not use the meeting as a forum to attack the Japanese, and there were no PLA officers present.

Shaping Future Sino-Japanese Security Relations. Japan will almost certainly begin the next century worrying about and watching a growing Chinese presence increasingly dominating the western horizon. China will squint back, continuing to covet the best that the relationship with wealthy Japan can bring to China and fearing the worst that Japan might bring about. What is now competition between Asia's richest and largest countries will shift toward competition between two rich (or at least developed) countries, one very large and the other not so large. That change in China's status may assuage to some degree the animosity and envy that China harbors for a country it feels is morally undeserving of good fortune.

A continued exchange of visits of senior officials may make China more tolerant of Japanese actions that it currently considers unacceptable, such as visits by cabinet officials each year to the Yakusuni shrine where Japan's war criminals are honored. The Japanese foreign minister was in China in August 1998, a visit surprisingly free of rancor. Ostensibly, the worst floods in half a century in China recently caused the indefinite postponement of the scheduled September 1998 visit of Chinese President Jiang Zemin to Japan. (Suspiciously, the postponement was announced just after Tokyo had rebuffed a reported Chinese request to echo the "three no's policy" concerning Taiwan that President Clinton elected to state publicly near the end of his June-July 1998 visit to China.)[68] According to the Japanese foreign ministry, that would have been the very first visit to Japan of a Chinese president![69] There have been and will be other visits of varying import, such as the little-noticed meeting of the leaders of the Chinese and Japanese Communist Parties in April 1998, the first meeting in 32 years after party ties were broken during the Chinese Cultural Revolution. If both countries weather the ongoing Asian financial crisis without suffering economic devastation, trade and investment will continue to bond the two countries and on balance be a positive factor in the security relationship. In all these aspects, the overall bilateral relationship is on a generally upward trajectory, even if the slope is hardly steep.

The picture is far less certain with respect to military-to-military relations. Intransigence by the PLA might wane with future generations of PLA senior officers who will be younger, better educated, more worldly, and more professional officers. They may conclude that sustaining the intense hatred for Japan and its armed forces does not serve China's interests. For now, however, the PLA tradition of hating the Japanese seems to be surviving. This emotional feature of the relationship blocks communication and consequently may be retarding developments that might otherwise have taken place by this time.

The Taiwan Fulcrum. Two other factors examined earlier matter greatly: (1) Chinese concerns that Japan will build a powerful military, and (2) what Japan would do if China used military force against Taiwan. The former is likely to simmer through the early decades of the next century, but the latter may boil over at any time and reduce East Asia to a battleground. There is ample reason to be relatively sanguine about keeping the lid on Japanese military expansion. It could be very much harder to keep the lid on a Taiwan crisis if the cross-strait situation really becomes roiled. No expenditure or exercise of prudence, sagacity, caution, and preparedness are excessive to avoid this outcome. No decisions with respect to U.S.-Japanese security cooperation, TBMD, or U.S. military commitment in the region can ignore the Taiwan issue. It boils down to this: currently the only truly critical factor in China's security relationship with Japan is Taiwan, and the United States is right in the middle. With resolution of the "Taiwan problem," as it is often referred to on the Chinese mainland, the hue of security relations between China and Japan will shift from dark and ominous tones to a much warmer glow, even if hardly rosy. Then the more fundamental problem will appear in even more vivid hues. As long as China remains the outsider in the framework of East Asian security, it will be a troublemaker, seeking what it sees as its rightful place as a major part of the architecture.

Korea: Seeing Double and Enjoying the View.[70]

Chinese leaders are cautious about the process of change on the Korean Peninsula and the implications of that impending change for China. Despite outward composure, Beijing is increasingly concerned by the developments in North Korea, a concern undoubtedly intensified by the history of disruptions to China's security and stability that have originated in Korea. Chinese leaders are troubled that Pyongyang remains deaf to its suggestions for reform and more rational conduct—advice given with Asian gentility in the hope that it can be accepted more readily than if delivered with Western bluntness. However, most Chinese who follow the issue do not believe that collapse of North Korea is imminent or that reunification or reconciliation is inevitable. Some accuse the South Koreans and Americans who forecast an early demise of North Korea of engaging in wishful thinking. Although many observers believe China favors the indefinite division of Korea, it is not clear that Beijing has made an unequivocal choice of a preferred outcome of a change in status on the peninsula. However, Beijing objects strenuously to being publicly lumped into a box with Japan and seen as preferring permanent division of the peninsula in order to keep Korea weak and nonthreatening. Instead, Beijing suggests that the focus should be on preserving stability, not effecting change, and that a slow, deliberate course to some form of reunification in the distant future, possibly 20 to 50 years from now, would be reasonable.[71]

Delicately Balanced Dual Relations. Beijing has been particularly attentive to, and ingenious in, its relationships with its two near neighbors, the Democratic People's Republic of Korea (DPRK) and the Republic of Korea (ROK).

China has skillfully contrived a way to preserve good relations with its fellow communist (more fashionably referred to as *socialist*) state and yet proceed outright to establish dynamic economic and political relations with the South. There are many complexities, inequalities, and sensitivities to be dealt with carefully in this peculiar pair of relationships between such dissimilar countries, and Beijing must devote considerable attention to the task. Possibly the only aspect of the relationships that smacks of unity of view is the intense degree of dislike for Japan shared by all three. In this decade, first with burgeoning trade relations and then diplomatic relations in 1992, China's preference with respect to the two Koreas has undeniably shifted to place South Korea foremost. As might be expected, Beijing's careful choice of Seoul as the favored partner was done primarily for economic reasons. Somehow, however, China's leaders have met the extraordinary challenge and kept things reasonably cozy with North Korea while snuggling up to the South.

Nuclear Weapons in Korea—and the Japan Link. Chinese officials say that China wants a stable, nonnuclear Korean Peninsula. Beijing has expressed a preference for a Korean Peninsula nuclear-free zone. It wants a peninsula void of weapons of mass destruction (WMD) and the means to deliver them. Further, Beijing does not want suspicions about Korea to serve as an incentive or excuse for Japan to develop its own nuclear weapons, which would foster Beijing's abiding fear, the resurgence of military capability in Japan.

Reunification: Whether, When, and How. By reason of geographic proximity and political, social, and economic vulnerability to the potential repercussions, China has a vested interest in the outcome of change on the peninsula. Among the reasons Beijing is in no hurry for reunification or reconciliation is the recognition that precipitating a change between the Koreas has high risk, both for the Koreas and for China. Beijing does not want circumstances to arise in the Koreas that ultimately will threaten the Chinese

Communist Party. Questions of reunification and its timing are often finessed when raised with Chinese officials, but it is clear that China seeks a Korea that leans more toward China than toward the United States or Japan. Both Beijing and Pyongyang consider a lopsided reunification process done on Seoul's terms unappealing. Unification is a desirable goal, Chinese officials say, but left unsaid is that for now a North Korea that is troublesome and distracting to Washington is not altogether a bad thing for China. Beijing, naturally, wishes to avoid social and political tumult just across the Yalu and Tumen Rivers. It also does not want Seoul's attention and South Korea's resources drawn from China and redirected to resolving the problem of a collapsed, or maybe just helpless and hopeless, North Korea. Peace and stability on the Korean Peninsula are described as essential to China's continued economic growth.[72]

Military vs. Economic Considerations. Without saying so, China recognizes that the real potential for trouble on the Peninsula lies with Pyongyang, and that neither Washington nor Seoul is inclined to start a war. It has worked diligently to discourage foolhardy military adventures by North Korea and has retained at least the semblance of a security pact with Pyongyang. However, the primary focus of China's Korea policy has been on cultivating economic and other relations with the part of Korea that really matters to China: the prosperous and progressive South. This outlook has been blurred slightly as a consequence of the ROK's severe economic problems during the ongoing Asian economic crisis, but China can see that South Korea will come out of the crisis with its workforce, intellectual capital, infrastructure, and democratic methods largely intact. That is the aspect of the Korean Peninsula for which China now has affinity.

South Korean investment in and trade with Shandong Province, jutting out eastward to less than 250 miles from Seoul, and with China's economically needy northeastern provinces, adjacent to the Korean Peninsula, have provided considerable benefit where it was needed most.[73] By 1996, South Korea had invested $830 million in Shandong and $516 million in the rust belt of Northeast China. Two-way trade totaled almost $20 billion for 1996. As a consequence of this important investment and trade, China now has considerably greater anxiety over the full recovery of its important economic ties with South Korea than it does about the presence of American troops in the ROK or even the future presence of U.S. forces there. Military matters concerning the South are simply not on the front burner for China.

With respect to North Korea, China views that security relationship largely in economic terms as well. Ties between the PLA and the North Korean People's Army (KPA) persist but are neither close nor flourishing. Beijing's very long-term vision for North Korea, separate or unified, is that of an economic partner with China's neighboring areas. The Chinese envision mutually beneficial trade and investment relations with the North. Chinese interlocutors dismiss suggestions that preservation of another socialist state or having a buffer zone between China and U.S. forces in South Korea is of any consequence. They call these notions outdated remnants of "Cold War thinking." In other words, Chinese officials assert that China's approach to the matter of reunification is largely an economic issue. Consequently, the modalities of reunification or reconciliation, in Beijing's view, should be governed by their implications for the South Korean economy (in the near future) and the North Korean economy (in the quite distant future). Whether others see it as naïve or not, China dreams of a Korea where prosperity is contagious and readily spread to neighboring parts of China.

China's Actions in a North Korean Crisis. This attitude on the future of North Korea is reflected in Chinese assertions that Beijing will attempt to stay out of the fray in a political crisis or societal collapse in Pyongyang, and it expects the United States to do the same. The theory is that Chinese intervention would mean that Beijing would be mired in a mess without a visible end and burdened with Pyongyang's intractable political, economic, and social problems. Moreover, Beijing insists that its dictum concerning no foreign forces in another country applies to its own forces as well. Also at play is the fact that China wants its own reunification process with Taiwan to be free of outside interference. Setting a contrary precedent by "interfering" in North Korea would be strongly resisted. On the other hand, if Beijing sees imminent DPRK economic collapse, supposedly it will "pull out the stops" and attempt to help Pyongyang overcome the crisis by whatever means prove necessary.

Of course, these Chinese assertions, despite determined efforts to make the positions sound plausible, are suspect. Some observers doubt whether China would restrict the PLA to blocking the border in order to control refugees and keep military forces out of North Korea. Questions arise about China's likely response in the event of a fractured DRPK, if for instance a rump government in Pyongyang or a faction there asked for PLA support to bring order or to deter movement north by ROK forces. Doubts are even greater in a scenario where U.S. forces might move northward. Beijing surely does not want U.S. forces near its border. Surely if Washington should ask Beijing to exercise restraint in a Korean crisis, Beijing is virtually certain to ask much of Washington—probably with respect to Taiwan. It might seek stronger assurances concerning curbing arms transfers to Taipei and may demand a "fourth communiqué."[74] Despite these doubts, there is some solace to be taken from any assurances from Beijing about the reluctance to use the PLA as a means to try to solve problems in North Korea. There is merit in having Beijing repeat these assurances to international interlocutors.

There are also doubts about the asserted Chinese commitment to go to almost any lengths to avoid economic disaster in North Korea. Beijing has been all too ready essentially to buy as scrap or at bargain prices North Korea's dismantled industrial complex—loaded onto trucks and trains and carted north across the border. Further, Beijing has appeared quite reluctant to toss money down the black hole of the North Korean economy. Given its direct interests, China has appeared as rather miserly in the provision of emergency food aid, from time to time sending tens of thousands of tons of corn and small amounts of other grain when the needs were many times that. Other Chinese goods have been sold to North Korea when it might have been appropriate to provide these items free to its "socialist brethren." Often the prices have been concessionary, but equally often the demanded terms have been for cash transactions and not barter. As mentioned, Beijing has been disappointed and frustrated that Pyongyang has not instituted economic reforms. The alternative has been for China to continue patronizing trade subsidies and other aid that have kept North Korea alive but have not succeeded in correcting structural problems or contributed to a long-term solution. How hard China is really trying is an open question.

It also remains open to question how far China would really go to aid North Korea if Pyongyang were acting even less responsibly than at present and showed no inclination to change. The answer may well be that Beijing has not seriously confronted that question because most Chinese do not think the collapse of North Korea to be a likely scenario. They profess to believe that the North Koreans are highly resilient, possibly more capable of enduring hardship than even the Chinese themselves. To illustrate the point, the Chinese recall times of great difficulty in China, including the Great Leap Forward and the Cultural Revolution, that did not result in national collapse. This logic may be less compelling to many, but such convictions in China are probably strengthened with each successive year of severe hardship in North Korea that passes without the catastrophic results that many Westerners forecast. While China talks about saving the day if the North begins to go under, it largely looks to South Korea, Japan, and the United States to provide the major funding for such things as the fuel oil and light water reactors being provided under the October 1994 Agreed Framework. As the next century begins, China will continue to urge Washington to ease or eliminate restrictions on trade and investment and facilitate American business in the North. It will perpetuate the *status quo* by patiently continuing to provide moderate amounts of food aid and significant trade subsidies and to conduct "commercial transactions."

Learning to Like Multilateralism. In April 1996, Seoul and Washington proposed talks to include North Korea, South Korea, China, and the United States. Beijing was initially quite reticent about these Four-Party Talks, as they came to be known. Eventually, Chinese leaders urged a reluctant Pyongyang to accept the proposal and agreed to participate themselves. China's participation in the Four-Party Talks was another signal that Beijing has come to accept that its interests can be served by a multilateral approach. The prospects are now greatly increased that China will be a regular participant in talks of this nature.

Living With But Not Liking Alliances. As with the Japanese-U.S. security alliance, Beijing has elected not to challenge directly the South Korean-U.S. alliance. Instead, China maintains a balanced policy toward the Koreas. Utterances from Beijing emphasize its own concept for international security, without confrontation or alliances, that Beijing has established with Moscow. There are obligatory statements opposing foreign forces stationed in another country, but responsible Chinese officers say that Beijing will not oppose the continued presence of U.S. forces in Korea or the existence of the alliance, even after reunification, as long as that is the desire of the Korean government and people. In May 1998, a Chinese diplomat said forthrightly that Beijing was taking a more conciliatory position on U.S. forces. Beijing would not oppose their continued presence if they were welcomed by the host country and if their use were limited to only "bilateral matters."[75] Despite the Taiwan issue, China was conceding that a U.S. presence in Korea after unification was not anathema. Beijing's concern focuses on the *purpose* for the forces rather than whether they should be there.

In any event, Beijing has currently come to accept that the 37,000 U.S. troops in South Korea are tolerable. Beijing also seems to recognize that the American presence serves as a deterrent to imprudent action by the North and as a brake on actions by Seoul that might create instability or bring demands from Pyongyang that China act in its behalf. Chinese officials describe their treaty with Pyongyang as sufficiently ambiguous that Beijing can interpret the pact as it wishes. Further, Beijing seems to have made it clear that it will not come to North Korea's aid if Pyongyang initiates hostilities. Beijing frequently reminds Seoul that South Korean intervention in the North would likely exacerbate rather than resolve the problem.

Beijing's positions with respect to its treaty with Pyongyang and the presence of U.S. forces on the Korean Peninsula reflect some nuances of China's abhorrence of alliances. With respect to the pact with Pyongyang, the Chinese have essentially chosen to abrogate what might have been viewed under other circumstances as a firm commitment to come to the aid of North Korea in the event of hostilities. The Chinese did so because they (1) found Pyongyang to be an unreliable partner, (2) did not wish to have another government in a position to obligate China to enter into an armed conflict, and (3) did not want to have to cope with the complications inherent in alliance and coalition relations. In other words, China finds alliances to be encumbrances rather than advantages.

Beyond all that, China wants the freedom to condemn alliances on the basis that they tend to target some other country. In Asia, China feels that it has been an unspoken target of U.S. alliances, particularly in the post-Cold War environment. To the degree that Beijing can discredit and diminish the solidarity of alliances and appear to be taking a moral high road, the Chinese think they can diminish the threats they face in the region and enhance China's reputation as a responsible and forward-thinking member of the community of nations.

With respect to the South Korean-U.S. alliance, Beijing recognizes that strident objections to a continued U.S. presence on the peninsula would most likely be either ignored or counterproductive. Strong Chinese objections could arouse suspicions about why a purportedly peaceful China was protesting so vociferously. Further, China does not want to appear to be interfering in the internal affairs of another country by dictating to the South Korean people how they should arrange for their own security. In sum, China wants to distance itself from alliance entanglements, eliminate or neutralize alliances against China, and rid itself of the more subtle but troublesome complications that the existence of alliances in the region produce for it.

Prognosis. China expects to enter the next century with a divided Korea composed of a crippled North and an economically recovering South. It expects that the Chinese economy will continue to benefit from trade and investment from South Korea. Beijing does not expect North Korea to move militarily against the South because without the support of the PLA, an attack would be tantamount to suicide for both the North Korean state and the regime. By the time there is reconciliation or reunification, well into the future by Chinese calculations, Beijing strongly hopes that the security framework for the region will have been altered so that China will be able to see itself as an integral part of the Northeast Asian security architecture, not a target of alliances and no longer treated as a troublesome outsider. In that situation, the presence of U.S. forces in Korea and Japan will either be of little concern to China, or the forces will have been withdrawn because of domestic and political pressures in Japan, Korea, and the United States.

Taiwan Complications Intrude Again. As in so many other aspects of China's regional security situation in the coming years, the issue of Taiwan is inescapable. If the Taiwan issue remains unresolved, and especially if it remains volatile, Beijing will be less likely to consider U.S. forces and alliances in Asia a matter to be accommodated. Moreover, the PRC threat to Taiwan will be seen by other countries as a demonstration of Beijing's will to resort to force. This will provide a justification to keep capable U.S. forces in the region. While it is hard to justify the cost of the U.S. presence by a vague reference to preserving stability and reacting to unidentified future contingencies, a continuing PRC threat to Taiwan obviates the need to contrive some compelling new justification for U.S. forces to be in Asia, regardless of how valid the new reasoning might prove to be in the long run. The Taiwan problem, once more, serves as the spoiler for China's aspirations and as a major complicating factor in devising a new security architecture for the region, even when the issue seemed to be Korea.

Over the Boundary-Bothered South China Sea to ASEAN.

Beijing's motives with respect to the South China Sea may be questioned, but its increased attention to its southern periphery is clear. The most conspicuous example of that attention is China's presence and participation in ASEAN and the ASEAN Regional Forum (ARF) as a "dialogue partner."[76] Some accuse Beijing of participating in bad faith and argue that China does not intend to compromise on its disputes with ASEAN countries, especially with respect to sovereignty claims in the South China Sea. These voices also suggest that the PLAN is waiting over the horizon. In 1997, Carolina Hernandez, president of the Institute for Strategic and Development Studies (ISDS) in the Philippines, said, "You cannot discount the possibility that [China] will exercise the rights of a Middle Kingdom." She went on to refer to lingering doubts in ASEAN "about the possibly hegemonic ambitions of China . . ."[77] Discussions by the author with officials from ASEAN countries reveal concerns that China's aspirations for big-power status are fueled by its increasingly close relations and summit meetings with the United States. All the while, ASEAN interlocutors note, China is pushing for disbanding alliances and the reduction of the stabilizing U.S. influence. At the very least, there is no common view among ASEAN nations that China's role in the region will be favorable.

Mischief Reef: Part of the Pattern? Though striving to foster a reputation as a partner and good neighbor to the ASEAN nations, Beijing nonetheless built structures on Mischief Reef in the eastern part of the Spratly Islands near the Philippines. Following the February 1995 discovery of the Chinese intrusion on the islet claimed by both China and the Philippines, an international row ensued. Beijing asserted the structures there were to shelter fisherman and monitor weather conditions. Manila said they were to support PLAN operations. Chinese interlocutors have suggested that the construction was purely a military move and locally directed, i.e., that Beijing was not to blame. China has gone so far recently as to offer use of the facilities to Filipino fishermen.[78] After 3 1/2 years, in November 1998, Manila once more complained of Chinese activity there. Beijing responded with the same disingenious explanations about facilities for fishermen.

Since 1995, other minor spats that smack more of comic opera than serious conflict have ensued around a couple of islets and reefs. China has backed off each time, suggesting that local forces may act out of turn but that cooler heads in the central government will prevail. Meanwhile, over the years Beijing has offered to negotiate Spratly Islands issues multilaterally and proposed to put aside sovereignty issues and proceed with joint economic development in the area. Even so, the other claimants remained unconvinced of China's long-term intentions.

Renunciation of Force. To some observers, China's efforts appeared to be just more rhetoric from Beijing. However, at a December 1997 meeting in Kuala Lumpur (the first such meeting between just China and the ASEAN countries), then Chinese Foreign Minister Qian Qichen announced that *all* claimants had agreed to put aside regional differences and pursue joint development. Qian said:

> There is no tension in the South China Sea despite the realities of our differences born from our historical legacy. But through regional cooperation, we have agreed to put aside the issue of sovereign claims and pursue joint development.[79]

Malaysian Prime Minister Mahathir, who had earlier expressed reservations about the Chinese proposal, said: "Everybody agreed that any dispute should be settled through negotiations in a friendly manner without threat or use of force. So I think that is progress."[80] Disbelievers still abound, but Beijing is trying very hard to convince ASEAN and the outside world of its good intentions with respect to cooperative economic development in the South China Sea.

A New Approach by Beijing? One factor fueling the disbelief is concern about the ultimate resolution of the disputed claims. There is an ominous note in China's formulation that the disputes will be shelved while economic development proceeds, and Beijing has not made definitive moves to ease those concerns. Indeed, a March 1998 article by Professor Ji Guoxing of the authoritative Shanghai Institute of International Strategic Studies restated the basis for China's claims:

> China stands for the settlement of the disputes in the Spratlys in accordance with international law and the U.N. Convention of the Law of Sea. When ratifying the U.N. convention, China stated it would negotiate with its neighboring countries "for the delimitation of each other's maritime jurisdiction on the principle of equity in accordance with international law." Now that the countries concerned have a common basis and a unified criterion for the settlement, they could engage in friendly negotiations, taking the related stipulations in the Convention for an equitable, objective and workable formula of settlement. **In seeking an equitable solution to the disputes, all relevant factors such as historic title, island entitlements, continental shelf rights, proportionality, geomorphological features, and economic interests**

should be balanced in the delimitation. [Emphasis added.]⁸¹

As the fourth anniversary of the Mischief Reef incident approaches, China continues naval operations in the South China Sea and persists in consistent protests of perceived violations or disregard of its claimed sovereignty, conceivably to strengthen its claims under international law. However, China has not built structures on other reefs, set up new outposts or troop garrisons, or challenged the small garrisons of other claimants. China has not threatened to use force or refused to renounce the use of force in the South China Sea to protect its asserted sovereignty. Beijing's most outrageous recent actions have been to propose, in April 1998, the development of a tourist resort on Yongxing, the largest of the Paracel Islands (less than 150 miles southeast of Hainan), and to repair or rebuild the structures on Mischief Reef—after notifying Manila of its intention do so.⁸² The first action, involving Yongxing, evoked a sharp rebuke from Hanoi, which continues to claim the Paracels.⁸³ The PLA is not likely to relinquish easily its valuable foothold there, especially given the military airfield it built on Woody Island.

The more intriguing issue is whether, if challenged somewhere in the South China Sea, Beijing will adhere to its commitment to abjure the use of force. This test will be all the more meaningful because China, alone among the disputants, has the forces needed to carry out an island-grabbing action in the South China Sea or dislodge an occupying force. If China does not use force in such a situation, it will almost certainly reflect a decision by Beijing that China's best interests are served by pursuing solutions through other means or by avoiding confrontation. The trend may be in that direction. Over the last few years, China has pursued an agenda of broad cooperation with the ASEAN countries rather than winning isolated spats over islets by employing heavy-handed military means.

Evolving Perceptions of China. China continues to seek a pre-eminent role in Southeast Asia, as elsewhere in East Asia. Beijing, however, abhors having the term *hegemon* applied to it and strives to employ its size and influence in ways that accomplish the purpose but avoid the appellation. China's cooperative participation in the various ASEAN fora seems to have produced some results. Certainly ASEAN considers Beijing before it acts. In January 1996, Singapore's former Prime Minister Lee Kuan Yew opposed India's full membership in ASEAN on the grounds that China would "resent" the move by ASEAN.[84] The following month, Lee said if the United States and its stabilizing effect were gone in 20 years, "Asian leaders will take care not to antagonize China." Already by 1996 Beijing had ASEAN countries exercising caution and expressing concern for the effects on China of their actions. However, China's concerns were being taken into account by ASEAN largely because it was to be feared. The sense was primarily one of conciliation, hardly a partnership among equals.

In the following months, Beijing sought to mollify its ASEAN neighbors, agreeing to multilateral negotiation of Spratlys issues and cooperative measures concerning navigation, shipping, and communications in the South China Sea. Jusuf Wanandi, Chairman of the Center for Strategic and International Studies in Indonesia, said in mid-1997,

> [China] still has to learn how to behave [in the region]. But I don't think, in the longer term, China will be a bully at all. With her opening up and her integration into the society regionally and globally, she will become an important and a responsible partner.[85]

Optimism began to replace obligation as the theme in ASEAN attitudes toward China, although there remains considerable diversity among these nations with respect to their views of Beijing's intentions.

Other events in mid-1997 contributed to a change of tone in the relationship between Beijing and ASEAN. The

ASEAN leaders, to the chagrin and dismay of American officials and others in the international community, decided to promptly admit Myanmar (Burma) to ASEAN. China and Myanmar were, of course, very close, and Beijing drove home that point when in the same month it concluded a broad economic and trade agreement with Yangon (Rangoon)—very soon after U.S. economic sanctions had been imposed on the unelected government of Myanmar.[86] ASEAN took an approach that undoubtedly pleased China since Myanmar's internal affairs and pressure from Western dialogue partners did not stop membership. Carolina Hernandez, president of the Philippine ISDS, said, "We don't want to be told by Western powers on what to do. We feel we have earned a right to play an independent role in the region."[87] Through press reports, however, Beijing was reminded that ASEAN membership was seen as a means to draw Myanmar away from its close political and arms relationship with China. Hernandez also commented on this aspect of the decision to admit Myanmar: "It's important in the view of ASEAN countries to have Burma included so that the resources and capabilities of Burma do not get under the control of only one power, and you know China is a rising power."[88] The admission of Laos to ASEAN in the same year did not cause as much comment, but the purpose was the same.

Beijing's Redoubled Offensive to Win Over ASEAN. China's most senior leaders then sought to convince ASEAN of China's good intentions. In August 1997, Li Peng, then the Chinese premier, described five proposals for promoting relations with the ASEAN countries: "respecting each other, treating each other as equals, strengthening dialogue, intensifying consultation, and seeking common economic development." Li said, "The potential for our economic cooperation is indeed enormous, areas broad and prospects highly promising."[89] A few months later, in mid-December 1997, Chinese President Jiang Zemin proclaimed "the beginning of a new stage of development in China-ASEAN relations." "China will never seek hegemony," Jiang said. "China will forever be a good neighbor, a good partner and a good friend with ASEAN countries." He went on to urge the leaders of the nine ASEAN countries to "give priority to our economic relations and trade, scientific and technological cooperation between our two sides."[90]

ASEAN is an important target for Beijing's efforts. With nine nations as members and Cambodia soon to be admitted,[91] it represents all the countries of the subregion, a half-billion people, compared to a bit over the one-third billion people in the European Union. Its total economy is roughly two-thirds that of Japan's.[92] There are other reasons for Chinese interest in ASEAN. Put bluntly, it is hard for Chinese leaders not to love an organization that shares Beijing's views on avoiding intrusions in the internal affairs of other countries. ASEAN endeared itself to Beijing when it ignored widespread disapproval and brought Myanmar into its fold, ignoring U.S. and international pressure over Yangon's authoritarian actions. "The purpose of ASEAN is not to bring nice guys into a club. The purpose of ASEAN is to live at peace among ourselves," is the way Dr. Tan Sri Noordin Sopiee, chairman of the Malaysian Institute of International and Strategic Studies, put it in response to criticism of ASEAN at the time of the decision on Myanmar. At the July 1998 ASEAN foreign ministers meeting in Manila, the policy of noninterference in the internal affairs of member states was reaffirmed when a Thai proposal for "flexible engagement" was rejected. The ministers agreed on "enhanced interaction" on drug enforcement, the spread of smoke from fires, and terrorist activities. Undoubtedly, Beijing, once more, was happy with ASEAN's rejection of the Thai proposal.

The ASEAN ARF, the organization's body to discuss security issues, is also important to Beijing. The ARF planned at its 1994 inception to move from discussion of defense matters, to preventive diplomacy, to conflict resolution. But it has hardly gone beyond the first step. It was not until mid-1997 that national defense officials began to participate with their foreign ministers in the deliberations. At an ARF mid-year working meeting in Beijing in early 1997, consensus could not be reached even on whether bilateral alliances made a favorable contribution to the region.[93] Chinese Vice Foreign Minister Chen Jian's words at a press conference following the 1997 meeting demonstrate how Beijing, through its dialogue partner status, was able to promote its agenda of disparaging alliances:

> There were efforts made to have the meeting acknowledge that such alliances play a constructive role in regional peace. . . . We do not think it is correct to regard bilateral military alliances as the basis for maintaining regional security or the ARF as a supplement to such alliances.[94]

Beijing appeared to support the ASEAN concepts of mutual, cooperative, multilateral solutions and to accept the idea that security in the region could be a win-win proposition.

As a reflection of this, the consensus of the participants at this meeting was that economic development had become the focus of all countries and that expanding regional economic and trade interaction would establish a strong safety net for the Asia-Pacific region.[95] The economic crisis hit only months later, undermining for a time the strength of that safety net, but Beijing can still count on ASEAN leaders, especially Malaysia's Mahathir, to remind the Americans of the value of ties among understanding Asian nations and to join it in swipes at Washington. Foremost however, China through its links with ASEAN and its role in the ARF can exercise influence, consolidate opposition to U.S. alliances and defense policy, promote its reputation as a responsible member of the community of nations, and represent itself as a constructive force in the region.

Burying the Hatchet with Vietnam? Beijing's relations with the capitals of ASEAN are diverse and complex. China re-established diplomatic relations with Vietnam in 1991, after a gap of more than a decade following the PLA's disastrous 1979 invasion to "punish" Hanoi. Exchanges of visits by senior officials and military leaders from the two countries have become routine. Unquestionably, the most spectacular of these was then-Premier Li Peng's prominent attendance at Vietnam's Eighth Communist Party Congress in June 1996. The following month Vietnam's Army Chief of Staff Lieutenant General Pham Van Tra visited Beijing and discussed regional security and military cooperation. In August 1996, the very next month, the PLA Chief of the General Staff General Fu Quanyou returned the visit. Then a month later, high-level talks were held in Hanoi on border disputes and maritime area issues. In the summer of 1997, Do Muoi, Vietnam's party chief and most senior official, accepted President Jiang Zemin's invitation to visit Beijing. In June 1998, the Vietnamese Army chief again visited Beijing to talk with PRC Minister of Defense General Chi Haotian.

Bilateral border disputes and tiffs over oil drilling and fishing rights have continued between China and Vietnam, but these disagreements have been handled routinely. Regular talks on the land border issue are being held, with an optimistic forecast that all issues will be resolved by 2000. China has withdrawn survey and fishing vessels from disputed areas when Hanoi has protested through diplomatic channels. This suggests that Beijing continues to "test the waters," but that China does not persist when challenged. This approach resembles its reaction over the last 3 years to complaints from Manila over South China Sea disputes. One interpretation is that Beijing is not trying to get its way in the South China Sea by throwing its weight around. Another explanation is that, because of Vietnam's substantive claims, it is useful for China to begin seeking negotiated settlements there. If China settles these claims, then Hanoi might not lead a coalition of the other ASEAN states. In any case, China is not pressing its claims by force and gives the impression of being conciliatory.

Beijing Watches Jakarta. In mid-1998, political chaos and rioting in Indonesia included mob attacks on well-off ethnic Chinese,[96] repeating a pattern established 3 decades earlier. The question then became whether Beijing, with far more capabilities at its disposal than in the 1960s, would threaten or even hint at any action directed at Jakarta. Apparently no action was contemplated, not even evacuation by air or sea of those ethnic Chinese fearing imminent murder, rape, assault, looting, and burning of property. Beijing's constraint was punctuated by protests at the Indonesian Embassy in Beijing, a reminder to Jakarta that China was concerned. Demonstrations in Beijing are not permitted without the approval of the Chinese government. Mob action against ethnic Chinese in Indonesia continued at least through November 1998, but Beijing has stuck to its policy of noninterference, while using demonstrations and protests to remind Jakarta it was watching.

Beijing's passivity may not seem remarkable on the surface. However, it is interesting to reflect on alternative outcomes. Were Beijing in the mood to pursue territorial claims to the area that encompasses the valuable Natuna natural gas field north of Kalimantan, this period of chaos in Indonesia would have been an opportunity to make a grab.[97] Indonesia's military was distracted and unable to react effectively to protect natural gas operations run by Esso in an area claimed by Indonesia 150 miles east of Indonesia's Natuna Island. China might have concluded that its interests would be served by confiscating facilities within the limits of its historic claims, asserting that these assets should be used to pay reparations for the heavy losses sustained by ethnic Chinese abused in Indonesia. Perhaps deliberations in Beijing do indeed contemplate economic security considerations in the South China Sea in a nonaggressive light. Although Indonesian oil production is waning, Beijing almost certainly sees the advantage in preserving its own access to oil imports and not creating antagonism in the country that controls the straits through which oil from the Middle East flows to China.[98]

Beijing and the Indian Ocean. China and Myanmar are very different in size and population but have much in common. The two "regained independence" in the late 1940s, have endured a history since then of social volatility and authoritarian rule, have remained largely poor and developing nations, and are forced to tolerate a nearby India with which neither has particularly good relations. In recent years, relations with India have been focused in a debate over the nature of Chinese facilities on Myanmar's Coco Islands, between the Andaman Sea and the Bay of Bengal less than 50 miles north of the India's Andaman Islands. Allegations voiced by New Delhi and others have ranged from the existence of a PLA surveillance station on the island to the establishment of a naval base from which the PLAN could conduct submarine or warship operations, which would threaten India. Yangon and Beijing deny such allegations but do not explain persistent reports about Chinese military activity on Coco Island.[99]

The PLAN has not demonstrated a capability to conduct clandestine submarine operations from a base approximately 2,500 miles from its nearest base in China—the submarine base at Yulin on the southern tip of Hainan. Nor is there evidence of support for such operations by the presence of a submarine tender. However, electronic monitoring of Indian naval and air operations, or a more general form of electronic surveillance from Coco Island, is feasible. Interestingly, the other countries of ASEAN have not publicly objected or inquired about the alleged PLA presence. Perhaps the ASEAN countries do not mind having someone else big and with growing military sophistication watch the flank that faces giant India.

As Beijing looks to the future regarding its interests in the South China Sea and among the ASEAN countries, it need not be pessimistic. It does not confront the prospects of an inevitable and endless series of confrontations over rocks, reefs, islets, and possible oil deposits. China seems likely to remain the biggest frog in the South China Sea pond, but for now it shares the pond. Moreover, it has used the ARF as a forum to advance its views on economic security, cooperative security, and the five principles of peaceful coexistence. As in its new relationship with Russia, China has also found support among ASEAN nations for its railings about the evils of U.S. hegemony and military alliances that presuppose an adversary. This perspective on China and ASEAN may not be the popularly accepted view of the Chinese outlook, but it seems to make sense and to serve Chinese interests far better than the assertive alternative. Whether China will continue its moderate position and realize its aspirations in the 21st century is an open question, but Beijing seems to be committed to this course.

Beyond the Himalayas to the Subcontinent: India and Pakistan.

The May 1998 nuclear detonations set off by India and Pakistan had at least one positive effect. If Beijing had any serious doubts concerning the perils of proliferation, the tests drove home the point that a nuclear arms race in South Asia served no country's interests, especially not those of China. Washington's years of cajoling Beijing, imposing sanctions on Chinese companies, and painfully extracting agreements from Chinese negotiators could no longer be dismissed by Beijing as efforts by the Americans to cram their own concerns down Asian throats. China's President Jiang Zemin said, "This [the South Asian nuclear tests] will inevitably endanger the peace and stability of South Asia and the world at large and have a big impact on the international non-proliferation regime. . . ." "I wish to point out that nuclear testing is against international trends, no matter whether the test is conducted by India or Pakistan," Jiang continued. He urged both countries to relinquish their nuclear weapon programs and unconditionally accede to the Nuclear Non-Proliferation Treaty (NPT) and Comprehensive Test Ban Treaty (CTBT).[100]

Amidst this supposed conversion from profligate proliferator to ardent nonproliferator, it was easy to forget the long road to Chinese accession to the NPT, a treaty that dates back to 1968. China became a party to it only in 1992. Largely ignored in 1998 was the fact that China set off its final detonation in July 1996, *after* the text of the CTBT had been agreed upon. Further, China was among the most obstinate of the CTBT drafters, throwing up one obstacle after another as it all the while tested warheads for its new missiles and assisted Pakistan. A statement from the Chinese foreign ministry expressed outrage over India's tests:

> The Chinese government is deeply shocked by this and hereby expresses its strong condemnation.... The international community should adopt a common position in strongly demanding India immediately stop its nuclear development program. [The tests displayed] outrageous contempt for the common will of the international community for the comprehensive ban on nuclear tests.[101]

The decision by Beijing to react harshly was not a foregone conclusion. Beijing had spent years denying that it has provided nuclear weapons and ballistic missile assistance to Pakistan, denials which few accepted but in which Islamabad and Beijing persist. Beijing had been similarly attentive to finding ways to skirt commitments to Washington and the world to do better with respect to proliferation or to curb dubious sales of "dual-use" items by Chinese entities to Pakistan. Neither India nor Pakistan, by these nuclear tests, had violated international agreements to which they were parties. Beijing's decision about how to react was made all the more difficult by the Chinese position on interference in another country's internal affairs. For 2 days or so, Beijing did not react to the Indian tests, reflecting the difficulty of its internal deliberations. Then, probably influenced by international pressure, Beijing came down unequivocally on the side of a commitment to a standard of international behavior. Moreover, it adhered to that position through Pakistan's tests, a much more sensitive decision for Beijing. India, and then Pakistan, had violated what had come to be accepted by the responsible members of the community of nations as a worldwide moratorium on nuclear testing. China passed the test of international responsibility by backing normative restraints on nuclear proliferation.

This decision by Beijing was all the more significant, given China's close ties with Pakistan and history of confrontation with India. The decision seems to reflect a significant shift in Beijing's security perspective on South Asia, although this shift was not as abrupt as might appear to be the case. China had for years been retreating from overt nuclear and missile cooperation with Pakistan, if for no other reasons than that Washington both brought pressure to bear and made persuasive arguments. However, China also seemed increasingly concerned about its international reputation, and in Beijing the number of officials and bureaucrats who argued that non-proliferation was responsible policy grew, as did their influence.

Moreover, Beijing was not inclined to condemn India, despite their disagreements. China's relations with India, including security matters, had taken a decidedly positive turn, starting with Rajiv Gandhi's 1988 visit to Beijing. Jiang Zemin in the mid-1990s became the first Chinese president to go to New Delhi, a visit that produced agreement to reduce troops and weapons along the two countries' disputed Himalayan borders. The improving relationship was not ruptured by the widely noted scathing outbursts of India's new defense minister, George Fernandes, after the Hindu Bharatiya Janata Party (BJP) led a coalition and took over the government in early 1998. Fernandes labeled China as India's biggest potential threat and accused Beijing of aiding the Pakistani missile program and stationing threatening aircraft in Tibet.

Despite these loud accusations by the colorful Fernandes, Beijing did not cancel a visit to India by PLA Chief of the General Staff General Fu Quanyou. BJP leaders managed temporarily to tone down the rhetoric in preparation for Fu's visit. A foreign ministry spokesman said,

> [The] Government of India remains committed to . . . the development of a friendly, cooperative, good-neighborly and mutually beneficial relationship with China, our largest neighbor. Both sides have agreed to build a constructive and cooperative relationship oriented towards the 21st century. . . . We see our relationship as one in which the two sides would be responsive to each other's concerns. Eliminating differences and promoting understanding would contribute to the development of good neighborly relations. . . .[102]

But the vociferous Fernandes spoke out again when the PLA general went home. Fernandes ratcheted up the level of rhetoric further after India's nuclear tests, saying that China presented an imminent nuclear threat that had forced India to develop nuclear weapons. Beijing denied the charges but did not overreact. Now that the nuclear dust has settled, both India and Pakistan are more soberly considering what they have wrought. Fernandes is singing a different tune:

> If China and the U.S. can have a strategic partnership which makes them de-target their nuclear missiles . . . despite the several issues that divide them, there is no reason why India and China cannot have a . . . closer relationship, while they work towards resolving outstanding disputes between them. . . . We have a shared past . . . both are proud of their civilizational heritage.

After blaming the Indian press for distorting his earlier characterization of China as a threat, Fernandes added, "We will take whatever measures are needed to be taken to see that we get on to the discussion table and see that we bring our relationship on to an even keel."[103] Fernandes glibly ignored that he had been the primary boat-rocker.

This anecdote about Fernandes does more than describe recent events in the Sino-Indian security relationship. It illustrates that Beijing and New Delhi—after a brief war in 1962, enduring disagreements, scathing condemnations, and India's nuclear challenge to China's ally, Pakistan—are pursuing the rapprochement commenced precisely a decade ago. Sino-Indian trade is not significant; geographic barriers to that are hard to surmount. Beijing seems not to be driven by economic factors in this case, but it is simply not inclined to teach India a lesson, as it did in the past. It is interested in perpetuating the progress that has been achieved on confidence-building measures in disputed areas, including mutual and balanced force reductions and other promising results stemming from the border talks that began in 1981. Over almost 2 decades, China has steered a long-term course for good relations with India. Despite the inevitable difficulties that will arise, Beijing appears intent on maintaining that course. Regional stability is something in which China now has a very big stake.

Moreover, Beijing is not inclined single-mindedly to stand behind Islamabad, savoring any opportunity to get at New Delhi. Pakistan has suffered China's verbal wrath. As understandable as Pakistan's nuclear tests were in the eyes of many Chinese, Beijing did not to need the threat of U.S. sanctions to enforce its new rules about controlling the sales of dual-use technology. China, of course, will not abandon Pakistan, and it is not likely to try to broker the Kashmir dispute. But it may well pursue more balanced relations on the South Asian subcontinent. Its policies for South Asia will be far less likely to involve roguish behavior or quibbling on interpretation of Missile Technology Control Regime (MTCR), viewed by many experts to be a search for loopholes. India and Pakistan have provided China with a lesson on what constitutes responsible behavior in the world, where China wants to be accepted as a major power and key player.

Through the Strait of Malacca—and All the Way to Iran and Iraq.

Economic security for China, like Japan and the United States, is largely dependent on access to crude oil. China is far from wholly dependent on oil imports, but it depends heavily on supplies from Iran, Indonesia, and, within the bounds of U.S. sanctions, Iraq. China became a net importer of petroleum products in 1993 and a net importer of crude oil starting in 1996.[104]

Although China has loosened price controls on domestic crude oil, cracked down on rampant domestic theft of crude oil, and begun an intensified oil search in the Lop Nur nuclear testing area of Qinghai Province, its crude oil needs are beyond domestic or regional production capacity.[105] Imported crude oil topped 35 million tons in 1997, 60 percent more than in 1996;[106] and for the first quarter of 1998, consumption was up 18 percent over last year.[107] Beijing has given up hope of meeting demand through domestic production. Prominent in its global search[108] is a 1997 $1.2 billion deal with Iraq to develop the huge Ahmad oil field—after United Nations (U.N.) sanctions have been lifted.[109] Iraq's oil minister, Lieutenant General Amer Mohammad Rashid, was in Beijing in May 1998 as part of Baghdad's effort to have the U.N. sanctions lifted.[110]

The intensity of China's quest for oil indicates recognition that its status as a net importer is almost certainly irreversible. In August 1996, there was no more enthusiastic proponent than China for easing the plight of the Iraqi people brought about by post-Gulf War sanctions. China promised that it would actively assist in providing humanitarian aid to Iraq under the U.N. oil-for-food program. During that same month, China was discussing with Iraqi officials the conduct of seismic studies and oil field development in Iraq, with contract negotiations reportedly underway.[111] Three months later, major oil exploration contracts were reported.[112] In September 1996, Beijing protested the strike on Iraq by 44 U.S. cruise missiles and, urging restraint, objected to the threat of an attack by massed U.S. armed forces.

In January 1998, the speaker of the Iraqi parliament was in Beijing. On that occasion, then Chinese Foreign Minister Qian Qichen said, "China calls on the world community to give a just and objective evaluation over

Iraq's implementation of relevant U.N. resolutions. . . ." Beijing displayed at least a glint of the "objectivity" it was calling for when Qian added, "China . . . hopes that Iraq will continue cooperating with the U.N. Special Committee in order to alleviate and finally lift the U.N. sanctions."[113] Later in the month, nonetheless, China joined Russia in the U.N. in calling for certification that Iraq had completed the dismantlement of its nuclear weapon program.

In February 1998, China and Russia again opposed an attack on Iraq because of Baghdad's intransigence with respect to U.N. weapons inspections. Xinhua reported that Foreign Minister Qian told U.S. Secretary of State Madeleine Albright by phone, "China does not favor the use of force against Iraq."[114] Later that month, then U.S. Ambassador to the United Nations Bill Richardson met with Qian in Beijing. Qian continued to oppose the use of force but, according to Richardson, acknowledged that Iraqi defiance of the inspections was a grave matter.[115] The Chinese government took a similar position in November 1998, actively encouraging Iraq to cooperate with the United Nations Special Commission (UNSCOM) inspection regime but opposing the use of force.

Beijing has demonstrated repeatedly that its relations with Baghdad extend beyond principled objections to the use of force; they are oil-fired. Certainly, there are other reasons for China's opposition to the application of force by the United States inside Iraq. China is sympathetic with countries that claim to have been oppressed and victimized by Western powers, and it opposes any precedent for the use of U.S. or U.N. forces in striking a country that has proven obstinate. Nevertheless, China focuses narrowly but optimistically on the coming decades when, after sanctions are lifted, large-scale exploitation of Iraq's expanding oil fields can be carried out by China. Beijing's security relationship with Baghdad is defined by the economic implications of oil, and Beijing will likely be tempted when sanctions are lifted to see if arms sales and nuclear technology will strengthen China's ability to ensure it gets the share of Iraq's oil that it desires.

In the case of Iran, arms sales and the transfer of nuclear technology have been central features of a relationship also designed to ensure that China's rising demand for oil can be met into the next century, when consumption will quickly pass 50 million tons per year and continue upward. Prominent among the weapons sold in recent years to Iran have been the C-802 and C-801K shipborne and air-launched antiship cruise missiles (ASCMs), subsonic in speed but with considerable range and capability. The transfer of these missiles did not violate the provisions of the MTCR, but the sales incensed the Pentagon. They may now have become a concern to Beijing, as China appears to have realized that the flow of oil from the Persian Gulf may be more imperiled than protected by Iranian patrol boats and aircraft armed with these missiles.

There were other salient aspects of China's support of Iran. Beijing complained vociferously in early 1996 about the D'Amato law, which permits the United States to sanction foreign companies investing in Iran (and Libya) because of their connections with terrorists. It was also troublesome to American defense officials that Chinese Defense Minister General Chi Haotian met his Iranian counterpart in August 1996 in Beijing to discuss improved military relations. Chinese leaders seem determined, at least, to make a show of support for Iranian causes and for improving bilateral relations. Then, to the surprise of many, at the October 1997 Jiang-Clinton summit meeting in the United States, Jiang promised to stop missile sales to Iran and also to cease nuclear technology transfers.[116]

Such assurances of future good behavior from China have often been subject to interpretation, so it was heartening when, in January 1998, Chinese Defense Minister Chi reaffirmed to U.S. Secretary of Defense William Cohen that neither ASCMs nor nuclear technology would be transferred to Iran.[117] Later reports that U.S.

intelligence had uncovered plots by Chinese companies to circumvent Beijing's commitment to Washington suggested, however, that the words were empty. U.S. National Security Adviser Sandy Berger reportedly wrote to his Chinese counterpart about the issue. An unidentified U.S. official said the Chinese government had intervened and halted the transactions.[118]

Washington seemed to have created a rift in relations between Beijing and Tehran, but the seriousness of the rift is uncertain. However, Beijing is not likely to give up so easily in its quest for oil from Iran. China's Vice Premier for Trade Li Lanqing visited Tehran in May 1997 and discussed expanding economic cooperation between China and Iran.[119] Of greatest import was the acceptance by China of an Iranian proposal to equip a Chinese refinery so that it could process high-sulfur-content Iranian crude oil. Li said this would allow China to buy more Iranian oil.[120] It remains to be seen whether, despite Beijing's reticence in arms sales, the oil relationship will survive. Tehran may find Beijing to be a fair-weather friend, but probably it will understand why China yielded to American pressure in some areas. If the security relationship cools further, it would be because China can obtain sufficient oil elsewhere.

Preserving Economic Security vis-à-vis Iraq and Iran. China does not yet have the navy to protect the sea lanes over which its oil comes from the Middle East. Ironically, China depends on the U.S. Navy to ensure freedom of navigation for the oil tankers that are essential to China's steadily growing economy. China must wend its way through perilous Iranian and Iraqi channels of intrigue and American nonproliferation "minefields." Sales of Chinese arms are counterproductive, even when used as inducements to those nations that are considered pariahs by other countries that have modern arms to sell. Thus, China has to contemplate its security concerns among these states on its far southwestern periphery in new and different terms, realizing that its security there is tied to China's new life blood: oil.

A Final Look Around.

China sees itself emerging as a major regional power and important global player. Among other things, Beijing will seek peaceful borders; insist on an appropriate role for China in Northeast Asian security; pretend, at least, to have learned humility in the South China Sea; balance its relations in South Asia and on the Korean Peninsula; and hope to master the technique of getting oil without giving arms in Southwest Asia. In all of this, weapons and troops mean much less than it seemed they would only a decade or so ago. A similar situation will apply to other countries of the region. Cancelled and postponed arms purchases by China's neighboring states, as a consequence of the Asian financial crisis, pale in security significance to the manner in which those nations will restore their competent workforces to productivity and to robust interdependent economic relations. A modernized PLA is a minor component of China's regional security calculi. Only with respect to Taiwan, not a peripheral state by Beijing's definition but a renegade province, is a formidable PLA truly a prominent part of the current picture. Even in this cross-strait contest, the odds are not bad for those who are willing to gamble that economic considerations will prevail and ultimately produce a lasting solution across the Taiwan Strait.

There is considerable evidence that China means much of what it says in the July 1998 Defense White Paper. Beijing is devoting more "quality time" and attention to its peripheral environment and doing so, although not perfectly, in ways that tend to build economic bonds rather than sow seeds of distrust and trepidation. Beijing will likely continue to be seen by Washington and others—especially Taipei—as obnoxious; but as Washington has demonstrated over the decades, it is very hard to be both big and powerful and still universally adored. Nevertheless, China is learning at least the jargon of multilateralism, confidence-building, and how to be a pre-eminent power while dodging epithets such as "hegemon" and "bully." China's impressive national economic success, as contrasted with its mediocre military modernization, may serve to reinforce the tendency in Beijing to believe that economics is the most important component in China's comprehensive national power and that military power is, at best, only complementary. That raises the intriguing question of how this new Chinese attitude might be affected were the economy to take a big tumble, as has been the case with several of China's neighbors. For now, examination of the odds of that occurring can be postponed for a future endeavor. At present, Beijing is making a convincing case that security relations on its periphery in the 21st century will turn on matters of economic security and interdependence, elements of national power where China is increasingly competent.

ENDNOTES - CHAPTER 2

1. The words *peripheral states* are used in the title of this paper in the sense of the countries that form a rough perimeter around the largest country in Asia, China, and not in the sense that these states are of minor relevance or importance. Taiwan is discussed extensively but is not afforded a separate section, as are the states or groups of states that are treated fully. There are two reasons: (1) This paper is intended as an attempt to view the periphery from Beijing's perspective. The government in Beijing, of course, does not see Taiwan as a *state*. (2) The Taiwan issue has received the fulsome coverage and attention it deserves in other writings, including both papers presented at the 1998 Wye River PLA Conference, where this paper was initially presented, and the 1996 PLA Conference at Coolfont, West Virginia, which was devoted to the Taiwan issue and cross-strait relations. The papers from that 1996 conference, including one by the author, appear as chapters in James R. Lilley and Chuck Downs, eds., *Crisis in the Taiwan Strait*, Washington: National Defense University Press, September 1997.

2. Information Office of the State Council of the People's Republic of China, *China's National Defense*, a White Paper, Beijing, July 1998, p. 1.

3. Information Office of the State Council of the People's Republic of China, *China: Arms Control and Disarmament*, a White Paper, Beijing: November 1995, Foreword. Available on the Internet at *www.chinanews.org/White Papers*.

4. 1998 White Paper, Chap. I, pp. 7-8.

5. *Ibid.*, p. 5.

6. *Ibid.*, Chap. IV, pp. 36-38.

7. 1995 White Paper, Chap. VI.

8. Private conversation between the officer and the author in the spring of 1998.

9. 1998 White Paper, Chap. I, p. 5.

10. *Ibid.*, pp. 4-5.

11. *Ibid.*, p. 3.

12. *Ibid.*, p. 5.

13. 1998 White Paper, Chap. IV, p. 34.

14. *Ibid.*

15. *Ibid.*, p. 37.

16. *Ibid.*, Chap. I, p. 7.

17. *Ibid.*, p. 8.

18. *Ibid.*

19. *Ibid.*, Chap. IV, p. 33.

20. *Ibid.*, p. 34.

21. The Xinjiang Uighur Autonomous Region composes about one-sixth of the area of China and holds important oil reserves and other natural resources. It is also the gateway to oil and gas fields in the Central Asian Republics.

22. Former Chinese Foreign Minister Qian Qichen in an April 1996 interview with *Reuters* said, "We are opposed to terrorist and separatist activities by some fundamentalists because religion and politics are two separate issues." He said Chinese officials were aware of the spread of Islamic extremists and that Beijing had joined forces with its heavily Muslim neighbors in the former Soviet Union. Of China's total

population of over 1.2 billion, about 16 million are Muslims of various ethnic minorities.

23. Hans now compose about 38 percent of the Xinjiang population of almost 17 million. Uighurs have been reduced from almost 80 percent before 1949 to as little as 48 percent now, although some think that number is as large as 60 percent. There are probably almost 200,000 Uighurs living in Kazakhstan and another 300,000 in other Central Asian countries.

24. Benjamin Kang Lim, "China Sings Praises of Cops Killed by Separatists," *Reuters*, Beijing, August 14, 1998.

25. Kazakhstan is by far the largest and most important of the bordering Central Asian countries. Its population of 16 million is roughly the same as that of Xinjiang; its area of slightly more than a million square miles is not quite twice that of Xinjiang.

26. Oleg Shchedrov, *Reuters*, Beijing, April 26, 1996; *New York Times* News Service wire report, Shanghai, April 27, 1996.

27. *Associated Press*, Almaty, Kazakhstan, December 14, 1996.

28. Gareth Jones, "Kazakh Activists Urge Chinese Respect for Uighur Rights," *Reuters*, Almaty, Kazakhstan, January 15, 1998.

29. Mike Collett-White, "Kazakhs, Chinese Vow Closer Ties, More Trade," *Reuters*, Almaty, Kazakhstan, July 4, 1998.

30. *Ibid.*

31. *Ibid.* The Collett-White article from Almaty reported on the meeting of the "group of five," the signing of the agreement by Jiang and Nazarbayev, and that Beijing has taken Kazakhstan more seriously as a potential trade partner since signing oil production and transport deals worth $9.5 billion last year. President Nazarbayev, it states, stressed that Jiang was firmly committed to the ambitious oil projects, which Western executives have dismissed as economically unviable. Nazarbayev is quoted as saying, "The biggest contract between Kazakhstan and China was signed by the oil company of the Chinese republic. This was called the project of the century. Today I confirmed with, Jiang,its importance for China."

32. Shchedrov.

33. Benjamin Kang Lim, *Reuters*, Beijing, November 10, 1997.

34. "China, Russia: Text of Sino-Russian Joint Statement," Xinhua in English, April 23, 1997, in *Foreign Broadcast Information Service-China* (henceforth *FBIS-CHI*)-97-079, April 23, 1997.

35. *Reuters*, "Russia, China FMs Discuss Security Issues," Beijing, July 22, 1998.

36. Robert Burns, *Associated Press*, Washington, January 14, 1997.

37. "China, Russia: Text of Sino-Russian Joint Statement."

38. *Ibid.*

39. Aleksandr Platkovskiy, "Rodionov Urges Chinese to Struggle Against Hegemonism," *Izvestiya*, April 16, 1997, p. 3.

40. "China, Russia: Text of Sino-Russian Joint Statement."

41. Alastair Macdonald, *Reuters*, Moscow, January 4, 1996.

42. *Ibid.*

43. Patrick E. Tyler, *New York Times News Service*, February 1996.

44. The rumors and uncertainty concerning the status of the Su-27 deal are circumstantial evidence of the problems that exist with respect to payment amounts and terms in arms sales from Russia to China. The fact that neither side chose to dispel the uncertainty with a definitive statement adds credibility to the assertion herein that cost and terms are a matter of considerable contention.

45. *Reuters*, Moscow, April 11, 1996.

46. *Reuters*, Beijing, January 11, 1996.

47. The year-long operation in Cambodia, UNTAC, in 1992-93 consisted of two contingents of 608 personnel each, almost all of whom were in civil engineering units. The 2-year-long operation in Mozambique, ONUMOZ, involved a total of 154 personnel in three contingents, almost all of whom were involved in transport activities. These data are taken from the Japan Defense Agency White Paper Defense *of Japan 1997* published in Japan by *The Japan Times*, Ltd. in July 1997, p. 277.

48. Although the issue of sovereignty has gotten prime attention in the confrontations over Diaoyutai, it should be noted that the catalyst for the confrontation in the summer of 1996 was the earlier presence off

the islands of a Chinese oil exploration ship. This was seen as a provocation and threat by the Japanese, especially the right-wing zealots who exacerbated the situation by constructing a navigation beacon on the island, but the economic implications of China's interests are revealed thereby. It is noteworthy that, similarly, Beijing's flurry of activity in the South China Sea corresponded to widespread optimistic estimates of oil reserves in the area of the Spratly Islands. As surveys and drilling have failed to produce significant oil and prospects have seemed less promising, China's attitudes and actions with respect to the Spratly Islands disputes have become more benign, even conciliatory.

49. Chen Yali, "U.S.-Japan Alliance not conducive to peace," *China Daily*, May 26, 1997.

50. Japan Defense Agency, White Paper entitled Defense *of Japan 1997* published in Japan in English by *The Japan Times*, Ltd., in July 1997, p. 286-289. Reference 18 in this volume is the full-text unofficial translation of the April 1996 document entitled "Japan-U.S. Joint declaration on Security—Alliance for the 21st Century."

51. In 1994, then-U.S. Assistant Secretary of Defense for International Security Affairs Joseph Nye pointed out that the guidelines for U.S.-Japanese defense cooperation were dangerously out of date.

52. Patrick E. Tyler, *New York Times*, April 19, 1996.

53. Tokyo NHK General Television Network broadcast the following report on April 9, 1997:

> Prime Minister Ryutaro Hashimoto, in his meeting with the Liberal Democratic Party's [LDP] Policy Research Council Chairman Taku Yamasaki and other senior members, explained a view that this fall's review of the Japan-U.S. cooperation guideline will address possible emergencies not only on the Korean Peninsula but also across the wide area surrounding Japan. At the meeting, questions were asked regarding review of the guidelines and other issues, saying: "Although assumptions are being made on the basis of an emergency on the Korean Peninsula only, should one not consider including the defense of the so-called sea-lanes as well?" In response, the prime minister said: "In Diet debates on the current Japan-U.S. security arrangements, questions were asked only on issues relating to the Korean Peninsula. But, I ventured not to limit the issues on the Korean

Peninsula. The Spratly Islands and Taiwan should also be considered subjects for debate." In this way, the prime minister explained the view that Japan-U.S. defense cooperation should be reviewed while assuming emergencies not only on the Korean Peninsula but also in the Spratly Islands, Taiwan and other areas surrounding Japan.

Reuters, Tokyo, August 19, 1997, quoted Chief Cabinet Secretary Seiroku Kajiyama as saying during a news conference: "The 'Far East' covered in the U.S.-Japan Security Treaty covers the area north of the Philippines . . . that includes the Taiwan Strait and the Korean peninsula." "I am not aware that the revision includes a change in the fundamentals of the security pact," Kajiyama reportedly said.

54. Paul Eckert, *Reuters*, Dalian, China, September 7, 1997.

55. *Associated Press*, New York, September 4, 1997.

56. Paul Eckert, *Reuters*, Shenyang, China, September 5, 1997.

57. Eckert, September 7, 1997.

58. *Ibid.*

59. Japan Defense Agency White Paper.

60. Brian Williams, *Reuters*, Tokyo, April 18, 1996.

61. *Reuters*, Beijing, April 18, 1996.

62. Chen Yali.

63. *Ibid.*

64. Private conversations by the author with Japanese defense specialists in the first half of 1998 revealed their belief that Beijing is attempting quietly to subvert political and public support for TBMD in Japan. Experts in Tokyo and Washington suggest, also privately, that the rather small Japanese budget allocations set aside for study of the TBMD issue are token amounts and are in reality evidence of lack of support for, or at least uncertainty about, the TBMD program. In addition to the effects Chinese arguments may have had, there are in Japan "political concerns" that TBMD's reach, the coverage the missiles provide by virtue of their inherent range, would provide incidental protection for Korea, thereby violating Japanese constitutional constraints. Also, there are doubts about whether the extremely

expensive system will work well, if it is, indeed, developed and fielded or put to sea.

65. *Kyodo News Service*, "Tokyo To Postpone Missile Defense Decision," Tokyo, March 1, 1997, in *Foreign Broadcast Information Service-East Asia* (henceforth *FBIS-EAS)*-97-041.

66. Eckert, *Reuters*, Beijing, September 4, 1997.

67. *Reuters*, "Japan Defense Chief Tours China Naval Base," Shanghai, May 2, 1998.

68. *Kyodo News Service* issued a report from Tokyo, August 19, 1998, stating that a senior Foreign Ministry official said Tokyo thought it unnecessary to accept Beijing's reported request to include the "three no's policy" in a joint statement the two governments were preparing for Chinese President Jiang Zemin's [now-postponed] visit to Japan during September 6-11, 1998.

69. Jiang Zemin's 1992 visit to Japan was as General Secretary of the Chinese Communist Party. The postponed visit was rescheduled for November 25-30, 1998, and was to include calls on Emperor Akihito and Prime Minister Obuchi.

70. Eric A. McVadon. For an examination and analysis of China's concerns, interests, strategy, and aspirations for the Korean Peninsula, see the author's paper prepared for the 1997 PLA Conference at Wye Plantation. This paper, "Chinese Military Strategy for the Korean Peninsula," is a chapter in *China's Military Faces the Future*, David Shambaugh, ed., AEI Press and M.E. Sharpe, 1999.

71. This distant time frame was offered by a moderately senior but well-informed PLA officer in 1997. The officer is well acquainted with his country's official position with respect to Korean issues.

72. In a late-August 1997 interview, a PLA general officer, cognizant of his government's positions with respect to Korea, gave top priority to China's continuing economic development among the factors in formulation of Beijing's policies with respect to the Korean Peninsula. He emphasized that, above all, peace and stability there are essential to China's achieving this goal.

73. McVadon, "Chinese Military Strategy for the Korean Peninsula," Tables 1 and 2. These tables and the preceding text provide the figures for South Korean investment in China.

74. The "three communiques" on U.S.-China relations were issued in Shanghai in 1972 (by President Richard Nixon), in 1978 (by President Jimmy Carter), and in 1982 (by President Reagan). President Clinton avoided a "fourth communique" in his 1998 visit to China.

75. A Chinese diplomat in Washington asked the author in May 1998 if he had noticed Beijing's "toned-down" approach to the issue of continued presence of U.S. forces on the Korean Peninsula, even after major change there. The new component of the Chinese position was the pointed emphasis on limiting the use of the forces to "bilateral matters." This term was apparently borrowed from Chinese statements about what the U.S.-Japanese alliance should be.

76. The PRC, United States, and several other countries participate as "dialogue partners" but not as full members of ASEAN.

77. Rene Pastor, *Reuters*, Singapore, June 4, 1997.

78. Manila in early August rejected Chinese Foreign Minister Tang Jiaxuan's late July offer. *Reuters*, "China says Spratlys sovereignty 'indisputable'," Beijing, August 6, 1998.

79. "Countries unite on Spratlys claim," *Star Malaysia*, Kuala Lumpur, December 17, 1997.

80. *Ibid.*

81. Ji Guoxing, "China Versus South China Sea Security," *Security Dialogue*, Sage Publications/PRIO, Vol. 29, No. 1, March 1998, as excerpted in Pacific Forum Center for Strategic and International Studies (CSIS) PacNet #17, April 24, 1998.

82. Ruben Alabastro, "Computer glitch helped spark Spratlys row—Manila," *Reuters*, Manila, November 9, 1998. A 13-day delay in receipt of the message from the Philippine embassy in Beijing resulted in Philippine discovery of the work only 1 day after the notification was received. Manila protested, with Defense Minister Mercado accusing Beijing of conducting a "creeping invasion." The comic opera of Spratly spats involving Manila continued unabated.

83. Only China, Taiwan, and Vietnam claim the Paracel Islands. Six countries, the three mentioned plus the Philippines, Brunei, and Malaysia, claim all or parts of the Spratly Islands. Of course, Taipei's claims in the South China Sea have mirrored those of Beijing. The author is not aware of changes of sovereignty claims by Taipei after abandoning its position a few years back that it was the legitimate government of all China, including the mainland.

84. Jawed Naqvi, *Reuters*, New Delhi, January 4, 1996. India is a "dialogue partner" in ASEAN meetings.

85. Pastor.

86. Washington had imposed economic sanctions on the SLORC in May 1997: Bill Tarrant, *Reuters*, Kuala Lumpur, June 1, 1997.

87. Tarrant.

88. *Ibid.*

89. Christina Toh-Pantin, *Reuters*, Kuala Lumpur, August 22, 1997.

90. "China will never seek hegemony – Jiang," *Reuters*, in *Hong Kong Standard*, December 16, 1997.

91. Cambodia's entry into ASEAN has been delayed as a consequence of the political strife there. Cambodia and Papua New Guinea attended the July 24-29, 1998, meeting of ASEAN foreign ministers in Manila in the status of observers. Reports of reconciliation between Hun Sen and the younger Sihanouk led to speculation in late 1998 that Cambodia might, once more, be near to acceptance into ASEAN.

92. Noordin Sopiee, "Fulfilling Dream of Regional Unity," PacNet #24, Pacific Forum CSIS, Honolulu, June 13, 1997. The economic comparisons were obviously derived from figures pre-dating the on-going Asian economic crisis.

93. The bilateral agreements in Asia primarily involve the United States. The Five-Power Defense Arrangement (FPDA), composed of Singapore, Malaysia, the United Kingdom, Australia, and New Zealand, is the only multilateral defense arrangement in the region. It was formed in 1971 after Malaysia had suffered a confrontation with its large neighbor Indonesia. Although the FPDA conducted exercises near the Spratly Islands while China was intimidating Taiwan with its exercises in early 1996, all attention was directed to the two U.S. Navy carrier battle groups that had been dispatched to the area of Taiwan.

94. Mary Kwang, "ARF Talks End with No Consensus on Bilateral Alliances," *Straits Times*, Singapore, March 9, 1997.

95. *Ibid.*

96. The more than eight million ethnic Chinese in Indonesia, 4 percent of the population, control a large portion of the economy and national wealth.

97. The Natuna gas field, but not the island of Natuna, appears to fall within the rather imprecise dashed lines that appeared on Chinese maps of the South China Sea.

98. This rather fanciful scenario is presented not because it seemed a likely course of action for Beijing to take during the height of the Indonesian crisis, but rather because, when we consider it, we conclude, significantly, that it was indeed a very unlikely course for the Chinese government, as we have come to perceive it in recent years, to take.

99. A PLA presence on a Myanmar island would also violate the Chinese fundamental position opposing foreign troops on the soil of another nation.

100. "China urges India, Pakistan to stop nuke programme," *Reuters*, Beijing, June 22, 1998.

101. Justin Jin, "China, Gloves Off, Attacks India," *Reuters*, Beijing, May 14, 1998.

102. "India Moves to Mollify China Over Defence Minister," *Reuters*, New Delhi, May 6, 1998.

103. Narayanan Madhavan, "India Says Can Get Close to China Despite Hurdles," *Reuters*, New Delhi, May 8, 1998.

104. Neil Fullick, *Reuters*, Singapore, January 26, 1998.

105. Neil Fullick, "China takes big step toward open oil market," *Reuters*, Singapore, June 5, 1998.

106. Fullick, January 26, 1998.

107. Fullick, June 5, 1998.

108. Unconfirmed reports have China seeking oil-related contracts in Iran, Kuwait, Saudi Arabia, the United Arab Emirates, Canada, Papua New Guinea, Peru, Sudan, and Thailand.

109. *Reuters*, Beijing, November 25, 1998.

110. *Associated Press*, Baghdad, May 25, 1998. Of course, Beijing is also investing in a pipeline with Kazakhstan.

111. *Reuters*, Beijing, August 18, 1996.

112. *Reuters*, Beijing, November 11, 1996.

113. *Reuters*, Beijing, January 6, 1998.

114. Scott Hillis, "China Tells Albright It's Uneasy Over Iraq Crisis," *Reuters*, Beijing, February 5, 1998.

115. Scott Hillis, *Reuters*, Beijing, February 14, 1998.

116. The latter step facilitated implementation of the Nuclear Cooperation Agreement between the United States and China, thus allowing U.S. companies to compete in China's burgeoning nuclear power industry.

117. A PLA general officer with considerable experience in dealing with Iran told the author in August 1997 that Beijing had decided not to provide Tehran with assistance in the construction of a nuclear reactor planned for a site near the border with Iraq. He said that the proximity to the border had been the stated reason, but that Iran's support for Islamic fundamentalists in the Central Asian Republics and in Xinjiang had made the decision to halt nuclear cooperation with Tehran easier to make.

118. "China Foils the Spread of Nukes . . . Probably," *Christian Science Monitor*, March 12, 1998.

119. China was reported in 1996 to be a major supplier and contractor for the Tehran subway system.

120. *Associated Press*, Beijing, May 4, 1997.

CHAPTER 3
PLA CAPABILITIES IN THE 21st CENTURY: HOW DOES CHINA ASSESS ITS FUTURE SECURITY NEEDS?

Michael Pillsbury

INTRODUCTION

With the Asian financial crisis and the floods in China, it hardly seems urgent to address the future warfighting capabilities of the People's Liberation Army (PLA).[1] But China's military planners are patient, long-term strategic thinkers, so despite the current problems, I will still provide some comments on the topic. This chapter is divided into six sections. Its purpose is to present a "net assessment" of how China may see its future military capabilities.

Section One continues a discussion, begun in the introduction, about errors to be avoided in estimating future Chinese military capabilities. *Section Two* describes the way that the open souces of information available in China assess the future security environment, including the likelihood of war and the future trends in military capabilities of the major powers. *Section Three* narrows the focus of this chapter to China's quantitative estimates of Comprehensive National Power (CNP) for 2010 and 2020, based on books by the Academy of Military Science and the Academy of Social Science, including a discussion of why some Chinese analysts claim these national power "scores" can predict the outcome of future warfare. *Section Four* identifies debates among the Chinese military about long-term modernization goals. *Section Five* lists China's military investment allocation priorities and attempts to link some of these investment decisions to the defense debate, suggesting that the shape of the PLA by 2020 can be affected a great deal by the debate among the three schools.

Section Six describes how Chinese military authors assess future American military capabilities to defend South Korea and Taiwan and to pursue a potential Revolution in Military Affairs (RMA). Easily offended or highly nationalistic American readers should skip this section.

What are some of the key issues in understanding what China's military capabilities may be in the first 2 decades of the 21st century? In spite of the hazards of straight-line projections of China's current forces to 2010 or 2020, many still use this estimative method to arrive at a picture of future capabilities. This chapter argues that it is also important to know in detail the objectives that China's leaders seek to pursue through military modernization. Happily, Western analysts of the Chinese military may have a better chance to get right the issue of China's modernization goals than whether China's military technology programs will succeed. After all, China's leaders continue to proclaim the validity of Sun Tzu and to repeat Deng Xiaoping's guidance *tao guang yang hui* (conceal our capabilities and bide our time). China is unlikely to raise its level of transparency by inviting the U.S. defense attaché to visit the research and development (R&D) programs in fields such as counter-stealth radar, laser weapons, electrodynamic railguns, anti-satellite interceptors, precision guided missiles, and many other weapons designed to focus on U.S. vulnerabilities. I believe that it is relatively easy to determine that China lacks items on the Militarily Critical Technologies List, but by paying attention to Chinese open sources, especially books and professional journals that deal with long-term future modernization goals, we can make some sound judgments about China's military future.

Choosing Among Estimative Methods for China's Future Capability.

This chapter concludes that China's future military capabilities will be based on factors that are impossible to estimate beyond 2010. Some of these factors cannot even be estimated accurately today. They include quantitative estimates of the fundamentals of military power such as the future size of China's defense budget, its future industrial base, its access to advanced military technology, and "non-equipment" factors such as the quality of its future officer corps. Of course, it is possible to estimate that a certain specific Chinese force structure may come into existence by 2010 by using straight-line projection. Even though this is an error-prone estimative method, it is quick and simple and perhaps can fool the gullible who have no idea how their own nation makes defense modernization decisions. For example, an intelligence analyst could simply use the current numbers of Chinese ships, tanks, aircraft, and other key indicators, then multiply these units by China's growth rate (say, 8 percent a year), perhaps adding a few new weapons systems known to be in development and retiring a few judged to be obsolete by 2010. Indeed, some in the U.S. intelligence community used such an approach on the Soviet Union for many years, even when it produced incorrect results. The erroneous assumption is that China is on "autopilot" in pursuing its military modernization. A more likely assumption is that China's leaders will debate and adjust their military programs (perhaps many times) between now and 2020. If so, then we must try to understand these debates and these adjustments rather than straight-lining, or making up long lists of obstacles that the Chinese can "never" overcome.

In a book published in 1998, a much better and more realistic approach than straight-lining has been suggested by John Culver who wisely points out that "most prudent analysts of the Chinese military rule out very few scenarios."[2] Culver's recommended approach proceeds from two important facts. First, he states that,

> . . . a survey of analytical documents prepared by the U. S. intelligence community over the past decade reveals a tendency toward "optimistic" assessments of developmental

weapons programs or changes in the force structure of the Chinese military.

In other words, American analysts have tended to overestimate China's capability to improve its forces and should be cautious not to repeat this mistake. This chapter argues that one factor in China's slow modernization has been a debate among the military leaders about their goals, a debate that includes at least three "schools" of thought, three sets of scenarios for future warfare China may face, and three corresponding preferences for defense allocations. Unfortunately, in spite of the evidence of these Chinese "schools," some specialists continue to impute "unified rational actor" decision-making to China as if Graham Allison, the Kennedy School of Government, and the seminal book, *Essence of Decision*, never existed.

I also agree completely with John Culver's second point, namely that,

> . . . in the course of examining the spectrum of development possibilities of the Chinese military in the next 10 to 20 years, two possibilities at the extreme end of the spectrum stand out: China could continue to make halting progress . . . or, China could break completely with the past and exhibit unprecedented abilities to integrate a new level of technology into its military. Either of these development trends is possible (as are any number of alternatives falling between these points on the development spectrum. . . .

Culver's prudent view of the range of choice that China faces suggests a potential policy challenge. The United States and other major powers (especially Japan and Russia) will have influence (if they wish to apply it) to shape China's future military capability. Along with Henry Kissinger, Culver and I and many others are impressed by the wide range of future Chinese military capabilities that may hypothetically develop in the next 10 to 20 years. Kissinger recently pointed that American options will not be lost by failing to confront China soon:

Undoubtedly, if China continues to grow at the rate of the past 20 years, it will become perhaps the most powerful country in Asia. Its impact on its neighbors would magnify. But do we really want a showdown now . . . ? [W]ere Beijing, at whatever juncture, to pursue hegemonistic policies it would have to contend around its borders with many states of considerable strength. A wise America could forge a determined resistance among them.[3]

Two Common Errors in Estimative Methods.

Unfortunately, Culver's views are not universally held, inside or outside the U.S. Government. Many analysts of Chinese capabilities are overly (perhaps obsessively) concerned with identifying **the obstacles that China faces** in developing its future military capabilities to the exclusion of finding factors that will help China's military modernization. It sometimes seems to me that some analysts of the Chinese military try to outdo each other to see who can imagine the most potent obstacles that China cannot possibly overcome for "decades." Strangely, perhaps for half-conscious ideological reasons, these same analysts shy away from considering even the most obvious benefits and advantages that China may enjoy as a technological latecomer. They seem to ignore that Japan, in the economic field in the 1950s and 1960s, benefited from catching up from behind. Excessively dwelling on the obstacles that China faces and ignoring China's advantages as a technological latecomer is a serious error. Analysts who doubt that obstacles can be overcome should read General Mi Zhenyu's book, *National Defense Development Strategy*, which lists the latecomers' advantages and urges China to exploit them. It seems to me rather strange for some analysts to display an almost cocky certainty that they can identify so well the obstacles to China's modernization and can identify so few advantages, especially in light of China's well-known secrecy about military affairs. As Ambassador James Lilley told the Senate Intelligence Committee on September 18, 1997:

> The other thing that clouds the issue is the Chinese superb practice of deception—when capable, feign incapacity. This is the way they operate. They'll throw up smoke screens. They'll take you to backward factories. They'll lead you down the garden path, and you'll always get some gullible person coming back saying their military is backward. For example they'll use obsolete tanks. That's because that's what the Chinese wanted them to see.

Analysts of the Chinese military who make long lists of obstacles are bad enough, but I fear more those analysts who neglect or even completely ignore the intentions and policy preferences of the Chinese military leadership. To estimate China's future military capabilities, it seems to me that a basic starting point should be to understand **what China's leaders think** they ought to try to develop. There is an especially perverse version of this error. It is committed by analysts who apparently assume the Chinese leadership to be robots in lockstep, incapable of disagreeing with each other about what goals for military modernization should be pursued. In one of the most useful analytical findings in many years, Dennis Blasko pointed out in 1996 that there seemed to be no Chinese Doctrine of Local War, in spite of the fact that quite a few Western analysts had been proclaiming a "new" doctrine of Local War for a decade.[4] A similar major contribution was made by Ellis Joffe in *The Chinese Army After Mao*,[5] when he shrewdly warned analysts of the Chinese military that there had been no formal termination or epitaph for Chairman Mao's doctrine of People's War, but that it had evolved in a very Chinese manner into something quite different.

What is the solution to the shortcomings of estimative methods? Are straight-line projections the only solution? Should we keep piling up examples of obstacles? Can we ever learn what doctrine and goals are guiding China's military modernization? Despite China's veil of secrecy, two modest steps may be worth consideration: greater exploitation of open sources and greater comparison of China with other cases, including historical cases.

SECTION ONE: U.S. DEFENSE DEPARTMENT NET ASSESSMENT

What is strategic or net assessment?[6] Does China do it differently than the United States? Net assessment is sometimes confused with intelligence analysis of foreign forces and international trends. The difference is that net or strategic assessment is an analysis of the *interaction* of two or more national security establishments both in peacetime and in war, usually ourselves and a potential enemy. It is the interaction of the two belligerents that is the central concept, not an assessment of one side alone.

A number of lessons from U.S. experience may help understand how China performs strategic assessment. The practice of strategic assessment in the U.S. Department of Defense in the past 25 years has been divided into the following six categories of studies and analyses:

(1) efforts to measure and forecast trends in various military balances such as the maritime balance, the Northeast Asian balance, the power-projection balance, etc.;

(2) assessments focused on weapons and force comparisons with efforts to produce judgments about military effectiveness;

(3) historical evaluations of lessons of the past;

(4) analyses of the role of perceptions of foreign decision-makers and even the process by which foreign institutions make strategic assessments;

(5) the search for quantitative analytical tools; and

(6) identifying competitive advantages and distinctive competencies of each side's military force posture, highlighting important trends that may change a long-term

balance, identifying future opportunities and risks in the military competition, and appraising the strengths and weaknesses of U.S. forces in light of long-term shifts in the security environment. This sixth form of study is the "net assessment" approach.[7]

Sources of Errors in Strategic Assessment.

In historical analysis, it is possible to examine what the senior leaders on each side did to "assess" the outcome and nature of the coming wars in the time prior to their outbreak. In fact, a widely praised explanation for the causes of war is precisely that the strategic assessments of opposing sides were in conflict prior to the initiation of combat—one side seldom starts a war believing in advance it will lose. Thus, we may presume there are almost always miscalculations in strategic assessments according to the nature of the national leadership that made the assessment. China may make its own miscalculations, and we should be alert to this possibility.

An insightful set of seven historical examples of strategic assessment in 1938-1940, which was produced for the Office of Net Assessment of the Office of the Secretary of Defense, has identified a number of serious assessment errors in Britain, Nazi Germany, Italy, France, the Soviet Union, the United States, and Japan.[8] A number of lessons drawn from these examples are relevant to any effort to understand how the Chinese leadership conducts strategic assessment of its future security environment.

First, it is a mistake to examine **static, side-by-side, force-on-force comparisons** of numbers of weapons and military units without trying to analyze the way these weapons and units would actually interact in future combat. The static use of counting numbers and units was at fault in the French military assessment of a potential German attack in 1939. The military balance, measured in quantitative terms between the German forces opposite France and the French forces involved in that theater, was almost equal, even slightly favoring France. The armored fire power of France and its allies exceeded that of the Germans by one-third. Force-on-force comparisons used by the French before the war did not reveal that (1) the Germans would achieve a four-to-one advantage by massing forces in the sector in which they achieved a breakthrough, (2) the Germans could make rapid, deep penetrations to destroy rear areas in France, and (3) the German air force would completely neutralize French air power and achieve absolute air superiority. Only a strategic assessment focusing on the qualities of the interaction of the two belligerents would give any indication of the outcome of the war.[9]

Second, the failure to define correctly **who will be a friend and who a foe in wartime** is critical to the outcome. Therefore, the question of international alignments or alliances cannot be ignored. Professor Paul Kennedy points out that Britain's pre-war planning completely failed to identify the role the Soviet Union could play as a second front in the war against Hitler. The French error was similar: French security thinkers failed to consider the scenario that Germany might first conquer France's East European allies, eliminating France's alliance, before attacking France directly.

Third, it is a mistake to deduce from an opponent's peacetime training exercises, published military doctrines, and peacetime military deployments what may be **the way forces actually conduct themselves in a protracted war** that goes beyond the original plan of war because the longer a war, the more time for factors involving the entire national society and economy to be brought into play and the less important the initial deployments, doctrines, and plans. Professor Stephen Rosen of Harvard University had found that, between August 1939 and June 1940, the U.S. Navy senior leadership's strategic assessments of the adequacy of U.S. military capabilities paid little attention to how a future war might unfold. It mainly satisfied U.S. Navy peacetime criteria, using simple comparisons of the number of U.S. Navy and Imperial Japanese Navy ships "... [with] no sense of the possible wartime interaction between the two fleets let alone between the two nations."[10]

Fourth, it is a mistake to **mirror image the assumptions of other nations.** As Andrew Marshall wrote in 1982 about assessing the former Soviet Union,

> A major component of any assessment of the adequacy of the strategic balance should be our best approximation of a Soviet-style assessment of the strategic balance. But this must not be the standard U.S. calculations done with slightly different assumptions. . . . rather it should be, to the extent possible, an assessment structured as the Soviets would structure it, using those scenarios they see as most likely and their criteria and ways of measuring outcomes . . . the Soviet calculations are likely to make different assumptions about scenarios and objectives, focus attention upon different variables, include both long-range and theater forces (conventional as well as nuclear), and may at the technical assessment level, perform different calculations, use different measures of effectiveness, and perhaps use different assessment processes and methods. The result is that Soviet assessments may substantially differ from American assessments.[11]

A fifth mistake is **geographic scope** or "big picture" problems. U.S. errors in the period between the two world wars were "big picture" problems. Although the United States eventually developed five alternative scenarios (RAINBOW I to V), it initially mistakenly believed it had only one potential enemy in the Pacific (Japan) and therefore assumed that, because of the Anglo-Japanese alliance of 1904, the United States might be forced to fight England in the Atlantic. Then with the rise of Hitler, 15 years of American assessments had to be discarded when the strategic focus shifted to winning first in Europe, while staying on the defensive in the Pacific.

A sixth mistake may be to neglect **open sources.** The most relevant comparison for better understanding China from among these pre-World War II case studies may be the study of the secretive Soviet Union of 1940. As Professor Earl Ziemke describes Soviet secrecy in 1940:

> The Soviet net assessment process cannot be directly observed. Like a dark object in outer space, its probable nature can be discerned only from interactions with visible surroundings. Fortunately, its rigidly secret environment has been somewhat subject to countervailing conditions. . . . Tukhachevsky and his associates conducted relatively open discussion in print.

Ziemke's description of the Soviet assessment process resembles in a few ways the Chinese process, including the "open discussion in print" of some assessment issues. It is apparent from Ziemke's account of the way in which Soviet strategic assessment was performed in the 1930s that a number of similarities, at least in institutional roles and the vocabulary of Marxism-Leninism, can also be seen in contemporary China. The leader of the Soviet Communist Party publicly presented a global strategic assessment to periodic Communist Party Congresses. The authors of the military portions of the assessment came from two institutions which have counterparts in Beijing today and were prominent in Moscow in the 1930s: the General Staff Academy and the National War College. Another similarity was that the Soviet Communist Party leader chaired a defense council or main military committee and, in these capacities, attended peacetime military exercises and was involved in deciding the details of military strategy, weapons acquisition, and war planning. As the leader of a party based on "scientific socialism," the leader was expected to pronounce openly the Party's official assessment of the future. Sensitive details obviously had to remain secret, but open sources could provide at least an outline of the assessment.

SECTION TWO: CHINA'S CURRENT STRATEGIC ASSESSMENT

Four superb books have laid the foundation for future efforts to understand China's perceptions of its security environment and the Chinese assessment process—David Shambaugh's *Beautiful Imperialist,* Gilbert Rozman's *The Chinese Debate on Soviet Socialism,* Allen Whiting's *China Eyes Japan,* and Carol Hamrin's *China and the Challenge of the Future.*[12] They stress the unique premises used by Chinese analysts during the 1980s and the process of debate among both analysts and the senior leadership in Beijing.[13] Some premises are:

- China's commitment to its version of Marxism rules out the use of Western international relations concepts to assess the future security environment. This ideology prohibits using certain concepts to assess the future. Deng Xiaoping's national security adviser on the State Council, Huan Xiang, wrote in 1987 that "bourgeois theories of international relations" were to serve the interests of imperialist foreign policies.[14] One well-known Chinese analyst observed that "differing from western international relations theorists such as Hans Morganthau, *China's theory of international relations is based on dialectical and historical materialism.*"[15] Textbooks of international relations in use in China, such as a recent book by Liang Shoude and Hong Yinxian, emphasize the interpretations of Marx, Lenin, Mao, and Deng.[16] Liang asserts that the foreign policies of nations depend on whether the bourgeois or the proletariat is in power.

- *Chinese textbooks state that bourgeois states are greedy and constantly plot war and intervention; they are blocked from this course only by the socialist states who desire peace and development. Students in China from high school on are examined on these principles.*

Liang headed the commission that drafted the national syllabus in international politics for all universities. The Chinese have explicitly rejected Western international relations theory, including the school of thought known as Realism or Neo-Realism, which began to be discussed in 1982 in China.[17]

- Consistent with their ideology, Chinese analysts have rigid views about the causes of war. *In contrast to Western research that suggests miscalculation and misperceptions may be the leading cause of war,*[18] *Chinese analysts assert that "scrambling for resources" causes war.* "Economic factors are . . . the most fundamental cause triggering war."[19] Such a narrow view may make it difficult for Chinese analysts to appreciate the role of miscalculation and misperceptions in causing war.

A Multipolar World.

What geopolitical features of the future do Chinese authors consider significant? Four questions are often addressed. Which nations will be the most powerful by 2020? What kinds of international alignments will form? What kinds of war may occur for which China should prepare? How will the RMA affect the relationships among the major powers?

The Current Assessment, 1986-1998. China's current assessment of the future security environment is based on the kind of calculations Sun Zi and the Warring-States strategist would recognize. The current assessment was issued *before* the collapse of the Union of Soviet Socialist Republics (USSR) and the end of the Cold War. It can be dated to early 1986. It is characterized as a "new era" of transition that will last several decades. During this period, many "local wars" will be fought (as large as Korea in 1950 or the Gulf War) as a "redivision of spheres of influence" takes place. It was reaffirmed as recently as August 28, 1998, in *Liberation Army Daily*, when Jiang Zemin told a group of Chinese ambassadors that the future structural pattern of "multipolarity" will restrict "hegemonism" and evolve gradually but inevitably.

Bosnia is one example, because in Chinese documents the Bosnia conflict is frequently called a "struggle between the United States and the European Union for domination of Europe." NATO enlargement, which China opposes, is another example of this "struggle to re-divide spheres of influence."

> Trends From 2000 to 2030:
>
> - A turbulent transition era of many Local Wars over natural resources.
>
> - U.S. hegemony declines toward global multipolarity of five equal powers.
>
> - Japan and Europe re-divide the former Russian and U.S. spheres of influence.
>
> - U.S. security alliances fade ("Cold War relics") as China's Five Principles are observed.

The outcome of this transitional period of "turbulence" will have the following eight features.

- After the transition period is complete, there will no longer be any "superpowers," but instead a "multipolar world" in which five major nations will each have roughly equal CNP.

- The nations that will do "best" in competitive terms during the transitional period will pursue "peace and development" and enhance their economic competitiveness. By avoiding Local Wars, they can decrease defense expenditures and avoid the damage of warfare. Chinese authors frequently assert that the collapse of the USSR and the decline of the United

States are due in large part to extremely high defense spending and declining competitiveness in CNP.

- Today's "sole superpower" is in severe decline. The United States risks declining so rapidly that it may not even be one of the five multipolar powers and may fall to the level of a mere "regional power." This continual decline of the United States in the decades ahead is an important feature of the Chinese assessment, so this study provides more details on this subject than on China's views of other major powers.

- After the transition to the multipolar world, a new "world system" will emerge to govern international affairs and that will probably resemble the current Chinese proposal for Five Principles of Peaceful Coexistence. The Chinese authorities assert that world politics since the 1800s always has had a "system" or a "strategic pattern." Under those rules, there is a competition among powers that includes a global division of spheres of influence. Chinese historical textbooks discuss (1) the "Vienna System" of 1815-70, (2) an intermediate system when Germany and Italy each unified and Japan launched the Meiji Reform, (3) the "Versailles System" of 1920-45, (4) the "Yalta System" of 1945-89, and (5) the present "transition era."

- The new Chinese-style "world system," based on the Five Principles of Peaceful Coexistence, will be much better, they assert, because there will be harmony, no "power politics" and no more "hegemony."[20] This harmonious world requires a transition away from the capitalism of the major powers toward some type of "socialist market economy." Just as China has modified the doctrines of Marx, Engels, Lenin, and Stalin to produce what Deng Xiaoping called "Socialism with Chinese Characteristics," so will the

United States, Germany, Japan, and Russia ultimately develop their own socialist characteristics.

- Some Chinese military authors believe that there is now underway an RMA that will radically change future warfare. Five recent Chinese books assert that the United States will not exploit the RMA as well as other nations in the decades ahead.[21] China's generals "plan to be better, to be ahead of everyone... and become latecomers who surpass the old-timers."[22]

- A major global nuclear war is highly unlikely for 2 decades. This official forecast is a sharp change from the forecasts of Chairman Mao that a global nuclear war was inevitable.[23] Therefore, China claims to have cut its defense spending from more than 6 percent of Gross National Product (GNP) in the 1960s and 1970s, to between 2 and 3 percent when the current assessment came into force by the mid-1980s, and down to about 1.5 percent of the GNP in the 1990s. This claim by China that it has drastically reduced defense spending, which included cutting the PLA's size from seven million to three million, is based on China's expectation to remain above the fray of "local wars" during the turbulent transition era ahead.

- There are many global forces at work creating turbulence (*luan*, a Chinese word which also may be translated as chaos), including the potential for nationalist, militarist takeovers of Japan and India. The "main trend" in the world, however, is toward "peace and development," but "potential hot spots exist which could lead to the involvement of major powers and regional powers in direct military confrontation."[24] Even in Asia,

Although the Asia-Pacific region has been relatively stable since the end of the Cold War, there are also many uncertainties there. If certain hot-spot problems are not handled properly, they may cause conflicts, confrontations, and even war in this region, thus wrecking the peace, stability, and prosperity of the region.[25]

Within the framework of this strategic assessment, China's analysts discuss a number of subjects in their journals and books.[26] For example, the question frequently arises concerning the manner that current events fit into the framework. Some Chinese authors see the following current examples of the "turbulent period of transition" as suggesting that former spheres of influence are being re-divided. While not all Chinese would agree with all these findings, the examples listed below demonstrate how the framework of the assessment of the future is applied in practice.

- First, the United States is exploiting Russian weakness by enlarging NATO in order to increase its domination of its European NATO allies.

- Second, the United States ("its hegemonistic ambitions further inflated") is forcing Japan to increase its financial support for U.S. bases and forces in Japan under the guise of the Defense Guidelines.[27]

- Third, the United States arranged the Bosnian settlement at Dayton to further dominate its European NATO allies.

- Fourth, Japan is seeking to embroil the United States and China in a struggle that will weaken both Washington and Beijing.

- Fifth, some in the United States are fearful of China and seek to contain or block China's gradually increasing influence by promoting the "China threat theory." This is wrong because "China has neither the strength nor the will to compete with the United States and other big powers in global affairs."[28]

- Sixth, Central Asia may be the location of political struggles and wars among the big powers as the former Soviet sphere of influence is re-divided.

Calculating Geopolitics: Lessons from the Warring-States Era.

China's military authors refer often to certain similarities between the geopolitics of the Warring-States era and the coming multipolar world structure. A representative article states that the classic book Sun Zi's *The Art of War* was "the product of the multipolar world structure in China 2500 years ago," that "there are a surprising number of similarities between Sun Zi's time and the contemporary multipolar trend," and that "in the 1990s, the world entered a multipolar era very similar to the time of Sun Zi."[29] The Warring-States period of ancient China is little known in the West. It was the source of the classic lessons of Chinese statecraft.[30] Unfortunately, there is no guide for Westerners to Chinese traditional statecraft. According to interviews with Chinese military officers, the style of statecraft is embedded in Chinese culture just as the West has its own history, its own literature, and its own Bible stories.[31] Two studies by the late Herbert Goldhamer sought to outline some of the content of Chinese statecraft and China's unique perceptions, but this work has not been continued.[32]

One of Goldhamer's insights relevant to this study is his emphasis on the fact that China's ancient statecraft demanded efforts to calculate the future. He points out that ancient China's first minister was called The Universal Calculator; that the philosopher Han Feizi demanded that strategy be based on cost-benefit calculations; and that the philosopher Mo Zi persuaded an enemy general to surrender by showing he could calculate through a "seminar game" what the battle's outcome would be, if fought.[33] The Warring-States era already had the equivalent of General Staffs, which calculated the strengths and intentions of players in this multipolar world;[34] Sun Zi warned that victory depended on the calculations and estimates of enemy strength and weaknesses that had been made in advance by advisers in the temple council; Mo Zi taught his students the future could be known.[35] Two of ancient China's greatest advisers on statecraft, Lord Shang and Li Ssu, warned of the need for calculating the future in a multipolar strategic environment. Li Ssu wrote a famous memorandum to the ruler of Qin, the man who would unify China and become its first emperor, warning that "this is the one moment in ten thousand ages. If your Highness allows it to slip away . . . there will form an anti-Qin alliance."[36] With regard to calculating the future, Goldhamer suggests that political writings from ancient China contained "principled predictions," not just intuition or guess work. For example, another famous adviser in Qin, Lord Shang warned that the price for neglecting quantitative calculations would be that even a state with a large population and a favorable geographical position "will become weaker and weaker, until it is dismembered. . . . The early kings did not rely on their beliefs but on their figures."[37] The subject of Chinese statecraft in a multipolar world, explored by Goldhamer, remains important to China's process of strategic assessment, especially judging by the sharp increase of Chinese military publications about the relevance of ancient statecraft in the last few years.[38]

Ancient Chinese Strategists and Comprehensive National Power.

Although the phrase "comprehensive national power" was invented in 1984, it has cultural roots in Chinese ancient statecraft. In his book, *Grand Strategy*, Wu Chunqiu, at the Academy of Military Science, provides examples from Sun Zi's *The Art of War,* Wu Zi's *The Art of War,* and *Guan Zi* to show how "the discussion of warfare in Chinese ancient literature embodies . . . national power thinking."[39] He writes that "China's wise ancient strategists never advocated only relying on military power to conquer the enemy, but emphasized combining military power with non-military power related to war in order to get the upper hand." Sun Zi identified "five things" and "seven stratagems" which governed the outcome of war. Wu Zi wrote about six conditions which, if the other side's strength was greater, meant war should be avoided. Wu Chunqiu writes, "These six points . . . are relatively complete, they simply are the epitome of [today's concept of] comprehensive national power."

According to Wu Chunqiu, calculating CNP can aid a nation not just for war but also to "coordinate a political and diplomatic offensive, to psychologically disintegrate the enemy forces and subdue them." Wu states,

> Victory without war does not mean that there is not any war at all. The wars one must fight are political wars, economic wars, science and technology wars, diplomatic wars, etc. To sum up in a word, it is a war of Comprehensive National Power.[40]

Section Three of this study explores CNP forecasts.

Avoiding War with Warring-States Strategy.

Within certain political limits, Chinese authors can examine the challenges that China will face and suggest alternative strategies. The director of the China Institute of Contemporary International Relations' (CICIR) foreign policy center, Dr. Yan Xuetong (Ph.D. Berkeley), has cautioned that the ruling American hegemon can be kept from using force to contain China's rise as long as certain policy goals are maximized. These are annually increasing exports up to 9 percent and avoiding simultaneous confrontation with the United States and two other powerful nations. Using an imaginative table of probabilities, Dr. Yan predicts that China can avoid war for at least 10 years by adopting these two policies. However, his assessment shows that as China's annual share of export markets decline and as the number of powerful nations that China confronts increases, the probability

China will become involved in wars increases rather sharply. Dr. Yan adds that because of American covert support for Taiwan independence, he cannot estimate if war with the United States can be avoided for more than 10 years.[41]

SECTION THREE: CALCULATING COMPREHENSIVE NATIONAL POWER

Two contending scientific teams in Beijing, one from the military and one from the civil sector, have calculated estimates of the CNP scores of the major powers in 2010. Both teams claim to use very sophisticated quantitative methods which, they explain, had to be developed due to the deficiencies in the methodological techniques that are used by the West and Japan to measure future growth rates in national power.

The military team's quantitative results are consistent with the orthodox Chinese view that a multipolar world structure is emerging and that U.S. hegemony is ending. In particular, according to the military estimate, the U.S. quantitative power score by 2010 shows a decreasing gap between the United States and the other major powers, and by 2020, the U.S. score will equal China's national power score, assuming China's power growth rate continues to be 5.8 percent, double the U.S. rate of 2.7 percent. Germany and Japan will also have higher CNP growth rates than the United States and will become the third- and fourth-ranking world powers after the United States and China in 2020. If these growth rates are extended another decade or so, China, Japan, and Germany will all three equal or surpass the United States in CNP, but the United States will remain ahead of Russia (which is not scored due to uncertainty) and India, the sixth power in rank order of CNP.

The civilian team's results contradict the orthodox view in China about an emerging multipolar structure. The most striking contrast is the assessment of China. The civilian team does not rank China equal to the United States by 2020, but instead, merely number eight in the world, with a projected power score of only about half of the U.S. score by 2010 and 2020. A second contrast is that the civilian team's quantitative results place Japan not number four in the world by 2010, but equal to the United States in 2010. Japan pulls ahead of the United States by 20 percent in 2020. China in 2020 will still rank only seventh in the world, trailing not only the United States and Japan, but Germany, France, Italy, and even South Korea in CNP.

Interestingly, military power is only 10 percent of the total, in spite of the claim by some authors that CNP scores can determine the outcome of wars. Figure 1 shows the relative CNP of five nations, including the United States and China, in 1989, 2000, and 2020.

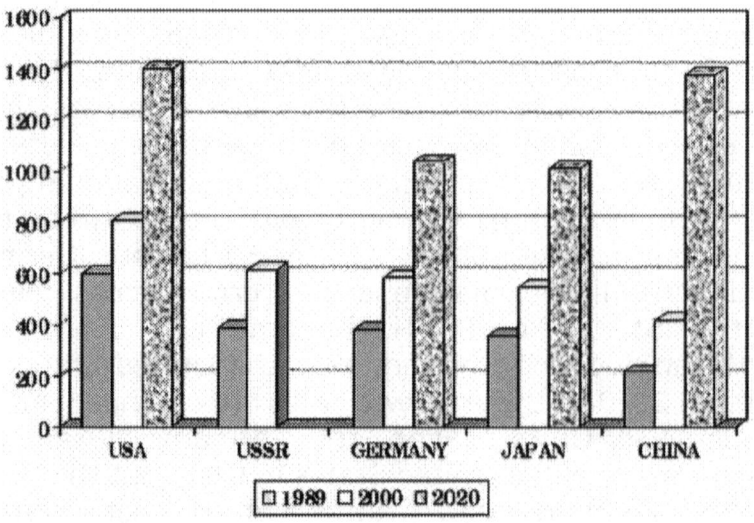

Figure 1. Comprehensive National Power Scores, 1989-2020.

National Power Factor	Weighted Coefficient
Total Comprehensive National Power	1.00
Natural resources	0.08
Economic activities capability	0.28
Foreign economic activities capability	0.13
Scientific and technological capability	0.15
Social development level	0.10
Military capability	0.10
Government regulation capability	0.08

SECTION FOUR: FUTURE PLA CAPABILITY: "SCHOOLS" OF FUTURE WARFARE

There is evidence that China's leadership cannot decide among several future paths that have been proposed by policy analysts and is therefore allocating resources among three distinct paths. Two of these paths represent reforms. Advocates of the two reform schools seemed to be arrayed against a third group of conservative traditionalists who have been losing their share of the allocation of defense investments. The muted debate among these schools may affect defense resource allocations. This section describes the three schools; the next section suggests what kind of future defense investments each school may prefer.

What Kind of Wars Could Affect China?

Since 1994, several dozen articles have appeared in the Chinese press and in military journals that purport to discuss China's current and future defense strategy. These articles are not all in agreement. At least three, and possibly more, schools of thought may be distinguished.

In the first school, authors refer to the enduring validity of Mao's concepts of People's War.[42] These authors imply that the 21st century may well see the outbreak of another

> People's War Scenarios:
>
> - The enemy—United States, Russia, or Japan—will invade and seek to subjugate China.
>
> - The war will last many years.
>
> - China's leaders will move to alternative national capitals during the war.
>
> - China's defense-industrial base will arm millions of militia in protracted war until the enemy can be defeated by the main army.

world war, a major invasion of China, or the use of nuclear weapons.[43] This "Maoist" school of thought is less frequently seen in Chinese military journals than a second school of thought, which can be termed "local war."

Local War is identified by the authors' call for China to prepare not for a protracted People's War with national mobilization, but for a quick, smaller scale "Local War under high-tech conditions" or simply Local War *(jubu zhanzheng)*. Such a war would be limited in scope, duration, and objective. These authors frequently cite a speech by Deng Xiaoping to the Central Military Commission in 1985 to explain the origins of the concept. Deng's speech flatly decreed that the world would not be seeing a world war or a major nuclear war for "a long time to come." In the decade since that speech, more than 30 conflict scenarios have been examined in articles by Chinese authors from this school of thought. In interviews of Chinese military officers the author conducted, it seems that the term "local war" is not a good translation of the concept that the Chinese authors have been discussing. Rather, Local War seems to include a broad range of scenarios, encompassing, in fact, almost any war smaller in scale than a global war or a major nuclear war.

> Local War Scenarios:
> - The opponent will not be a superpower.
> - The war will be near China's border.
> - The war will not be a deep invasion.
> - China will seek a quick military decision.
> - Rapid reaction forces will defeat local forces of Japan, Vietnam, India, Central Asia, Taiwan, Philippines, Malaysia, or Indonesia.

The third school of thought probably dates only from 1994 and is represented by a few books and a number of articles. However, its proponents include several generals who occupy or are recently retired from high positions in China's most influential military institutions. This third school of thought recommends that China prepare for future warfare along the lines of concepts first discussed by Russian and American authors who forecast a potential RMA.

Chinese writers in 1995 repeatedly referred to the "third military technical revolution" without actually citing the Soviet military journals which in the past decade have been discussing the same subject. What was new in 1995 in Beijing was not the subject itself, which had been discussed in books such as General Mi Zhenyu's *Chinese National Defense Concepts*.[44] It was the enthusiasm for the subject that was different. In October 1995, the official media announced a national conference had been held to discuss the implications of a potential revolution in military affairs.

Soviet military science and its Chinese counterpart explicitly require the use of "scientific" forecasts about the changing nature of future warfare. In other words, it is mandated by "military science" that strategists concern themselves with the search for the emergence of "revolutionary" changes in warfare brought about mainly by technological change rather than falsely assuming that mere evolutionary trends will continue.

> Revolution In Military Affairs Scenarios:
>
> - The opponent will have advanced weapons, satellites for communications and reconnaissance, stealth aircraft, nuclear weapons, and nanotechnology—perhaps the United States, Russia, or Japan.
> - China must close an "information gap."
> - China must network all forces.
> - China must attack the enemy C^3I to paralyze it.
> - China must pre-empt enemy attacks.
> - China must use directed energy weapons.
> - China must use computer viruses.
> - China must use submarine-launched munitions.
> - China must use anti-satellite weapons.
> - China must use forces to prevent a logistics buildup.
> - China must use special operations raids.

According to the shared Chinese and former Soviet concepts, "military science" studies operational art as well as specific approaches including "the conditions and factors that determine, at any given historical moment, the nature of a future war."[45]

There seems to be no American counterpart to Chinese "military science" and its related requirement to anticipate military revolutions and to "experiment scientifically" with organizations, exercises, and prototype equipment. Rather, American studies of military innovation tend to emphasize the somewhat accidental role of the relatively rare individual genius who invents a new concept, pushes a new doctrinal idea, or changes resource allocations together with his organizational allies.

Like the RMA school, the Local War school also borrows Soviet and American concepts. After the Gulf War in 1991, authors writing about Local War incorporated many aspects of the American Gulf War strategy into their concept of this type of conflict. More than 40 books were published by the Academy of Military Science and the National Defense University, drawing on examples from the Gulf War in order to illustrate how China's concept of Local War should be implemented in the 21st century. Most of this writing focused on how the Chinese military may have to defend against an American-style Gulf War offensive action. In a similar fashion, the main Chinese military newspaper, *Liberation Army Daily*, has published in the last 5 years several hundred articles attempting to describe Local War doctrine and Chinese military exercises designed to cope with a "high-tech enemy." These articles and books leave little doubt that the weapons, equipment, and uniforms that will be possessed by this "high-tech enemy" will be the forces of the United States or its military allies.

These three schools of authors cannot be easily reconciled. With a limited budget, it is hard to prepare for all three types of future warfare. The neo-Maoist or People's War school seems to recommend that China be prepared for a long war of many years at a low level of intensity in which space can be traded for time, territory will be surrendered initially, and the population will be mobilized for guerrilla warfare against the invader and in support of the regular Chinese armed forces. The authors of the Local War school advocate preparing for a short warning attack in which the decision will come quickly, with no opportunity to mobilize the nation for a multiyear People's War. They explicitly describe future "local" warfare as concluding within a matter of days or weeks, allowing no time to mobilize the population. There will instead be an intense tempo. Success will almost certainly require China to consider pre-emptive strikes against the enemy near or beyond China's borders in order to achieve an "early, decisive victory."

Since the early 1980s, foreign scholars have declared in a series of articles that Local War has become the official strategic doctrine of China. These conclusions may have been premature. Not only have the neo-Maoist articles continued to appear, but in interviews conducted by the author, senior Chinese military officers declared that Local War doctrine had not been written for China's armed forces, nor has it been formally adopted by the Central Military Commission, at least as of 1998. This divergence between published articles and military exercises, on the one hand, and the lack of an authoritative declaration that Local War is the national strategy constitutes a major puzzle.

Further complicating the confusion is the fact that in the last 3 years, observers have noted an increase in the press attention to China's nuclear forces being further developed, a direction that does not seem connected to Local War doctrine. Additionally, a series of books and articles have appeared advocating a Chinese blue water navy, another direction that also seems to have no linkage to the Local War doctrine. Some PLA naval authors assert that Local War at sea covers two large zones of "active defense." Within the first zone out to the "first island chain," there are three levels, each with its own naval forces providing a "multi-level in-depth defense at sea." The sea space between the People's Republic of China (PRC) coast and the "first Pacific island chain" has three levels:

(1) out to 50 miles, which is defended by radar, missiles, and large coastal patrol boats such as missile speedboats and fast gunships, and where laying mines and clearing enemy mines is very important;

(2) from 50 to 300 miles from the coast, which is defended by missile destroyers and corvettes, including ship-based helicopters;

(3) from the Korean Peninsula to the Ryukyu and Spratly Islands, which is defended by submarines with advanced missiles and naval attack planes.[46]

The "second island chain" that the Chinese navy aspires to patrol extends along a line from the Aleutians through Guam and the Philippines. However, these "island chains" are not discussed by PLA navy (PLAN) authors who write about the RMA.

As if this were not enough confusion, since 1994 the third RMA school of thought has been vocal in advocacy pieces that do not directly attack Local War theory, but state that China must exploit a potential future RMA in order to avoid a growing gap in its military capabilities as compared to America, Russia, and Japan. At least 30 articles have appeared advocating development by China of the capability to conduct information operations, massive long-range precision strikes, attacks on enemy satellites in space, and efforts to paralyze an enemy's command and control system by non-nuclear attacks on his homeland.

Institutional Affiliations of the Three Schools.

These three schools may be seen as independent, or even linked, viewpoints which any individual could hold. They may also reflect the institutional biases of the "homes" where the schools' authors work. RMA advocates (who tend to be senior colonels and a few major generals) seem to be employed by the Academy of Military Science (AMS) or the large components of the Commission on Science, Technology and Industry for National Defense (COSTIND) complex, such as the China Aerospace Corporation, and its research institutes, such as the Beijing Institute of System Engineering. This is not surprising since COSTIND and the research institutes focus on technology for their livelihood. The Local War authors occupy most of the highest leadership positions of the PLA and also are employed at the National Defense University, which trains almost all future generals. The authors of the People's War school seem to be senior party officials, members of the General Political Department, and senior militia and People's Armed Police (PAP) leaders who spent most of their careers in a politicized, Maoist environment.

The three schools may also to some extent reflect the current state of China's existing force structure, its efforts in doctrinal development, the equipment in its inventory, and the types of conflict scenarios used as points of reference. According to a concept proposed by Dennis Blasko, the relationship of the three schools to one another and to Chinese force structure can be visualized as a triangle or pyramid composed of three tiers.[47] This relationship is depicted in Figure 2.

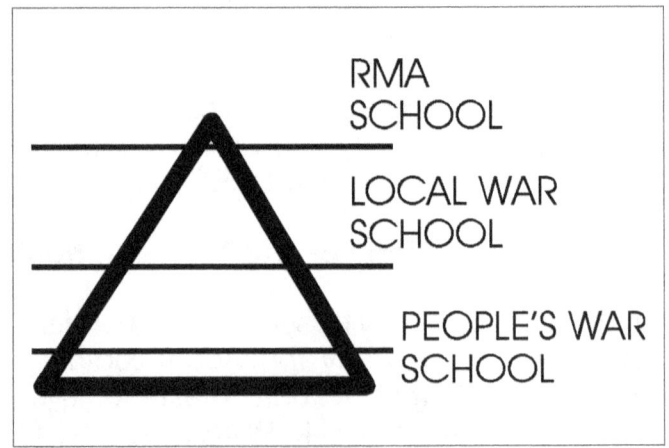

Figure 2. Blasko Pyramid.

People's War: The Pyramid's Base.

The base of the pyramid consists of the People's War school—the vast majority of the PLA today. The military thought of Mao Zedong provides the theoretical foundation for this school.[48] This doctrine is mainly defensive and has little utility beyond the borders of China, but a considerable portion of all Chinese military writing still must pay homage to the heritage of People's War. Probably about 80 percent of the PLA is best suited to fight a People's War and is equipped with weapons designed in the 1950s and 1960s that would be museum pieces in many countries. This school relies upon the use of "existing weapons to defeat an enemy equipped with high technology weaponry." These forces are trained to defend the mainland, its adjacent seas, and air space from invasion. They would fight alongside the militia and swallow up an invader, using concepts devised by Mao 60 years ago and slightly modified to account for "modern conditions." Stratagem and deception are particularly important in People's War. Logistics for these forces depend almost completely on the militia and a supportive, friendly local populace.

Local War School: The Pyramid's Middle Tier.

The second tier of the PLA pyramid is the Local War school. It requires fully trained and equipped forces that can react rapidly to problems on China's periphery. Maybe 15 percent of all army, navy, and air force units fall into this category and have the requisite preparation. The writings of Deng Xiaoping contain the theory that justifies this school.[49] In the 1980s, as the PLA began its modernization program, it developed rapid reaction units, experimental forces, and what has been labeled the "Doctrine of Local War." Local War is understood to be a limited war on the periphery of China that will be short but intense, utilizing advanced technology weapons, with units fighting in a joint and combined arms effort. It envisions an element of force projection (i.e., the ability to transport combat forces to and, when necessary, beyond China's borders), but by definition is regional, not global, in nature. Some rapid reaction and experimental units, but by no means all, have been the recipients of the numerically-limited imports of Russian hardware reported so vigorously by the media. Many units in this category still are equipped with outdated indigenous equipment and, like the Peoples' War school, must devise ways to use their existing weapons to defeat a high-technology opponent. This segment of the PLA probably receives more training opportunities than do units dedicated to fighting a People's War. China usually regards Local War as its "next war"; the Persian Gulf War is often a point of reference for this school. China has no combat experience in this type of conflict. At this time, the development and dissemination of doctrine on how the PLA will fight such a war is limited. The number of units actually prepared to live up to these modern standards is problematic, but this portion of the PLA is expected to grow in the future.

The RMA Advocates: Pyramid's Narrow Top.

The RMA school is represented by only a very small portion of the PLA strategists in its premier academic institutions, officers in what was COSTIND and who are now probably affiliated with the General Armaments Department, some of its strategic missile units in what is known as the Second Artillery, and a few other units equipped with modern cruise missiles.

Three Mutually Exclusive Scenarios.

Different types of conflict scenarios emerge from each school of thought. In interviews with Chinese military officers, there are distinctive premises and assumptions made by each of the three schools of thought about Asian conflict scenarios. From the viewpoint of the People's War framework, the most significant and likely scenario is the takeover of a major power by a leader who is viewed by the Chinese as a madman bent on the invasion of China to "turn China into a colony." Whether Russian, Japanese, or American, this madman could successfully carry out the first phase of his invasion and penetrate several hundred miles into China along several axes of advance.

This school is obviously vulnerable to allegations that the Chinese are still planning to "fight the last war." The example of a 7-year war against the Japanese invaders with a loss of over 20 million Chinese lives occurred during the lifetime of all Chinese military officers over the age of 50.

This school of thought is particularly committed to the need to maintain a defense mobilization base and defense industry for production of weapons in the deep interior of China where an alternative command center and national capital would be established for the years required to repulse the madman's invading forces. Figure 3 shows the main points of a People's War scenario.

In contrast to the People's War school, the Local War school of thought focuses on entirely different scenarios. Its concern is to repel enemy forces that infringe on Chinese territory or maritime resources. These authors refer to islands already occupied by China's enemies and China's disputed borders with nearly all its neighbors, including North Korea. They are also concerned about separatists in Tibet and western China who may receive terrorist or military support from China's enemies.

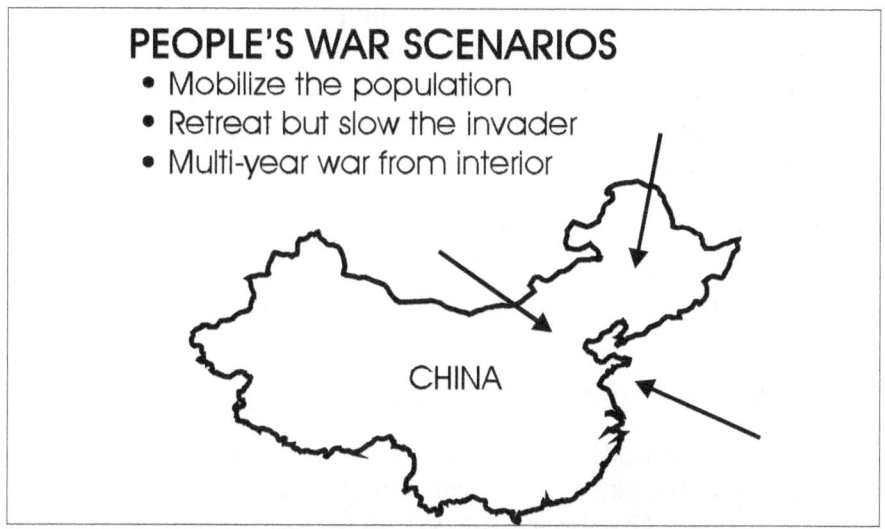

Figure 3. People's War Scenarios.

Chinese military authors have never repudiated the writings of Chairman Mao. The highest leaders still proclaim that People's War is the essence of China's military thinking.

Local wars may not be small, but they are conceived as being fought for limited objectives. The Local War authors include China's conflict with Vietnam in 1979 and with the United States in northern Korea in 1950-51 as examples. In February and March 1979, China mobilized at least 400,000 ground forces to achieve superiority over the 100,000 Vietnamese troops (mainly militia) and used more than 1,200 tanks and 1,500 heavy artillery pieces in support of the attack. No air or sea forces were involved. China suffered as many as 50,000 casualties with 10,000 deaths. The Chinese offer of a Chinese withdrawal from Vietnam in return for a Vietnamese withdrawal from Cambodia was rejected by Vietnam.[50]

In Korea, China sent 260,000 troops to secretly surround and ambush a smaller American and South Korean force of 140,000, nearly achieving a 2:1 superiority. As this "local war" continued, a massive Chinese offensive in April 1951 cost 70,000 Chinese casualties. By mid-1951, 700,000 troops on the China-North Korean side faced 420,000 United Nations (U.N.) troops. By the conflict's end in 1953, China lost an estimated 400,000 dead.[51] The proximate cause of Chinese intervention in Korea, as stated by China's spokesman, was

> The American imperialists . . . directly threatened our northeastern borders. . . . The aim was not Korea itself but to invade China . . . to save our neighbor is to save ourselves . . . only resistance can make the imperialists learn the lesson.[52]

Figure 4 shows points associated with Local War doctrine.

The third school of thought, which concerns itself with a potential RMA, seems to envision conflict scenarios very different from the first two schools. For example, in his article "The Challenge of Information Warfare," General Wang Pufeng, after quoting Andrew W. Marshall, urges that China develop three new missions: a strategic reconnaissance and warning system, a battlefield information network that brings all military branches into a

Figure 4. Local War Scenarios.

Most Chinese authors in the past decade discuss Local War doctrine.

single network for combat coordination, and long-range precision strike systems, including tactical guided missiles. In an implicit rebuke to Local War analysts and neo-Maoists, General Wang emphasizes that "in comparison with the strength of its potential enemies, the information technology and information weapons of the Chinese Armed Forces will all be inferior for quite some time." He also warns about the need to be the first to exploit a revolution in military affairs:

> Those who perceive it first will swiftly rise to the top and have the advantage of the first opportunities. Those who perceive it late will unavoidably also be caught up in the vortex of this revolution. Every military will receive this baptism. This revolution is first a revolution in concepts.[53]

Other articles by this RMA school stress "the submarine will rise in its status to become a major naval warfare force" with the "appearance of underwater arsenal ships (perhaps a reference to submarines capable of launching cruise missiles) and underwater mine laying robots." Space warfare will be conducted by navy ships and ground-based weapons which can destroy satellite reconnaissance and other space systems. Tactical laser weapons will be needed for anti-ship defense. Long-range precision strikes at sea will cause "both sides to strive to make lightning attacks and raise their first strike damage rate."[54]

Chinese RMA Articles on Future Warfare:

- United States Will Fail to Exploit the RMA
- RMA requires New Measures of Effectiveness
- RMA requires New Operational Concepts
    — Pre-emptive Information Warfare
    — Long-Range Precision Strikes
    — Primacy of Submarines
    — Stealth and Counter-stealth
    — Nanotechnology Weapons
    — Robots
    — Directed Energy Weapons

One theme of this RMA school is the need to change the measures of effectiveness used to design and develop military equipment and weapons. One analyst proposed that future weapons systems and military organizations be judged largely on the basis of the "intensity with which they use information technology." It is apparent from this author's proposal that Local War weapons and equipment now being procured in China would score at a very low level using the Information Intensity Measure of Effectiveness. Thus, this article is another harsh criticism of the recommendations of both the Local War and neo-Maoist schools.[55] Figure 5 shows likely scenarios, according to the RMA school.

How should foreign observers assess and understand these conflicting Chinese strategic writings? The Asian conflict scenarios implicit in the RMA school of thought involve China's future enemies possessing equipment and capabilities that are not possessed by Vietnam, Outer Mongolia, North Korea, India, the Central Asian states, South Korea, and Japan at this time. The missions of long-range precision strike, information warfare operations, and attacks against space satellite reconnaissance systems imply that advanced military powers, either Russia or the United States, are part of the conflict scenario.

These three Asian conflict scenarios seem mutually exclusive. Is there a "strategic debate" underway which has

Figure 5. RMA Scenarios.

In the 1990s, Chinese military authors began to address how the RMA will change the nature of warfare. Their scenarios envisaged attacks on China by a superpower.

not been resolved? Some authors refer to past debates on military strategy:

> In the 1980s there was a debate among Chinese military circles on the following questions: How to comprehend the exact meaning of "luring the enemy in deep"? Is it meant for battles or for the whole war? Should China fight a protracted or a quick war? Should China fight a full-scale war or a limited Local War?[56]

Implicit in these questions are the views of the Local War school, which in the 1980s probably was the "reform" view as opposed to the orthodox People's War view. The president of the Academy of Military Science (AMS) apparently sided with the Local War view. According to interviews in Beijing, the AMS actually "staffed" out the formation of the Local War concepts.

Yan Xuetong of CICIR continues the story to the late 1980s:

> After the Cold War a consensus has basically been reached on these questions among Chinese military circles, i.e., in order to ensure the safety of the country's economic achievements against war damages, the Chinese army must commit itself to the task of engaging the enemy outside of China's territory. Additionally, because wars China might be involved in during the post Cold War period will most probably be high-tech Local Wars, the Chinese army must acquire the ability of winning a high tech Local War so as to keep the enemy outside the country's territory.

Yan here introduces an evolution of the original Local War view that focused on border disputes—by the early 1990s, the view emerged that China must fight Local War beyond its borders. Yan writes:

> Consequently, a strategy of active defense that lays stress on enhancing the army's rapid response capability and readiness for any high tech Local War has become China's current military strategy for national defense. The objective of this

strategy is to prevent war from breaking out, or if failing that, to keep them outside of China's territory.[57]

Even with these insights about the 1980s, analysis in the 1990s remains difficult because the three groups under review decline to acknowledge each other. They do not "debate" in a Western sense of the word, and positions are not always clear cut. For example, People's War may be invoked to support the importance of information warfare. When outsiders inquire about apparent differences, Chinese authors decline to admit the existence of a debate, preferring instead to claim there is merely a difference in "emphasis" among authors.[58]

In fact, there are clearly sharp, mutually exclusive differences among the three schools: one that still champions Chairman Mao's People's War and "active defense" against likely opponents in the 21st century bent on invading China after a pre-emptive nuclear strike; one that (in the name of "Deng Xiaoping's new strategic thinking") wants China to follow aspects of Soviet military models for conventional warfare with a balance among ground, naval, and air forces ready to repel limited aggression on Chinese territory; and a third (new and small) school that has been inspired by the writings of Marshal Ogarkov and the Soviet General Staff Academy about a potential RMA which anticipates a world in the mid-21st century in which China will have the world's largest economy and be at least roughly equivalent in nuclear forces to Russia and America, a triangular nuclear equivalence never seen before, in which new measures of effectiveness will be needed to calculate the balance of military power.[59]

These three schools of thought among military authors have counterparts among the civilian defense and foreign affairs community.[60] As has been discussed in detail, the civilians pursue unique techniques of strategic analysis to determine where future conflicts may involve China's national interests. They use a set of analytical categories different from their Western counterparts and do not anticipate that the United Nations or other well-intentioned security organizations will be able to bring about much.

> An Example of the People's War School—Excerpt on Information Warfare:
>
> The concept of people's war of the olden days is bound to continue to be enriched, improved, and updated in the information age to take on a brand-new form . . . only by bringing relevant systems into play and combining human intelligence with artificial intelligence under effective organization and coordination can we drown our enemies in the ocean of an information offensive. A people's war in the context of information warfare is carried out by hundreds of millions of people using open-type modern information systems.

In general, space warfare appears to be an area for constructive debate among Chinese analysts. As would be expected, RMA advocates see space warfare as central to the outcome of future wars. However, the advocates of Local War and People's War theories seem to view space warfare as not particularly important to China. It was mainly important as part of the overall military balance that shifted back and forth during the Cold War competition between the United States and the former Soviet Union. Some have taken note of the history of American and Russian anti-satellite developments.

How do these analysts judge the future space balance?[61] Some have been extremely concerned about China's relative weakness in this area and have openly advocated a Chinese "space warfare headquarters" to command a future anti-satellite capability and ballistic missile defense to break the "superpower monopoly" of space, in spite of China's current diplomatic position that anti-satellite missiles (ASATs) should be banned and no weapons permitted in space.[62] *China Aerospace* has published drawings of a space station and space shuttle for the future.

Other more cautious Chinese officers at least agree that ASATs and space warfare are an important aspect of any strategic assessment. First, they look backward at the shifting balance in U.S. and Soviet efforts. Then they remark on the importance of China's enhancing its limited ability to manufacture satellites and to continue developing a robust launch capability at several sites with several reliable launchers. Both a manned space program and a Chinese space station are budgeted. Articles have discussed the need to reduce satellite vulnerability by using, for example, very small satellites, the need for anti-ASAT capabilities to defend Chinese satellites, and the need to develop a capability to strike first at enemy space capabilities.

SECTION FIVE: DIFFERENCES IN INVESTMENT PRIORITIES AMONG THE THREE SCHOOLS

Investments Recommended by the RMA Advocates.

The RMA visionaries (represented in numerous articles and five books in 1997) have been calling since at least 1993 for China to attempt to leapfrog the United States in the next 2 decades by investing in the most exotic advanced military technology and in new doctrines and new organizations along the lines of American and Russian writings on a potential RMA. Judging by the tone of the authors in this RMA school, they have not yet been very successful. Books by these authors have warned that if China tries to match U.S. military technology in the short term (rather than by leapfrogging), the result after 20 years will be that China will only fall further behind. This warning has not been heeded by the second and more influential school of thought described below.

Investments Recommended by the Power-Projection Advocates.

A second reformist school of thought, identified by its use of the concept of Local War or power-projection, has advocated evolutionary reforms. These evolutionary reformers are caught between the traditional conservatives who have the lion's share of the budget and the RMA advocates who appear to be championing what are seen as unrealistic goals in the eyes of the Local War reformers.

Local War advocates, while satisfied at the *current direction* of defense investment, seem discontent about the *level* of funding the central government is providing. They complain, for example, that all China's neighbors possess more advanced military technology. They complain of the too-slow pace of Chinese programs to develop aerial refueling, at-sea replenishment, airborne warning and control aircraft, a national command and control system, sufficient airborne and amphibious forces, an aircraft carrier program, and fighter aircraft. In the nuclear field, they express concern that U.S.-supplied theater missile defense will neutralize China's nuclear forces.

Investments Recommended by the People's War Advocates.

Those who advocate the importance of People's War and active defense still command the lion's share of Chinese defense investment. They oppose troop cuts and the purchase of foreign weapons systems. The PLA had seven million in the early 1980s, and only after major controversy was it reduced to today's three million, with a recent promise (debated for the past 5 years) that another 500,000 may be cut by 2000. The People's War school also prefers to maintain a disbursed national mobilization capability for wartime defense industry (including production of light arms and ammunition). The People's War school may not be completely antagonistic to the reforms of the Local War advocates in the direction of limited power projection, as long as the expense does not compromise the large standing army, does not undermine a suitable defense mobilization base, and does not lead to dependence on foreign weapons or foreign technology.

China's defense reformers of both the RMA and Local War schools need to free up resources by resolving the threats and challenges that the programs of the People's War school are designed to handle. Otherwise, conservatives will continue to dominate the defense investment process. For example, a China with a GNP equal to the United States and focused on the RMA or advanced power-projection forces would be a challenge to the United States. In contrast, a China focused on defense investments "turned inward" would be very different. Instead of pursuing an RMA or power-projection forces, China may decide to focus "inward" on:

- layered strategic air defense,
- enhanced underground defense complexes,
- extensive ground forces around the national capital,
- border defense forces,
- a large People's Armed Police and other forces for internal stability and counter subversion,
- inefficient defense industries located in interior provinces,
- fixed positional defenses for the largest energy project,
- hedges with air and land deployments in the north against the revival of Russian nationalism, and
- forces tied down opposite Taiwan preparing for a short-range amphibious invasion if Taiwan declares independence.

The following are probably very high priorities for defense investment, which must be sufficiently addressed before any additional resources may be allocated to the goals of the Local War and RMA advocates for power-projection forces or technological efforts to leapfrog the United States.

Investments in Defense of the National Capital Area.

China's leaders appear to have invested heavily to protect themselves and their national capital. As much as 40 percent of China's land, sea, and air forces may be deployed within 200 miles of Beijing. Many of the new S-300 missiles purchased from Russia have been deployed around the city. In addition, former Chinese officers have described a series of extensive underground bunkers that protect the national leadership in the Beijing area.[63] According to these officers, these investments date from the decision by Chairman Mao in the 1950s to build tunnels for protection against American nuclear attacks. This program of underground construction was extended in the 1960s to include underground tunnels north of Beijing designed to stop potential Soviet tank attacks along the main routes to Beijing.

To the degree that this priority has been successfully accomplished, resources would become available for new programs for RMA and Local War advocates. However, the purchase and deployment from Russia of S-300 missiles, or systems similar to the Patriot used by the United States to protect Tel Aviv during the Gulf War, suggest that the mission of strategic defense of the national capital can still command resources.

Investments in Denial and Deception.

China has invested heavily in concealment of major military installations of the army, navy, air force, missile forces, and national command centers. The Chinese appear to believe this investment continues to be effective, but requires upgrading. One former PLA officer stated that China's leaders would be astonished if an enemy could actually target these concealed and underground facilities and would invest heavily to ensure their secrecy. One indicator of this Chinese sensitivity has been China's complete refusal to permit foreigners to visit any sensitive military site that might be targeted in wartime, including recent requests from the U.S. Secretary of Defense.

This sensitivity has required extremely expensive investments. In the 1960s, Chairman Mao ordered the relocation and concealment of almost all of the Chinese defense industry into the interior of China where it would be supposedly out of range of the forces of the USSR and the United States. Extensive underground bunkers and even bases, together with the relocated interior defense industries, may have cost China the equivalent of several years of its GNP, according to Deng Xiaoping. This would amount, in U.S. terms, to trillions of dollars.

Key future priorities will include the following points.

- Maintain secrecy from U.S. targeting intelligence of all China's nuclear weapons and missile storage sites. The United States is assumed not to know these locations.

- Ensure that China's national command centers and vital C^3I nodes are sufficiently concealed and also sufficiently deeply buried to be invulnerable to attack by conventional U.S. munitions.

- Maintain sufficient military protection for the national leadership in its deep underground complexes in the capital, by deploying the most advanced surface-to-air missiles purchased from Russia, the largest share of ground forces in the entire nation, the largest share of air defense aircraft and radar sites, and the largest concentration of police forces within 200 or 300 miles of Beijing.

- Continue only limited dismantling of the defense industries in the interior provinces so that the capacity for national mobilization is not compromised too much.

One could speculate that China's leaders would react strongly to maintain the value of their 5 decades of investment in successful denial and deception of national military "targets." In other words, if China began to believe that its reliance on concealment to protect its nuclear deterrence as well as the bulk of its conventional forces was being compromised, enormous additional investment would be a high priority to restore this concealment. There would be a strong disbelief that the United States or any other power had the capability to "see through" what is probably this first line of defense. This field is a subject for debate in Beijing today, at least in general terms. Various articles in Chinese newspapers praised Saddam Hussein's underground palace complexes that have survived the Gulf War and advocated a program to *strengthen* China's underground defense complex.[64]

Investments in Internal Stability.

In the 1990s, Chinese military authors alluded to the need to continue to reduce the three million-strong army in order to reallocate funds for higher quality forces and technology. This is referred to as national guidance to implement the two "basic transformations" since 1994 from quantity to quality and from a low-technology to a high-technology force. There are three assumptions behind these two "basic transformations." First, there will be only low-level threats to internal stability. Second, lightly armed police will be able to handle these threats. Third, social and economic policies will not generate internal instability. Therefore, China can continue to:

- reduce its three million ground troops at a very gradual pace,

- maintain internal stability by transferring one million troops to the PAP,

- assume social stability will be maintained through appropriate economic and social policies, and

- assume there will be no successful foreign diplomatic and material support for unrest among minorities such as Tibetans, Muslims, Mongols, and human rights groups.

China would have to divert its planned allocations of defense investment away from the goals of the RMA and Local War advocates if the leadership began to doubt that internal stability could be adequately guaranteed by social policy, if there were an end to restraints on foreign subversion in Tibet, Inner Mongolia, Muslim Xinjiang, or if the effectiveness of the PAP in maintaining internal stability was somehow called into question.

Investments in Protection of Maritime Natural Resources.

Throughout the 1990s, Chinese military journals have featured warnings that China's national humiliation during the past century has been due to failure to develop naval forces able to protect China's maritime resources. However, other writings by civilians imply that Deng Xiaoping has successfully postponed the need to protect maritime resources because of his successful diplomacy. Foreign powers are not yet exploiting these resources and may not do so for a decade or more. Thus, the pace of developing naval forces need not be hasty. The driver here is based on the assumption that foreign "imperialists" will not begin to exploit natural resources on Chinese territorial claims.

This assumption may account for the modest pace of China's naval and power-projection forces. A challenge to this assumption would require a much more rapid pace and much more extensive defense investment in power-projection forces. A recent book by a Chinese military officer calls this assumption into question by asserting that Vietnam intends to begin exploiting energy reserves in the South China Seas and is illegally occupying nearly 30 Chinese islands there. At stake is the length of time China will have available to wait to acquire these resources. China's leaders will presumably accelerate their pace of investment in power-projection forces if they decide maritime resources will soon be irreversibly lost to other nations. Conversely, China could delay or decrease its development of power-projection forces if the threat to these maritime resources diminishes.

Investment to Protect the Three Gorges Dam.

Perhaps because the world's largest dam cannot be concealed and because of its high value as a target (it will supply up to one-third of eastern China's electricity), several Chinese military authors have addressed the need to defend it from a wartime attack, including a proposal to deploy extensive surface-to-air missile sites and even an anti-missile system around the dam. However, other military authors argue that it need not be defended because (1) no one will dare to violate international law by attacking it, (2) the water behind the dam could be released prior to any attack, and (3) such an attack is unlikely due to the world trend toward peace and development. It would appear this issue has not been resolved, but China will probably:

- rely on international law and not invest heavily in defense for the mega-power project at Three Gorges, but

- continue to debate the need for positional defenses for this high-value target.

Investments to Hedge Against Revival of Russian Nationalism.

China has invested heavily since the 1960s in fixed defenses against a Soviet invasion. According to interviews, diplomatic agreements with Russia and three new Central Asian states have greatly reduced the need for defense in the "Three Norths," the nickname of the three military regions that border on Russia. Reductions in the three million ground forces are expected to come from these three military regions. China will probably:

- ensure that the main axis of possible Russian armor attack through Northeastern China (Manchuria) continues to be garrisoned by the second largest concentration of ground forces and air forces in the entire nation, including depending on an extensive system of secret underground complexes 100 to 200 miles north of Beijing for ambushes, and

- continue to proceed slowly to reduce forces north of Beijing as long as Russia continues to agree to the current "strategic partnership" with China.

Investment in the Liberation of Taiwan.

Until 1996, China did not appear to be developing the capacity to conquer Taiwan by force. Nor did China deploy more than symbolic land, sea, or air forces within 300 miles of Taiwan. Indeed, the military command responsible for Taiwan (Fuzhou MR) since 1949 was dismantled around 1985. Similarly, there was little, if any, discussion of how to attack Taiwan in professional military journals. This began to change after the March 1996 missile incidents and deployment of two U.S. aircraft carrier battle groups to the area east of Taiwan. There is now some evidence of a debate about what military investments may be appropriate if force will have to be used to prevent Taiwan independence.

The People's War advocates would bring the least to this debate. The RMA advocates propose programs with long lead times so they would presumably have little to contribute to liberate Taiwan until after 2010. However, Local War advocates of power-projection forces could well justify their programs by the need to dissuade or conquer an independent Taiwan. If so, the more Taiwan independence seems probable to China's leaders, the more investments will have to be made in infrastructure opposite Taiwan and in forces appropriate to conquer an island of 20 million people that lies 100 miles off the mainland coast and that may be defended by the United States.

Conversely, the less the chances are that Taiwan will need to be liberated by force, the more resources will be available to the RMA advocates for long-term technology programs. At present, it appears that China will:

- continue to give relatively low priority to land, air, and naval forces deployed within 500 miles of Taiwan, and

- continue to debate what military investments may be necessary to liberate Taiwan in the decade ahead if reunification talks fail and trends toward independence continue.

Investment in Border Defenses Near India, Vietnam, and Central Asia.

Imagine the frustrating dilemma that faces the Local War advocates who seek to build modest power-projection forces to enhance China's defense of its borders. China has fought border wars with India in 1962 and Vietnam in 1979, but not lately. China's diplomats have since 1989 successfully improved diplomatic and trade ties with all of China's neighbors. Confidence-building measures have been agreed to with India, Russia, and three Central Asian nations. There is no longer a dramatic or compelling military threat to China's borders, at least in the short term.

This may explain why China continues to place a low priority on improving the quality and quantity of land, sea, and air forces appropriate to border defense along China's *land* frontiers. This aspect of the security environment may tend to free up Chinese defense resources for investments in maritime, air, and even space forces. Indeed, according to interviews and military journals, China appears instead to place a high priority on coastal and harbor defense of the key ports that serve the two largest cities of Beijing and Shanghai, historical avenues of approach used by foreign invaders.

Investment in a National Layered Air Defense System.

As noted above, after witnessing the performance of the U.S. Air Force in the Gulf War, senior Chinese authors have advocated construction of a nationwide air defense system. China may believe that its C^3 nodes and national rail system are vulnerable to U.S. air strikes. (With little air or sea lift, China depends almost entirely on its railroad trunk lines to transport its ground forces.) Traditionally, the strategic intersection of the sole east-west and north-south rail lines at Shijiazhuang constitutes a decisive point to be defended from an invader. Japan seized it. Russian airborne forces supposedly planned to seize it. The elite 38th Group Army defends it today. (This army was selected for experiments with new doctrine, technology, and organization in the 1980s.) Yet strategic Shijiazhuang, like many high-value targets in China, is without air defense.

Need to Monitor the Debates.

It is in the interest of the United States at least to monitor this debate and the competition for defense resources among the three schools. For example, the Local War or Power-Projection school may eventually pose a challenge to U.S. naval and air forces in the western Pacific. Over time, the Chinese have explicitly stated they intend to attain military influence out to the "first island chain" (roughly 500 to 1,000 miles from China) with their power-projection forces. They cannot operate in this area today. Yet Chinese authors emphasize that enormous natural resources await exploitation by China in this area. China's authors claim that in the past century China was humiliated by Japan and the Western imperialists because it lacked modern military technology. China particularly lacked advanced naval forces, and so it lost Taiwan province and other areas. Yet this school cannot obtain the necessary resources if the programs championed by the other two schools must also be funded.

In order to commit more resources to either power projection or to the development of RMA technology and doctrine, China must resolve or neglect a number of threats that will otherwise continue to claim the lion's share of defense investment. If these kinds of threats are reduced, then the RMA and Local War advocates can claim a larger share of defense resources. If China's economic growth rate continues to be three or four times faster than the U.S. economic growth rate (8 percent for China, 2.5 percent for the United States), then the estimates of Charles Wolf and the World Bank suggest that in the first quarter of the 21st century, China will have enormous resources with which to develop power-projection and/or RMA capabilities. In some scenarios, the level of Chinese defense investment could exceed that of the United States within 2 decades.

Much more would have to be known about China's secretive defense decision-making process before a thorough understanding could be achieved about why China's leaders may select one path instead of another. This is probably worth attempting. Whether the People's War (and Local War) advocates continue to dominate China's military investment decisions may become an issue of some importance to the United States over the long term.

SECTION SIX: CHINA'S NET ASSESMENT OF MILITARY CAPABILITY

Three Alternative Net Assessments of Japan's Military Power.

How would each of the three schools measure the military power of other nations? If it is correct to separate PLA analysts into three schools of thought, it then follows that their assessments of military power may also follow the very different main premises of each of these schools. We may speculate how each of the three schools would quantitatively assess future military power. The three schools might make very different calculations about Japan, for example.

According to interviews with knowledgeable Chinese analysts in Beijing, there is little doubt that Japan has been an opponent of China in a series of war games and other simulations over the past decade at the Academy of Military Science. One particular Chinese nightmare apparently is that Taiwan may not be reunified with the mainland by 2010, after which time Japan will be able to play a strategically important role in providing a nuclear or at least a conventional umbrella over Taiwan. Chinese analysts have developed a number of scenarios involving conflicts between Japan and its neighbors, including China:

- Japan in a Taiwan conflict,

- Japan in an Association of Southeast Asian Nations (ASEAN) conflict,

- Japan in a Korean Peninsula conflict.

An important part of any effort to appreciate the way that China sees the future world security environment is an attempt to reproduce the kinds of calculations that Chinese analysts may be using to calculate future defense requirements against Japan. Each of the three Chinese schools of strategic thought might go about measuring current and future Japanese military power differently.

There are probably sharp differences, perhaps by a factor of ten or more, among the three schools when it comes to measuring Japan's military capability. The People's War school seems to view Chinese superiority to Japan to be very large. Japan is assessed as completely unable to perform a land invasion of China by any route. In this sense, China's historical experience of 1590s, the 1894-95 war, and the war of 1937-45 have resulted in China successfully solving these past modes of vulnerability to a land invasion by Japan. This is seen as a great achievement by Chinese analysts. Of course, the scenario of People's War against an invading Japanese ground, sea, and air force benefits decisively by China being the sole possessor of nuclear weapons, by the assessed vulnerability of Japan to nuclear disruption because of population and industrial density, and by the need for any Japanese forces to cross North Korea or Taiwan (by sea) to repeat the damage of the 1580s, 1894, or the 1930s.

Local war theorists, however, probably see Japan today as roughly equivalent to China in all important indexes of military effectiveness in the most common scenarios that are deemed relevant. Some insight is possible about the kinds of calculations used by these theorists because of their approval of Soviet works on operations research that have been examined. Chinese translations of Soviet books from the 1960s are still used in China for these calculations, according to interviews. One indicator that is used is the life in years of a weapons system multiplied by its number which produces a kind of depreciation in the value of the score of the ground, sea, and air units using such weapons.

In sharp contrast to the first two schools, the third school of RMA advocates apparently calculates Japan to hold a potential of as high as a ten to one superiority over China in selected scenarios. Theorists in the RMA/future warfare group advocate the use of very different measures of military effectiveness based on the gap in information-processing capability of weapons, platforms, and units.

China's Assessment of Future American Military Capability.

Chinese military analysts use examples from the Gulf War to illustrate U.S. weakness. Many authors state that the outcome of the Gulf War would have been a U.S. defeat if Iraq had employed different tactics and exploited U.S. weaknesses. An overall assessment of the war comes from Vice-President of the Academy of Military Science Li Jijun who writes that, during the Gulf War,

> U.S. Armed Forces revealed many weak points. For example, the combat consumption was too great, and it could not last long. There was great reliance on the allied countries. The high-tech equipment was intensive and its key links were rather weak; once they were damaged, combat effectiveness was greatly reduced. Also **if the adversary of the U.S. was not Iraq, if the battle was not fought on the flat desert, if the Iraq armed forces struck first during the phase when U.S. armed forces were still assembling, or if Iraq armed forces withdrew suddenly before the U.S. armed forces struck, then the outcome of the war might have been quite different.**[65]

Other areas of U.S. weakness cited by Chinese analysts include the following points.

- The United States had insufficient means of transportation.

- U.S. munitions cannot damage deep underground bunkers.

- Various U.S. weapons systems have their own specific weaknesses.

- The United States did not have superiority in its efforts to destroy Iraqi tanks.

- The U.S. non-linear form of combat makes it vulnerable to being divided.

Chinese analysts believe Iraq failed to exploit critical U.S. vulnerabilities by:

- not making surprise attacks on U.S. airbases and the U.S. rear;

- permitting the United States time to build up logistics and to train for several months; and

- not employing pre-emptive "special measures" such as harassing attacks.

U.S. Forces Cannot Even Defeat North Korea.

Chinese military authors also appear to devalue the effectiveness of U.S. forces in a future Korean scenario. According to a colonel at the Academy of Military Science, several factors ensure U.S. defeat "if in the next few years a Korean War erupted." His main points are:

- The United States will not have 6 months to deploy and train forces. Instead, "the Korean People's Army will surprise attack South Korean air bases, ports, and communication lines."

- "U.S. casualties will not be as low as in the Gulf War.... On the Korean peninsula, the population is dense, with river networks and mountains, roads are few, unsuitable to armor... casualties will be extremely high."

- "North Korea's mountains are wrapped in clouds and mist, it will be difficult for the U.S. air force and high technology weaponry to give full play to their vast superiority."

- Temperatures of 40 degrees centigrade below zero "provide excellent conditions" for guerrilla warfare.

- North Korea will "not allow the United States to land in the rear."

- U.S. ground forces lack the numerical strength they once had. During the Korean War, U.S. troops numbered more than 400,000 at one point, but "the result was not victory." During the 1960s and 1970s in the Vietnam War, America had 663,000 forces and a great technical superiority, but "the result also was defeat." U.S. forces in year 2000 will be reduced 30 percent from current levels.[66]

U.S. Forces Will Fall Behind in the Competition to Exploit the RMA.

Chinese authors emphasize several problem areas that the United States faces in implementing the RMA and maintaining its leading position:

- the U.S. interservice rivalry,

- the U.S. decreasing defense budget,

- the U.S. existing investment in technology,

- universal availability of U.S. technology after its development,

- easily damaged U.S. information networks, and

- greater potential of other countries to innovate.

Several Chinese analysts suggest that China can exploit these U.S. weaknesses while pursuing its own development of the RMA. Chinese authors define RMA as they believe the United States does, emphasizing the potential invention of radical new forms of warfare, enhanced information warfare, networks of systems, and "digitized" combat forces. However, while Chinese analysts acknowledge America's current leading position, they describe future U.S. weaknesses and how they can be exploited. The extent of negative predictions about how the United States will implement RMA varies little among five books published by PLA authors at the Academy of Military Science in the last 4 years.[67] Several authors emphasize the greater potential of other countries in the area of innovation. With regard to China, Gao Chunxiang writes that U.S. weaknesses:

> . . . provide us with the train of thought in future information warfare on how to stay clear of the enemy's main force and strike at his weak points, avoid his strengths and attack his weaknesses, adopt his good points and avoid his short comings, use the indigenous to create the foreign, seek the cause to respond with a plan. On future information warfare, if we only dare to blaze new trails there will be no need to be afraid of anyone.[68]

General Wang Pufeng's writings estimate that it will take until 2050 for all U.S. forces to be "digitized" and part of a "system of systems," because of the slow pace to date and U.S. interservice rivalry.[69] According to Han Shengmin, the United States faces the following four major obstacles in "establishing a digitized battlefield."[70]

First, interservice rivalry—the Air Force and Navy do not want to join the Army's digital forces experiments and have a "negative-passive attitude." Both Houses of the U.S. Congress are also said to be obstacles. For example, "Senate Armed Services Committee, Air-Land Forces Subcommittee Chairman John Warner believes that 'troops still lack the technical skills to use digitized equipment in combat'." Another Senator says that "army troops are too reliant on digitized battlefields, and as soon as a digitized network is destroyed, they would be unable to fulfill their combat missions."[71]

Second, insufficient funds. The U.S. defense budget has been decreasing for many years, even recently for digital forces.

Third, the technology is too complex. "If you want to build a digitized battlefield, you must resolve the following six technical issues: converting sensors information into digitized coded form; processing digitized information; making digitized connections; joining digitized systems of different combat platforms; developing digital display equipment; and establishing digital links between troops and platforms."[72]

Fourth, information networks are easily damaged:

> The control nodes of information networks after being attacked are easily damaged, causing the entire system to break down.... Local network systems' security is poor, and they are easily subject to electronic attacks.[73]

Another important example is *America, Russia, and the New Revolution in Military Affairs,* by two officers at the Academy of Military Science, who argue that the United States will at first successfully innovate during the initial decade of the RMA but later will be surpassed by one (or more) vigorous nations. They explain that the United States will ultimately lose its status as a military superpower because it will fail to exploit the RMA for several reasons, including the following points.

- American military arrogance, growing out of the Gulf War, will inhibit fundamental innovation, especially in the area of new operational concepts which are crucial for RMA.

- Information technology and other new military technologies will be universally available through commercial enterprise and cannot be restricted by the U.S. Government, so the United States will lose its current advantage.

- Smaller defense budgets have historically produced more innovation than the giant U.S. budgets will.

- New, innovative "measures of effectiveness" tend to drive innovation, and nations other than the United States are experimenting more in this area, even when they have to buy weapons from more advanced nations.[74]

Chinese analysts also use the most recent public review of U.S. defense strategy, the Quadrennial Defense Review (QDR) in 1997, as the basis to suggest increasing military challenges the United States may not be prepared to face. First, there is the issue of homeland defense. Lu Dehong from the China Institute of International Strategic Studies writes, "It is the first time since the end of the Cold War that the United States emphasizes that the U.S. homeland is not free from external threats." Second, Lu points out that the United States is only making a modest effort to exploit the RMA. "How to balance investment in the present vs. future was the fundamental contradition facing the U.S. Department of Defense." The QDR examined three different strategic paths to solve this tough problem: the QDR chose a third path—to strike a balance between present and the future "that embraces the RMA in an evolutionary way. . . . Continuing to exploit the RMA has been adopted as the general principle of U.S. military development of the QDR."[75]

According to some Chinese military authors, *the United States already knows China can defeat it in 2020*. General Pan Junfeng states that the United States will not have formed a full information warfare force until the middle of the 21st century. He explains three ways that in future wars American computers can be very vulnerable.

> We can make the enemy's command centers not work by changing their data system. We can make the enemy's headquarters have wrong judgments by sending

disinformation. We can dominate the enemy's banking system and even its entire social order."[76]

General Pan states that the United States has already realized these three points and that the magazine, *Defense News*, on January 30, 1994, reported that war games took place at the Navy War College, Newport, Rhode Island, that pitted the Chinese military against the U.S. Navy in the Pacific. In these games, the Chinese forces defeated the U.S. forces. General Pan makes five suggestions:

- increase research on military doctrine;
- establish new operational theory;
- train high-quality officers with advanced degrees;
- establish combat "laboratories" and study six laboratories that the United States has created; and
- create *sha shou jian* or "magic weapon trump cards."[77]

China's Assessment of the China-Taiwan-U.S. Balance.

Chinese open-source writings describe Taiwan's military strengths and weaknesses, U.S. military strengths and (mainly) weaknesses, alternative scenarios for how the Taiwan problem can be solved, and a variety of operational details about the land, sea, and air battles that could be fought.

There is no guarantee that these open-source writings reveal actual Chinese plans. They probably do not. They do, however, suggest a framework for analysis of the problem of using force against Taiwan. This is obviously a major subject and requires further discussion. The dilemma, then, is that we have no certain knowledge of China's plans, but we do have some signs of how Beijing will approach its military problems with Taiwan and the United States. Analysts must keep an open mind, avoid ethnocentrisms, and avoid the dangerous course of systematically underestimating the Chinese.

ENDNOTES - CHAPTER 3

1. However, Paul Dibb, David D. Hale, and Peter Prince note in "The Strategic Implications of Asia's Economic Crisis," *Survival*, Summer 1998, p. 5, that the crisis will bring "a shift in the regional balance that favors China."

2. Hans Binnendijk and Ronald N. Montaperto, eds., *Strategic Trends in China*, National Defense University Press, 1998. All quotations from John Culver in this paragraph may be found on p. 69.

3. Henry Kissinger, "No Room for Nostalgia," *Newsweek*, June 29, 1998, p. 52.

4. Dennis Blasko, "Better Late Than Never," in C. Dennison Lane, Mark Weisenbloom, and Dimon Liu, eds., *Chinese Military Modernization*, London, New York, Washington: AEI Press, 1996, p. 131.

5. Ellis Joffe, *The Chinese Army After Mao*, Cambridge, MA: Harvard University Press, 1987.

6. Two colonels at the Academy of Military Science define "strategic assessment" as used by Sun Zi in the *Art of War*. Their new translation into English faults the well-known translation in 1963 by Brigadier General Samuel Griffiths for "serious errors," including using the word "estimates" instead of "strategic assessment." See Pan Jiabin and Liu Ruixiang, *Aft of War. A Chinese English Bilingual Reader*, Beijing: *Junshi kexue chubanshe*, 1993, pp. 123-124.

7. George E. Pickett, James G. Roche, and Barry D. Watts, "Net Assessment—A Historical Review," in *On Not Confusing Ourselves* Andrew W. Marshall, J. J. Martin, and Henry S. Rowen, eds., Boulder, CO: Westview Press, 1991, pp. 169-171.

8. Williamson Murray and Allan R. Millett, *Calculations: Net Assessment and the Coming of World War II*, New York: Free Press, 1992.

9. Rosen, *Assessing the Correlation of Forces. France 1940*, BDM Report for the Office of Net Assessment, June 18, 1979, pp. 296-297.

10. Stephen Peter Rosen, "Net Assessment as an Analytical Concept," in Marshall, Martin, and Rowen, eds., p. 288.

11. Andrew W. Marshall, "A Program to Improve Analytic Methods Related to Strategic Forces," *Policy Sciences*, November 1982, p. 48.

12. David L. Shambaugh, *Beautiful Imperialist: China Perceives America 1972-1990*, Princeton, NJ: Princeton University Press, 1991; Gilbert Rozman, *The Chinese Debate About Soviet Socialism, 1978-1985*, Princeton, NJ: Princeton University Press, 1987; Allen S. Whiting, *China Eyes Japan*, Berkeley: University of California Press, 1989; and Carol Lee Hamrin, *China and the Challenge of the Future: Changing Political Patterns*, Boulder, CO: Westview Press, 1990.

13. By 1986, an open-source article described many of the key tenets of the current assessment of a multipolar world structure. See Gao Heng, "Shijie zhanlue geju zhengxiang duojihua fazhan" ("Development of Global Strategic Multipolarity"), *Guofang daxue xuebao* Vol. 2, 1986, pp. 32-33.

14. Huan Xiang, Preface to the Chinese Translation of Dougherty and Pfaltzgraff, "Contending Theories of International Relations," *Shijie zhishi* (*World Knowledge*), No. 8, 1988, p. 12.

15. Wang Shuzhong, "The Post-War International System," in *As China Sees the World.—Perceptions of Chinese Scholars*, Harish Kapur, ed., London: Francis Pinter Publishers, 1987, p. 22.

16. Liang Shoude and Hong Yinxian, *Guoji zhengzhixue gailun* (*General Theory of International Politics*), Beijing: Zhongyang bianshi chubanshe, 1994.

17. See Chu Shulong, "Guangyu guoji guanxixue xueke jianshe de ji ge wenti" ("Several Issues Concerning the Establishment of the Subject of International Relations"), *Xiandai guoji guanxi* (*Contemporary International Relations*), No. 4, 1995, pp. 59-63; Yang Zheng, "Shixi guoji guanxixue de yanjiu duixiang wenti" ("A Tentative Analysis of the Object of the Study of International Relations"), *Xiandai guoji guanxi* (*Contemporary International Relations*), No. 4, 1995, pp. 64-67; and David Shambaugh and Wang Jisi, "Research on International Studies in the People's Republic of China," *Political Science*, Fall 1984, pp. 758-64. According to an interview in Beijing with Wang Jisi in June 1995, the first article on Western theory was by Chen Lemin entitled "Western International Relations Theory—in Research on International Problems," *The Journal of the CIIS*. Chu has a Ph.D. from George Washington University, Wang from Oxford University.

18. Arnold J. Toynbee, *War and Civilization*, New York: Oxford University Press, 1950, pp. 10-11.

19. Liu Mingde, "Changes in the Forms of War," *International Strategic Studies*, No. 2, 1992, p. 9.

20. Chen Xiaogong, a senior military intelligence officer and former U.S. Atlantic Council visiting fellow, has written that the question of the transition period will be "Should the world be built into a peaceful and stable place based on the Five Principles of Peaceful Coexistence, one which is beneficial to economic development in an absolute majority of countries?" In Chen Feng and Chen Xiaogong, "The World Is in the Transition Period of a New Strategic Pattern Replacing the Old," *Jiefang jun bao* (*Liberation Army Daily*), January 4, 1991, p. 3. Translated in *Foreign Broadcast Information Service-China* (hereafter *FBIS-CHI*)-91-021, January 31, 1991, pp. 11-15.

21. Chinese views of the RMA will be treated in detail in *Section Six*.

22. Mi Zhenyu, *Zhongguo guofang fazhan gouxiang* (*China's National Defense Development Concepts*), Beijing: Jiefangjun chubanshe, 1988.

23. Declassified quotations from Chairman Mao and other Chinese leaders illustrate China's strategic assessment in the 1970s. Mao's assessment predicted an inevitable Soviet-American war in Europe in which Soviet forces would drive NATO forces toward the Channel and result in a "Dunkirk," or evacuation under fire of the United States from continental Europe.

24. Pan Zhengqiang, "Current World Military Situation," *Renmin ribao* (*People's Daily*), December 23, 1993, p. 7. Translated in *FBIS-CHI*-94-005, January 7, 1994, pp. 27-29. General Pan is director of the Institute for National Security Studies of the National Defense University in Beijing.

25. Zhu Chenghu, "Focus Attention on the Converging Points of Interest of China and the United States," *Jiefang jun bao*, (*Liberation Army Daily*), June 19, 1998, p. 4. Zhu is deputy director of the Strategic Research Institute of National Defense University, Beijing.

26. See Xi Runchang and Gao Heng, eds., *Shijie zhengzhi xin geju yu guoji anquan* (*The New World Political Structure and International Security*), Beijing: Junshi kexue chubanshe, 1996; and Chen Qimao, ed., *Kua shiji de shijie geju da zhuanhuan* (*Major Changes in the World*

Structure at the Turn of the Century, Shanghai: Shanghai jiaoyu chubanshe, 1996.

27. Zhang Taishan, "New Developments in the Japan-U.S. Military Relationship," *International Strategic Studies*, No. 4, 1997, pp. 28-33.

28. Chen Peiyao, "Big Power Relations in the Asia-Pacific Region," *Journal of the Shanghai Institute of International Studies*, No. 3, November 1995, p. 1.

29. Liu Chungzi, "The Art of War and Contemporary Military Struggle," *Zhongguo junshi kexue, (China Military Science)*. Colonel Liu Chungyi serves in the National Defense University Strategy Department in Beijing.

30. The Warring-States era, 475-221 BC, was "the flowering age for the Chinese fable and exerted a definite influence on works of later centuries," according to K.L. Nu, *100 Ancient Chinese Fables*, Taiwan Commercial Press, 1993, p. 8.

31. Gao Rui, *Zhongguo shanggu junshi shi (Chinese Ancient Military History)*, Beijing: Junshi kexue chubanshe, 1995, p. 2, writes that the era is "extremely distant from modern times, but still shines with the glory of truth" and "the splendid military legacy created through the bloody struggles of our ancient ancestors . . . [today] has a radiance even more resplendent."

32. Herbert Goldhamer, *The Adviser*, New York: Elsevier, 1978; Herbert Goldhamer, "Reality and Belief in Military Affairs: A First Draft," June 1977, Santa Monica, CA: Rand Corporation, 1979.

33. Goldhamer, *The Adviser*, pp. 130-132.

34. Goldhamer, "Reality and Belief in Military Affairs," pp. 32-33.

35. Huang Yingxu, "Manyi Zhongguo gudai junshi sixiang zhong de minben jingshen" ("Chinese Ancient Military Thought on People's Spirit"), *Zhongguo junshi kexue (China Military Science)*, Spring 1996, pp. 121-125. Colonel Huang describes the change from divination to calculation in Spring and Autumn era. He is a research fellow in the department of Mao Zedong Military Thought at the Academy of Military Science.

36. Goldhamer, *The Adviser*, p. 121.

37. *Ibid.*, pp. 135-136.

38. A forthcoming study for OSD Net Assessment discusses Chinese military writings published since 1993 on the contemporary relevance of ancient Chinese statecraft, including these books: *Sanshiliu ji gujin tan tan (Ancient and Modern Discussions on the Thirty-Six Stratagems); Zhisheng taolue-Sunzi zhanzheng zhixing guanlun (Strategies of Superiority—Sunzi's Views on Knowledge and Action in War); Bu zhan er qu ren zhi bing—Zhongguo gudai xinlizhan sixiang ji qi yunyong (Conquest without Combat—Ancient Chinese Psychological Warfare Thought and Usage); Zhongguo lidai zhanzheng gailan (An Outline of Warfare in Past Chinese Dynasties); Quanmou shu-Shujia yu yingia de jiaoliang (Power Stratagems—A Contest of Losers and Winners); Sunzi bingfa yu sanshiliu ji (Sunzi's The Art of War and The Thirty-Six Stratagems); Zhongguo gudai bingfa jingcui (The Essence of the Ancient Chinese Art of War); Sunzi bingfa de diannao yanjiu (Computer Studies on Sunzi's The Art of War); Ershiwu li junshi moulue gushi jingxuan (A Selection of 25 Stories on Ancient Military Strategy).*

39. Wu Chunqiu, *Guangyi da zhanlue (Grand Strategy)*, Beijing: Current Affairs Press, 1995, p. 98.

40. *Ibid.*, pp. *17-18.*

41. Yan Xuetong, "Zhongguo jueqi de guoji huanjing pinggu" ("An Assessment of the International Environment of China's Rise"), *Zhanlue yu guanli (Strategy and Management)*, No. 1, 1997, pp. 18, 23. The table is from page 20.

42. A recent endorsement of People's War appeared January 9, 1998, in *Liberation Army Daily* which quoted Defense Minister Chi Haotian who, at the National Defense University, stated that "under high tech conditions, we still need to insist on People's War." Chi said that People's War "is the product of historical and dialectical materialism."

43. For examples of Chinese writing on People's Warfare, see Liu Sheng'e and Mao Lin, *Xiandai jubu zhanzheng tiaojian xia de renmin zhanzbeng (People's War Under the Conditions of High Technology Warfare)*, Beijing: Guofang daxue chubanshe, 1996; Wang Pufeng, ed., *Mao Zedong junshi zhanlue lun (On Mao Zedong's Military Strategy)*, Beijing: Junshi kexue chubanshe, 1993; and Xia Zhengnan, *Mao Zedong junshi zhanlue lun (Mao Zedong's Military Methodology)*, Beijing: Junshi kexue chubanshe, 1995. See also the following six articles translated in CVFW: Chen Zhou, "Zhongguo xiandai jubu zhanzheng lilun yu Meiguo youxian zhanzheng lilun zhi butong" ("Chinese Modern Local War and U.S. Limited War"), *Zhongguo junshi kexue (China Military Science)*, Vol. 33, No. 4, Winter 1995, pp. 43-47; Fang Ning,

"Shilun woguo xin shiqi de guofang zhengce" ("Defense Policy in the New Era"), *Zhongguo junshi kexue* (*China Military Science*), Vol. 32, No. 4, Winter 1994, pp.43-49; Shen Kuiguan, "Gao jishu zhanzheng zhong yilieshengyou de bianzhengfa" ("Dialectics of Defeating the Superior with the Inferior"), *Zhongguo junshi kexue* (*China Military Science*) Vol. 32, No. 4, Winter 1994, pp. 105-109; Wang Naiming, "Jianchi jiji fangyu, shixing xiandai tiaojian xia renmin zhanzheng" ("Adhere to Active Defense and Modern People's War"), in *Deng Xiaoping zhanlue sixiang lun* (*On Deng Xiaoping's Strategic Thought*), Peng Guangqian and Yao Youzhi, eds., Beijing: Junshi kexue chubanshe. 1994, pp. 280-298; Wei Jincheng, "Information War: A New Form of People's *War*," *Jiefangjun ribao*, (*Liberation Army Daily*), June 25, 1996; Zhao Nanqi, "Xu" ("Deng Xiaoping's Theory of Defense Modernization"), in *Deng Xiaoping zhanlue sixiang lun* (*On Deng Xiaoping's Strategic Thought*), pp. 1-12, foreword.

44. Mi Zhenyu, *China's National Defense Concepts*, 1988.

45. Sokolovskiy, *Soviet Military Strategy*, Moscow, 1968, p. 18.

46. Chen Yung-kang and Chai Wen-chung, "A Study of the Evolving PRC Naval Strategy," *China Mainland Research,* September 1, 1997, pp. 7-10, 13-20.

47. Blasko, "Better Late Than Never," *passim.*

48. See Liu Sheng'e and Mao Lin; Wang Pufeng; and Xia Zhengnan.

49. Six representative articles on Local War by senior officers are Liu Huaqing, "Yi shi wei jian jiaqiang guofang xiandaihua jianshe" ("Defense Modernization in Historical Perspective"), *Zhongguo junshi kexue,* (*China Military Science*), No. 4, 1994, pp. 7-8; Fu Quanyou, "Wojun houqin xiandaihua jianshe de zhinan" ("Future Logistics Modernization"), *Zhongguo junshi kexue,* (*China Military Science*), No. I, 1994, pp. 2-10; Yang Huan, "Woguo zhanlue he wuqi zhuangbei de fazhan" ("China's Strategic Nuclear Weaponry"), in *Huitou yu zhanwang* (*Retrospect and Prospect: Chinese Defense Science, Technology and Industry*), Beijing: Guofang gongye chubanshe, pp. 157-159; Wu Jianguo, "Gaojishu zhanzheng zhong de he yinying bu rong hushi" ("Nuclear Shadows on High-Tech Warfare"), *Zhongguo junshi kexue,* (*China Military Science*), No. 4, 1995, pp. 107-109; Chen Benchan, "Woguo zhuangjiabing wuqizhuangbei fazhan de huigu yu zhanwang" ("Research and Development of Armour"), in *Huitou yu zhanwang* (*Retrospect and Prospect: Chinese Defense Science, Technology and Industry*), Beijing: Guofang gongye chubanshe, pp. 169-171; Ding Henggao, "Guofang keji gongye fazhan yu gaige ruogan

wenti de sikao" ("Reforming Defense Science, Technology and Industry"), *Zhongguo junshi kexue, (China Military Science*), No. 2, 1994, pp. 67-73. All are translated in Michael Pillsbury, ed. *Chinese Views of Future Warfare,* Washington, DC: National Defense University Press, 1997.

50. A proximate cause for this Chinese invasion was Vietnam's seizing a number of strategic hilltops inside China and shelling Chinese villages nearby in December 1978. Other factors were the Vietnamese navy's harassing Chinese fishermen, Vietnamese expulsion of at least 200,000 ethnic Chinese, Vietnam's invasion of Cambodia and liquidation of a pro-Chinese government there, and Vietnam's growing military alliance with the Soviet Union.

51. Harvey Nelson, *Power and Insecurity: Beijing and Moscow and Washington, 1949-1988*, Boulder, CO: Westview Press, 1989, p. 12.

52. The source is "Declaration of all Democratic Parties," November 4, 1950, in *The Great "Opposing America, Assisting Korea" Movement* Beijing: New China Bookstore, 1954, pp. 366-367. Later, General Wu Xiuquan at the U.N. Security Council described an American master plan to invade China that included bases and arrangement in Japan, South Korea, Taiwan, and the Philippines.

53. Wang Pufeng, "Yingjie xinxi zhanzneng de tiaozhan" ("The Challenge of Information Warfare"), *Zhongguo junshi kexue, (China Military Science*), No. I, 1995, pp. 8-18. Translated in CVFW, 317-326.

54. Shen Zhongchang, Zhou Xinsheng and Zhang Haiying, "21 shiji haizhan chutan" ("21st Century Naval Warfare"), *Zhongguo junshi kexue, (China Military Science*), No. I, 1995, pp. 28-32. Translated in CVFW, 261-274.

55. Chang Mengxiong, "21 shiji haizhan chutan", (Weapons of the 21st Century"), *Zhongguo junshi kexue, (China Military Science),* No. I, 1995, pp. 19-24, 49. Translated in CVFW.

56. Song Shilun, *A Preliminary Probe into Mao Zedong's Military Thought,* Beijing: Junshi kexue chubanshe, 1983, pp. 96-97.

57. Yan Xuetong, "China's Post-Cold War Security Strategy." *Contemporary International Relations,* No. 5, 1995.

58. An anthropologist has observed that Chinese involved in factional disputes carry on the conflict by denying to outsiders that the other factions even exist. Few Chinese analysts footnote other analysts or comment about the work of others in any article or book. See Barbara

Pillsbury, "Cultural Patterns in Chinese Factional Politics," *The China Quarterly*, 1974.

59. This new third school has no senior leader like Mao or Deng to serve as a patron as yet. It tends to cite American specialists about the RMA, including Andrew W. Marshall, without reference to Mao or Deng. It will be important if the speeches of President Jiang Zemin ever incorporate this school rather than continuing as they have for the past 5 years, to endorse a vague mixture of both the Mao and Deng approaches.

60. Each of the three schools of thought identified above—"People's War, combined arms, and information warfare-RMA—has certain themes which identify it. For People's War advocates, one clue is appeals for "defense conversion," or the production of commercial products, to assist with the politically correct goal of economic growth, but still carefully maintaining the capability to shift rapidly back to wartime intensity of production of weapons in order to arm the millions who will be mobilized to defeat the invader.

61. For a strategic framework, see Peng Guangqian and Wang Guangxu, *Jushi zhanlue jian lun* (*A General Discussion of Military Strategy*), Jiefangjun chubanshe, 1989, pp. 161-162; and Liu Mingtao and Yang Chengjun, *Gao jushu zhanzheng zhong de daodan zhan* (*Missile Wars During High Tech Warfare*), Beijing: Guofang daxue chubanshe, 1993.

62. Bao Zhongxing, "Concepts for Developing Space Forces," in *Thinking About Force Modernization*, Beijing: Guofang daxue chubanshe, 1988.

63. Interviews conducted by the author.

64. *Liberation Army Daily*, February and March, 1998, *passim*.

65. Li Jijun, *Junshi lilun yu zhanzheng shijian*, in CVFW, p. 227.

66. Zhen Xi, *Kelindun junshi zhanlue yu di er ci Chaoxian zhanzheng shexiang* pp. 66-68.

67. Wang Pufeng, *Xinxi zhanzheng yu junshi geming,* (*Information Warfare and the Revolution in Military Affairs*), Beijing: Junshi kexue chubanshe, 1995; Li Qingshan, *Xin junshi geming yu gao jishu zhanzheng,* (*The New Revolution in Military Affairs and High Technology Warfare*), Beijing: Junshi kexue chubanshe, 1995; Gao Chunxiang, ed., *Xin junshi geming lun* (*On the New Revolution in Military Affairs*), Beijing: Junshi kexue chubanshe, 1996; Zhu Xiaoli

and Zhao Xiaozhuo, *Mei-E xin junshi geming* (*America, Russia and The New Revolution in Military Affairs*), Beijing: *Junshi kexue chubanshe*, 1996; Han Shengmin, ed., *Zouxiang 21 shiji de waiguo jundui jianshe* (*Foreign Military Development Toward the 21st Century*), Beijing: Junshi kexue chubanshe, 1996.

68. Gao Chunxiang, p. 202.

69. Wang Pufeng, "Yingjie xinxi zhanzheng de tiaozhan" ("The Challenge of Information Warfare"), *Zhongguo junshi kexue* (*China Military Science*), No. 1, 1995, pp. 8-18. Translated in Pillsbury, *Chinese Views of Future Warfare*, pp. 317-326.

70. Han Shengmin, p. 47.

71. *Ibid.*

72. *Ibid.*, pp. 47-48.

73. *Ibid.*, p. 48.

74. Zhu Xiaoli and Zhao Xiaozhuo, *Mei-E xin junshi geming* (*America, Russia and The New Revolution in Military Affairs*), pp. 41-45.

75. Lu Dehong, "An Analysis of the U.S. New Report of the Quadrennial Defense Review, *International Strategic Studies*, No. 4, 1997, pp. 12-17.

76. Pan Junfeng, *China Military Science*, Summer 1996. General Pan is director of the Foreign Military Studies Department of the Academy of Military Science in Beijing. Similar suggestions for how China can exploit U.S. weaknesses and improve its position in the RMA are offered in Gao Chunxiang, pp. 199-202; and Wang Pufeng in *Xinxi zhanzheng yu junshi geming* (*Information Warfare and the Revolution in Military Affairs*), pp. 201-203.

77. *Ibid.*

CHAPTER 4
ADVANCED MILITARY TECHNOLOGY AND THE PLA: PRIORITIES AND CAPABILITIES FOR THE 21st CENTURY

Bernard D. Cole
Paul H.B. Godwin

Introduction.

China's military strategists and planners face an increasingly difficult dilemma as they prepare their defense modernization plans for the 21st century. Even as their armed forces are just beginning to acquire small amounts of the technologies, weapons, and equipment designed for war in the latter part of the 20th century, advances in military technology portend a potential revolution in the conduct of war in the 21st century. Extensive publications by Chinese military analysts amply demonstrate their understanding of the difficulties facing their armed forces as they grapple with the implications of advanced technologies for war in the next century.[1] Given the openness with which China's military leaders and analysts discuss the problems faced by their armed forces, this chapter focuses on four areas of inquiry.

First, we review the implications of advanced technology warfare, as assessed by Chinese military analysts in the years since the 1985 revision of China's national military strategy and particularly in the period following the 1991 Persian Gulf War. Second, we use the evaluations found in the *Militarily Critical Technologies List Part 1: Weapon Systems Technologies* (MCTL), released by the Office of the Under Secretary of Defense (Acquisitions and Technology) in June 1996, to assess China's military-industrial capabilities. Third, in order to determine the technological modernization objectives and priorities of the People's

Liberation Army (PLA), we look at the results of this assessment in conjunction with Beijing's acquisition of foreign military technologies and with analyses of the types of military operations that, according to translations of selected Chinese military journals, Chinese forces seek to conduct over the next decade. Finally, we analyze the kinds of feasible strategies and concepts of operations that are being contemplated by Chinese analysts as they search for specific technologies to offset the advantages of potential adversaries.

We do not assess the implications of advanced technologies for China's nuclear force modernization. Scholars such as Alastair I. Johnston have already thoroughly analyzed the implications, drawn by Chinese analysts, of the technology advances in this realm for Beijing's strategic doctrine and strategy.[2] Rather, we focus on the implications for China's conventional, general purpose forces.

Deficiencies in the technologies of warfare are far from a new plight for the PLA. A major facet of the PLA's doctrinal heritage is Mao Zedong's principle, developed during the struggle in the 1930s against a technologically superior Japanese army, that military forces can successfully compensate for their inferiority in the tools of war with ingenious doctrine and concepts of operations. Nonetheless, Beijing's 1985 revision of China's national military strategy and the implications of the Persian Gulf conflict raised questions within the PLA as to whether doctrinal and operational ingenuity can compensate for technological deficiency in the 21st century.

China's Changing National Military Strategy.

Revising China's national military strategy resulted in the most significant transformation of PLA missions since the founding of the People's Republic in 1949. Until 1985, continental defense against a massive ground assault was the PLA's primary military mission. PLA strategy and operations relied upon numerically superior forces absorbing an attack and then conducting protracted, attrition warfare to sap the enemy's strength and superior technology, leaving him weak and exposed to a counteroffensive that would eject him from China's territory. In the late 1960s, nuclear deterrence joined this core strategy as China deployed its first strategic forces.[3] The wars China fought in Korea and with India and Vietnam were "just outside the gate." As conflicts with bordering states, they were within the scope of a continental defense strategy. In this strategy, pride of place was granted to the ground forces with naval and air forces in secondary supporting roles. The PLA Navy's (PLAN) primary mission was coastal defense, while the PLA Air Force (PLAAF) was devoted to air defense of the homeland.

In 1985, the PLA was given a radically new strategic direction.[4] The potential military threat against China was no longer perceived to be a massive assault, possibly involving nuclear weaponry, designed to conquer China and overthrow its regime. Beijing's strategic assessment in 1985 saw the most likely future military threats as potentially intense, but politically and geographically limited, wars fought on China's periphery, including its maritime territories and claims.[5] It was the requirement to actively defend China's noncontinental territory that brought to the fore a new mission for the PLA—force projection across maritime and aeronautical space.

PLA Post-Gulf War Self-Assessment.[6] China's armed forces were wrestling with these new requirements as the Persian Gulf War erupted. Operation DESERT STORM brought about a new awareness of the extent to which technology had changed the conduct of war. For China's military analysts, Operation DESERT STORM manifested the advent of a probable Revolution in Military Affairs (RMA), based in large part on evolving information technology, such as microelectronics, space-based systems, and data processing. Following the Persian Gulf War, the manner in which the PLA characterized its most likely future conflicts was modified from "limited, local war" to "limited, local war under high-tech conditions."[7]

Particularly impressive to China's military analysts were the allies' capabilities in offensive air operations; surveillance, including space systems and unmanned air vehicles; precision-guided munitions, including cruise missiles for long-range over-the-horizon (OTH) precision strikes; and battlefield command and control. The brief 100-hour ground war against Iraq was seen as demonstrating that numerical superiority is no longer the key to military victory and that the offense now has a significant edge over defense in modern warfare.[8]

Although the display of military technology was impressive, the doctrine and operational art demonstrated by the coalition forces, as they exploited these new technologies for success on the battlefield, were deemed equally salient. For PLA analysts, the stunning victory of coalition forces was recognized as more than the result of advanced platforms, weapons, sensors, and improved training and doctrinal advances. The orchestration of joint warfare was understood to be the critical factor making combat effectiveness more than simply the sum of individual service capabilities.

These analysts find China currently disadvantaged in most areas of the technologies critical to near-term and future warfare. Also evident is the PLA leadership's understanding that China will not achieve the same broad-based technological level as the United States' armed forces and military industrial base any time in the near future. However, published analyses by Chinese military researchers evidence a systematic effort to identify more precisely those technologies within China's grasp that are critical to PLA ability to conduct war successfully in the future. A significant aspect of PLA research is the attempt to link selected advanced technologies with the analysis of potential strategies and/or military operations to counter a superior adversary. Those technologies that could offset distinct advantages held by the United States, and which also serve to support American allies, are specifically included in these inquiries.

Despite their understanding that advanced military technologies are changing the conduct of war, PLA authors continue to wrestle with a "mix" of technology and ideology. The icons of Mao's military theory, dependency on "the people" and "people's war," remain even though military strength is no longer measured in numbers. Despite the new emphasis placed on quality-rather-than-quantity forces voiced by all of China's military leaders, this continued obeisance to Mao Zedong suggests no small tinge of the Qing dynasty reformers as they espoused the principle of *zhongxue weiti, xixue weiyong*—Chinese learning for essence, Western learning for practical use. Despite the widespread understanding within China's military leadership that extensive reform is required to transform the PLA into a world-class combat force in the 21st century, military doctrines of the past still constrain reform and tend to place ideology before training and equipment in assessing combat capabilities.

Advanced Technologies and the Conduct of War. Advanced technologies of greatest interest and concern to the PLA are those contributing to significantly improved battlespace transparency, command and control of joint military operations, long-range precision guided munitions, and information warfare (IW). These technologies allow the commander to obtain and communicate near real-time information on enemy forces and permit the engagement of adversary forces at greater distances with increased accuracy under all-weather and night conditions. IW technologies are used to achieve information superiority over the battlespace by confusing and hindering the adversary's information collection, processing, and utilization while simultaneously defending one's own information-based systems and processes. IW capabilities are often referred to as the "soft" side of warfare in contrast to the "hard" capabilities of more conventional offensive and defensive systems.

These military developments mirror increasingly computer-intensive civilian communications and financial systems, transportation-control networks, and power grids. Disrupting these nominally civilian processes could well have serious deleterious effects on a country's ability to sustain a war. Thus IW has added a new dimension to the appreciation by PLA analysts of technology's role in future military conflict.

Advances in military technology demand changes in concepts of operations to exploit fully the advantages of military technology on the battlefield. Operation DESERT STORM'S demonstration of technology's increasing importance convinced Chinese analysts that the "battlefield" had expanded into space. It also showed that success in war was now crucially dependent on a coordinated plan of joint warfare that placed very high requirements on command, control, communications, computers, intelligence, and information (C^4I^2).

These implications of advanced technological warfare place especially serious demands on the PLA, a military force that lags a generation and more in the evolution of military technology and depends on a relatively unsophisticated population for its manpower. Chinese military analysts recognize that their armed forces must integrate new technologies into concepts of operations, battlefield tactics, maintenance processes, and logistical support without the experience the PLA might have gained if it had gone through earlier evolutions of these technologies.

Certainly there are potential benefits inherent in the requirement to make rapid, dramatic changes. The PLA's very backwardness may ease the leadership's task in shedding the baggage of entrenched organizational and operational principles. It may also mean that PLA operational commanders will resist change until the advantages of new technologies are clearly demonstrated. In either case, the PLA's lack of experience in the employment, maintenance, and logistical support of advanced military technologies will exact a double penalty as it transitions toward a 21st century combat force. First, leveraging technology through military operational capability is especially difficult because technology is advancing faster than it can be acquired, tested, developed, and applied in a military environment. Second, other nations' militaries will continue to advance, so PLA modernization efforts face moving technological goalposts.

Similar problems confront China's weapon-design teams and defense industries when they contemplate production of advanced-technology weapon platforms, sensor systems, and munitions. Design teams must *integrate* the various processes and technologies into coherent weapon platforms, such as ships, aircraft, tanks, etc. Systems and technology integration is a complex, demanding requirement at the heart of technologically advanced military effectiveness. Only slightly less critical is the precision required to manufacture advanced-technology systems, a capability not well established in China's industrial base.

China's defense industries parallel the PLA's experience in lagging a generation and more behind in the requirements for manufacturing advanced-technology military systems and munitions. These deficiencies can be overcome, but it could be many years before China's defense industries develop the consistent quality and precision in manufacturing required to move advanced-technology military items from the drawing board to the battlefield.

China's Military-Industrial Capabilities.

Can the Chinese military-industrial complex (CMIC) build what the PLA thinks it needs for the next century's high-technology warfare? The question is simple, but the answer is not. Mark Stokes has prepared what may be the definitive monograph on what China's military research centers are undertaking to fill the military's requirements,[9] but the question remains. Two decades of reform have sought to rationalize the CMIC and its associated research centers and universities, but priority has been placed on reducing China's defense burden, not on building a modern, effective defense research, development, and industrial base. Today, perhaps no more than 10 percent of the defense manufacturing plant is actually used for military production, with the remainder either idle or devoted to producing goods and services for the civilian market.[10]

Despite reforms initiated in the early 1980s, the CMIC remains the huge, lumbering, obsolescent behemoth built with Soviet assistance in the 1950s. Consisting of more than 2,000 enterprises, each with multiple factories employing three million workers, and encompassing more than 200 major research institutes with 300,000 engineers and technicians, the CMIC has not yet approached the research and production capabilities that mark a major military power.[11] Placing national defense fourth in the "Four Modernizations" investment priorities established in 1978 took its toll on the defense industries as well as the PLA. As late as 1994, Chinese sources state that 81 percent of military producers were losing money.[12]

The Commission on Science, Technology and Industry for National Defense (COSTIND), a successor to the National Defense Science and Technology Commission, was established to provide the cornerstone linking the PLA and the CMIC. COSTIND's failure is evident as military research, development, and production remain weighed down by a lack of centralized coordination and fragmented, almost feudatory, CMIC fiefdoms. This condition hinders the process of translating technological innovation into usable weapons and equipment.[13] But COSTIND, too, has already been reorganized in 1998 into a General Armaments Department (GAD) of the PLA and the "State COSTIND" (SCOSTIND).

Defense conversion has not resolved this problem. While it may facilitate the introduction of new technology, it may have exacerbated the situation as the CMIC entered the world of competitive civilian markets. Furthermore, by the early 1990s, defense conversion policies had created the situation where many plants no longer even wanted to undertake defense production. Peacetime military manufacturing in China involves small quantities with high production costs that leave the producer with little or no profit. Defense contracts often have to be subsidized with revenues from civilian production, which has led to PLA complaints that production plants seek to "guarantee profit, not military interests."[14] Defense research centers also suffered as central government funding was sharply reduced and institutes formerly restricted to defense-related research were required to commercialize their services. Frequently, civilian research and development projects took priority and had to subsidize military research.[15]

Despite the priority the PLA places on acquiring sophisticated military technologies, it should not be assumed that research and manufacturing, employing advanced technologies for civilian products, including imported technologies, automatically lead to "spin-on" for military applications. Infrastructure deficiencies, combined with the lack of experience in transforming dual-use technologies to military purposes, slow down whatever spin-on is derived from civilian or dual-use technologies. No doubt spin-on is taking place, but COSTIND's own daily newspaper complained as late as 1998 that converting defense industrial plants to civilian production in a very competitive market has not resulted in centralized, coordinated programs to exploit civil and dual-use technologies.[16]

While there may well be advances in specific research areas and production capabilities, sometimes referred to as "pockets of excellence," it remains to be determined whether this progress is the result of a focused, planned response to

21st century military requirements or simply research centers acting independently, without direction or coordination. Here again assessment is difficult because failed projects are the norm in this kind of research activity, and it takes many years, especially in the CMIC, to transform development projects into deployed systems.[17] The reorganization of COSTIND mandated at the Ninth National People's Congress in March 1998, as well as the formation of a new General Armaments Department (GAD) to constitute a fourth General Department of the PLA, implicitly acknowledges COSTIND's failure.[18]

Given the evidently poor state of China's indigenous research, development, and production capabilities, the quickest way to embark on acquiring advanced military technologies is foreign procurement.[19] Israel and Russia are currently Beijing's principal suppliers, with Moscow providing the most, but China also gets help from Italy and Great Britain. Israel is contributing to the J-10 advanced fighter project, while Russia has provided a wide variety of weapon systems and military technology. The most visible signs of an expanding military technology linkage with Moscow are the sale of four *Kilo*-class diesel-electric submarines, a reported contract for two *Sovremenny*-class guided missile destroyers, and the recent agreement granting licensed production of Su-27 multiple-role fighters following the sale of some 50 completed aircraft.[20] Italy is helping with avionics and shipboard systems, and Great Britain is assisting with airborne early warning.

These technologies and production capabilities are, however, at best 1980s genre. Entering the realm of 21st century technologies is far more complex—and expensive. This is especially so in the realms of digitization, information technologies, and the technologies required for military space operations. Yet it is in precisely these areas that many facets of 21st century warfare require the highest degrees of production precision and reliability. This high degree of precision and reliability is necessary because, once deployed, it is not possible to maintain or repair computers or artificial intelligence technologies in the space-based reconnaissance systems that are capable of providing real-time intelligence to battlefield commanders. Furthermore, these technologies must function in an extremely harsh environment after surviving the shock and vibration of the launch-phase of deployment. To what extent China is receiving foreign assistance in these obviously strategic technological capabilities is unknown, but even Moscow may be reluctant to provide assistance in such realms.

Assessing China's Military Technology Capabilities.

In the United States, the Department of Defense's (DOD) process for assessing militarily critical technologies for the MCTL involved 15 technology working groups (TWG)[21] which reviewed more than 6,000 technologies and identified 2,060 as militarily significant. Significance was determined by two sets of criteria: those that could (a) enhance threats by potential adversaries of the United States and (b) provided a measurable advantage to U.S. military systems. Ultimately, 656 technologies met the "militarily critical" criteria. Within the limits set by data availability, all the world's significant defense industries were evaluated. Although the MCTL is not a classified document, it may be assumed to include assessments based on classified data because each TWG included representation from the intelligence community as well as from industry and academe.

The TWGs assigned a numerical grade ranging from "0" to "4," reflecting their assessment of the capability of a state's industrial base to produce a specific technology:

"0" indicates that a state has *no capability* or that the TWG could not reach a consensus.

"1" indicates a capability in *only a limited set* of the critical elements of a technology.

"2" indicates a capability in *some* critical elements.

"3" indicates a capability in a *majority* of the technology area's critical elements.

"4" indicates that a country is believed to have the production capability in *all elements* of a technology area.

Only the United States is assessed as possessing all but two of the 84 production elements for the 18 technology areas critical to the development and production of superior weapons.[22]

Of the countries included in the MCTL, we have selected five, in addition to the United States, with which to compare China. Selection was based on the principle that each of the countries selected must possess the range of technological capabilities China is seeking to obtain. Japan, France, Germany, and Great Britain fit this criterion. Russia was included because its military technologies and defense industries were subject to considerable investment during the Cold War and could provide some technologies that China's defense establishment desires.

Compared with the other countries selected, China is relatively new to advanced military technologies, for it did not begin to develop a defense research and industrial base until the mid-1950s. This first step toward a modern defense establishment came to an end in 1959-60 when the former Union of Soviet Socialist Republics (USSR) essentially terminated all of its assistance. With the exception of the nuclear weapon, ballistic missile, and nuclear-powered submarine programs that had special status, internal political dislocation associated with the Great Leap Forward and the Great Proletarian Cultural Revolution left China's defense research and industrial base essentially stagnant. By 1978, when Deng Xiaoping as China's paramount leader initiated his reform programs, the defense industrial base was capable of placing only Soviet technologies from the 1950s into series production. Therefore, the DOD's assessment of June 1996 evaluated a defense technology capability that, with few exceptions, has emerged since 1978. Thus China's defense-industrial base does not have the depth and experience in developing and producing advanced military technologies that the other six countries used in this analysis possess.

We note at the outset that Beijing's deliberate lack of transparency about China's military capabilities means that any assessment of the CMIC must be viewed as tentative. Thus, although we use MCTL assessments of technologies when evaluating China's modern military capabilities and potential, we are aware that evaluations for more transparent states will be more reliable than those for China. Furthermore, an assessment published in 1996 most probably reflects data collected in 1994-95. Nonetheless, the 1996 MCTL, which forms the basis of our analysis, provides the most substantive and accurate body of data for analyzing China's defense industrial capabilities and potential, especially when used in conjunction with information from several other sources.

China's Production and Development Capabilities in Overview. China's overall comparative standing can be seen in Figure 1. In most of the 84 technology areas critical to the development and production of advanced military weapons China is weak, having all necessary production capabilities

Production Capability:	CHINA	U.S.	RUSSIA	JAPAN	GERMANY	U.K.	FRANCE
4	3	82	14	28	20	36	29
3	11	2	30	29	40	34	39
2	37	0	34	19	17	12	14
1	26	0	4	7	6	2	2
0	6	0	2	1	1	0	0
Total	82**	84	84	84	84	84	84

Legend:
Production Capabilities:
  0 = No Capability **or** no consensus
  1 = Limited
  2 = Some
  3 = Majority
  4 = All
  ** China was not evaluated in two technology areas.

Figure 1. Capabilities in the 84 Critical Military Technology Areas.

only for nuclear weapons and nuclear materials processing. Those areas where China has a majority of the production capabilities are in armaments and energetic materials, chemical and biological systems, materials technology, power systems technologies, and in theoretical models for signature control technology. In essentially all other areas of critical military technologies, China is extremely deficient.

Figure 2 provides another overview of China's capabilities to produce advanced military hardware. In none of the technologies essential for the manufacture of

Technology Areas	CHINA	U.S.	RUSSIA	JAPAN	GERMANY	U.K.	FRANCE
Advanced Fabrication and Processing	2	4	2	4	4	4	4
Bearings	2	4	2	3	4	3	4
Metrology*	1	4	2	3	4	4	3
Nondestructive Inspection and** Evaluation	1	4	2	3	4	2	4
Production Equipment	2	4	2	4	4	3	4
Robotics	1	4	2	4	2	1	2

Legend:
Production Capabilities:
  0 = No Capability **or** no consensus
  1 = Limited
  2 = Some
  3 = Majority
  4 = All

*State-of-the art hardware requires precision measurement for both development and manufacturing. The extensive list includes ships, aircraft, missiles, propellers, bearings, avionics, etc.

**Technologies essential for detecting problems in design and manufacture and in delivered hardware. Additionally these technologies can provide the basis for determining reliability and maintenance requirements.

***The level of this technology directly affects the cost, reliability, and level of military hardware that can be produced.

Figure 2. Manufacturing and Fabrication Technologies.

Armaments & Energetic Materials Technology	
Energetic Materials	3
Chemical and Biological Systems Technology	
Chemical/Biological Defense	3
Detection/Warning Identification	3
Materials Technology	
Armor & Anti-armor Materials	3
Electrical Materials	3
Structural Material	3
Special Function Materials	3
Nuclear Systems Technology	
Fission Reactor	
Nuclear Materials Processing	4
Nuclear Weapons	4
Power Systems Technology	
High Density Conventional Systems	3
Mobile Electric Platform Power	3
Sensors & Laser Technology	
Obscurants	4
Signature Control Technology	
Theoretical Models	3

Legend:
Production Capabilities:
 0 = No capability or no consensus
 1 = Limited
 2 = Some
 3 = Majority
 4 = All
*Strength is defined as having the capability to produce a majority or more (levels 3-4) of specific military technologies.

Figure 3. China's Strengths.

advanced military equipment does China rank higher than "some" production capabilities.

Looking at China's technological capabilities in greater detail, Figure 3 lists those areas where China is evaluated with a production capability of "3" or "4." Figure 4 indicates those technology areas where China is evaluated as possessing less than a majority of development and production capabilities, a level of "1" or "2."

Aeronautics Systems Technology
Fixed Wing Aircraft. 2
Gas Turbine Engines 2
Human (crew) systems 1

Marine Systems Technology
Propulsors and Propulsion System 0
Signature Control and Survivability 1
Subsurface and Deep Submergence Vehicles 1

Guidance, Navigation, and Vehicle Control Technology
Aircraft and Vehicle Control Systems 2
Inertial Navigation Systems. 2
Radio and Data-Based Navigation Systems 2

Directed and Kinetic Energy Systems Technology
Lasers, High Energy Chemical. 2
Supporting Technologies. 1

Weapons Effects and Countermeasures Technology
Induced Shockwave from Penetrating Weapons 1

Sensors and Laser Technology
Acoustic Sensors 0
Marine Active Sonar 2
Marine Passive Sonar 2
Marine Platform Acoustic Sensors. 2
Electro-Optical Sensors. 2
Gravity Meters 1
Lasers. 2
Magnetometers 2
Radar 1

Signature Control Technology
Materials 2
Design Concepts 2
Applications to Integrated Systems. 1
Manufacturing. 1
Logistics. 1
Testing 2
Computer Codes 1

Space Systems Technology
Computer and Electronics 1
Optronics. 2
Power and Thermal Management 1
Space Systems Propulsion 2
Space System Sensors. 2

Figure 4. China's Weaknesses.**

Information Systems Technology
- C⁴I² Systems 1
- CAD/CAM 2
- High Performance Computing 1
- Human Systems Interface 1
- Information Security 2
- Intelligence Systems 1
- Modeling and Simulation 0
- Networks and Switching 2
- Signal Processing 2
- Software 1
- Transmission Systems 1

Information Warfare Technology
- Electronic Attack 1
- Electronic Protection 0
- Optical Countermeasures 0
- Optical Counter-Countermeasures 0

Electronics Technology
- Electronic Components 1
- Electronic Materials 2
- Fabrication Equipment 2
- General Purpose Equipment 2
- Micro-Electronics 2
- Opto-Electronics 1

Manufacturing and Fabrication Technology
- Advanced Fabrication and Processing 2
- Bearings 2
- Metrology 1
- Nondestructive Inspection and Evaluation 1
- Production Equipment 2
- Robotics 1

Materials Technology
- Magnetic Materials 2
- Optical Materials 2

Electric Power Systems
- Pulse and High Power Systems 1

* Also applies to marine gas turbine engines for naval applications
** Weakness is defined as having the capability to produce only "none" or "some" (levels 0-2) of the specific military technologies.

Legend: Production Capabilities:
  0 = No capability **or** no consensus.
  1 = Limited.
  2 = Some.
  3 = Majority.
  4 = All.

Figure 4. China's Weaknesses.** (cont)

PLA Priorities.

Our analysis, however, is not concerned primarily with the CMIC's overall development and production capabilities, but with assessing China's advanced technology capabilities in areas of expressed interest to the PLA: those that contribute significantly to improved battle-space awareness, long-range precision strike munitions, command and control of joint military operations, and information warfare. These capabilities can be assigned to three broad operational areas generic to all combat operations—detection, location, and effective engagement, especially in a target-rich environment.

Detection technologies may soon be able to provide near real-time information on the total battle area from space through air to surface, to below the ocean's surface. Knowing precisely where the adversary's forces and command and control facilities are *located* allows a commander to prioritize and select targets. Locating the forces and facilities of the greatest significance to the battle allows a commander to employ joint forces in space and air, as well as on land and sea, to *engage* the adversary at the most advantageous time and place and with the most appropriate weapons.

Detection and location capabilities can place the adversary in a disadvantaged position, especially when they create a relatively transparent battlefield, which permits a commander to know engagement results in near real-time. We will be expanding on each of these mission areas and their associated technologies as we continue our analysis.

The three sets of technologies associated with these operational mission areas as defined in the MCTL are:

Detection:
Space Systems Technology
Sensors and Laser Technology
Guidance, Navigation and Vehicle Control Technology

Location:
  Sensors and Laser Technology
  Guidance, Navigation and Vehicle Control Technology
  Information Technology (C^4I^2, etc.)

Engagement (joint warfare)**:**
  Information Technology (C^4I^2, etc.)
  Directed and Kinetic Energy Systems Technology
  Information Warfare Technology
  Aeronautics Systems Technology
  Marine Systems Technology
  Signature Control Technology

In several areas, specific technologies fit more than one mission. Additionally, the technologies listed apply equally to offensive and defensive operations.

China's production capabilities in space systems are assessed in Figure 5. Space surveillance provides the military commander with critical information and capabilities. Beyond target detection and location, of particular value are weather information, the ability to provide precise navigation data, and robust command and

Production Capabilities:	CHINA	U.S.	RUSSIA	JAPAN	GERMANY	U.K.	FRANCE
Computer & Electronics*	1	4	3	1	1	3	3
Optronics**	2	3	3	3	2	2	3
Power & Thermal Management***	1	4	2	2	3	2	2
Propulsion****	2	4	3	2	1	1	3
Sensors*****	2	4	2	3	1	2	3

Legend:
Capabilities:
0 = No capability **or** no consensus
1 = Limited
2 = Some
3 = Majority
4 = All
*Emphasis on component reliability in high stress environments: high vibration, radiation, thermal cycling, etc.
**Emphasis on technologies enhancing target detection, identification, resolution, etc.
***Emphasis on efficiency, light weight, long duration and reliability.
****Emphasis on emerging chemical, low-thrust electrical and nuclear thermal technologies.
*****Emphasis on electro-optic sensors providing "real-time" intelligence.

Figure 5. Space Systems Technologies.

control for operational forces. The critical components of space reconnaissance are optronics, for these technologies determine the parameters for detection, identification, and resolution of targets. Where conditions do not permit sufficient clarity or detail, electro-optic sensors join with laser illumination to provide the essential data.[23]

Although China's interest in military surveillance systems is unquestioned, its ability to design and produce the space sensors central to wide-area reconnaissance is clearly limited. Beijing still defines its military reconnaissance satellites as "experimental." China's first generation of recoverable photo-intelligence satellites (FSW-1) of the mid-1960s had an operational life of 7 to 10 days. A later model, the FSW-2, could remain in orbit for up to 16 to 18 days. Two FSW-types were launched into low earth orbit in 1994. In March 1996, however, an FSW-type satellite did not return to its Sichuan basin recovery area, but instead made an uncontrolled entry into the South Atlantic.[24]

There may be more progress with the *Ziyuan*-1 (ZY-1). This commercial satellite joint venture with Brazil was scheduled to be launched in 1998, with an estimated orbit life of 2 years. However, by May 1999, this launch had not taken place. Given China's practice of combining civil and military functions, we assume that this satellite system will have military missions when it eventually becomes operational. The ZY-1, with three remote sensors, has a real-time transmission capability and a ground resolution power of 19.5 meters. This is less than most commercial systems and far less than a U.S. KH-12, which has a resolution power of 1.5 to 3 meters.[25] Thus, despite its 30-year experience with satellites, China's ability to successfully deploy space systems that have the ability to detect and locate targets in a wide battle area and that can provide commanders with real-time intelligence is evidently some years away.

As Figure 6 indicates, nor are China's sensors for air, ground, and maritime platforms particularly advanced. PLAN anti-submarine warfare capabilities (ASW), now referred to as Under Sea Warfare (USW) by the U.S. Navy, are limited by evident weakness in acoustic and other sensors. Similarly, China has only a limited capability in the electro-optical sensors used for terminal guidance in "smart" and more advanced "brilliant" munitions. In sum, the CMIC is demonstrably weak in essentially all areas of technology associated with precision locating and targeting.

Technology Areas:	China	U.S.	Russia	Japan	Germany	U.K.	France
Acoustic Sensors	0	4	2	1	1	2	2
Marine Active Sonar	2	4	3	3	3	4	4
Marine Passive Sonar	2	4	2	3	3	4	4
Marine Platform Acoustic Sensors	2	4	3	3	2	4	4
Electro-Optical Sensors	2	4	4	3	3	3	3
Gravity Meters	1	4	2	1	2	2	2
Lasers	2	4	4	3	3	3	3
Magnetometers	1	2	3	2	3	2	3
Obscurants	4	3	4	4	4	4	4
Radar	2	4	3	3	3	3	3

Legend:
Capabilities:
0 = No capabilities **or** no consensus
1 = Limited
2 = Some
3 = Majority
4 = All

Figure 6. Sensors and Laser Technologies.

Similar deficiencies in providing precise location of China's own and the enemy's military platforms are equally evident, as indicated by Figure 7. In 21st century warfare, continuous and accurate position data are required to maintain real-time reconnaissance of enemy forces and to permit effective coordination of highly mobile military forces in joint, non-linear warfare. China is deficient in these technology areas. Furthermore, both conventional and nuclear munitions rely upon precise guidance technologies for the accuracy required to fit the weapon's footprint to the target. Yet, here again China is lacking.

Technology Areas:	China	U.S.	Russia	Japan	Germany	U.K.	France
Inertial Navigation Systems	2	4	3	3	3	4	4
Aircraft & Vehicle Control Systems	2	4	3	2	3	4	4
Radio & Data-Based Referenced Navigation Systems	2	4	3	2	3	4	4

Legend:
Production Capabilities:
   0 = No capability **or** no consensus
   1 = Limited
   2 = Some
   3 = Majority
   4 = All

*Accurate positioning, attitude, pointing, and control of land, sea, air, and space forces are essential for coordinating highly mobile forces engaged in joint operations.

Figure 7. Guidance, Navigation and Vehicle Control Technologies.*

Deficiencies in navigation and guidance are exacerbated by poor command and control technologies, without which effective engagement of joint forces becomes extremely problematic. Figure 8 indicates that China's mastery of command and control technologies is inadequate.

Reliable and secure C^4I^2 systems are essential in military operations. Today and in the next century, the seamless integration of communications, intelligence, and information complements battle-space awareness, providing the commander with real-time decision-making capabilities. This is particularly significant because near real-time assessment of the *results* of an engagement is now becoming critical to dominating the battle-space and in gaining tactical and operational advantage over an adversary. China's continuing deficiencies in this critical area are reflected in the failure of its most recent second-generation military communications satellite, the DFH-3. Built as a joint venture with Germany's Daimler-Benz company and using some U.S. components, the satellite failed to become operational following its May 1997 launch. This was the second DFH-3 malfunction, the first occurring in 1994 when the satellite failed to achieve proper orbit. Because of these failures, COSTIND leased two receivers on the commercial Apstar-1A for military use.

Technology Areas	China	U.S.	Russia	Japan	Germany	U.K.	France
C^4I^{2}*	1	4	2	3	3	4	4
Information Security**	2	4	2	2	4	4	3
High Performance Computing	1	4	2	4	3	3	3
Intelligent Systems***	1	4	2	4	2	3	1
Networks & Switching+	2	4	2	4	4	4	4
Signal Processing++	1	4	2	3	3	3	4
Transmission Systems+++	1	4	2	4	4	4	4
Software	1	4	2	3	3	4	4

Legend:
Production Capabilities:
0 = No capability **or** no consensus
1 = Limited
2 = Some
3 = Majority
4 = All
*Command, Control, Communications, Computing, Intelligence and Information (C^4I^2) Systems
**Cryptographic and cryptoanalytic technologies essential for keeping data secure and breaking ciphertext in intelligence dissemination, global surveillance, computer and communications networks.
***Technologies (hardware & software) allowing systems to adjust their functionality without human operator intervention or preprogrammed logic.
+Technologies essential for maintaining communications at all times with all elements. They include radiation hardened telecommunications, optical switching, and equipment capable of operating in extreme heat or cold.
++Technologies associated with ensuring the accuracy and reliability of data transmission in environments with high levels of interference, including intentional countermeasures.
+++These technologies minimize third-party interception and neutralize electronic warfare capabilities used to disrupt accurate reception of transmitted information

Figure 8. Command and Control Technologies.

The Apstar communications satellite was built by Hughes Electronics and sold to a commercial communications company, APT of Hong Kong.[26]

The PLA's use of commercial satellites for both reconnaissance and communications demonstrates the overall pattern of weaknesses in China's military capabilities in space. Thus, when command and control deficiencies are combined with detection and location frailties, China's hopes for achieving early in the 21st century the capabilities demonstrated by the United States in the early 1990s are slim to none. Moreover, the use of leased commercial capabilities leaves the PLA vulnerable to having its information flow cut.

Countering High-Technology Adversaries. With these collective disadvantages, it is important to assess the ability of Chinese forces to disrupt the advantages held by technologically superior forces. Such an approach to future conflict not only fits the PLA's deeply-held doctrinal and operational tradition, but it can also be ascertained from Chinese assessments of their future strategy.

Of particular interest to China are the capabilities of high-energy lasers (HEL).[27] HEL systems can deliver energy at the speed of light and show promise of being able to provide rapid retargeting of platforms ranging from satellites to ballistic missiles to aircraft.[28] To achieve this promise, design is now focused on supporting technologies that will permit HEL systems to acquire and track targets, to conduct "kill" assessments, and then to move quickly and accurately on to new targets. To achieve these capabilities, the supporting technologies must allow the system to track one or more targets, to sustain the beam on target long enough to harm it, to evaluate the damage produced, and then, if the level of damage is sufficient, to reorient the beam to another target.[29] These are very complicated technologies to design, manufacture, and integrate into weapon systems. As Figure 9 indicates, China's assessed production capabilities, both in chemical lasers and the supporting technologies essential for effective engagement, are low, although clearly some progress is being made.

Chinese analysts also show a high interest in information warfare (IW),[30] sometimes referred to as "soft" warfare. IW is a combination of old and new missions, is

Technology Areas	CHINA	U.S.	RUSSIA	JAPAN	GERMANY	U.K	FRANCE
Lasers, High Energy Chemical	2	4	3	2	2	2	2
Supporting Technologies for Directed Energy Weapons	1	4	3	1	1	2	2

Legend:
Production Capabilities:
 0 = No capability **or** no consensus
 1 = Limited
 2 = Some
 3 = Majority
 4 = All

Figure 9. Directed Energy Systems Technologies.

linked to emerging information technologies, and has both offensive and defensive capabilities. Offensive missions seek to harm an adversary's information, information-based processes and systems, and computer-based networks. The modes of attack used to execute such missions are electronic warfare (EW), command and control warfare (C^2W), physical destruction, and deception. Although "hackers" have demonstrated the capability to break into unprotected computer-based information systems, the disruption of protected, hardened military systems is more difficult. Figure 10 indicates China's IW technology capabilities are limited.

Technology Areas	CHINA	U.S.	RUSSIA	JAPAN	GERMANY	U.K	FRANCE
Electronic Attack	1	4	3	2	3	3	3
Electronic Protection	0	4	3	2	2	2	3
Optical Counter-measures	0	4	4	2	3	4	3
Optical Counter-Counter Measures	0	4	3	2	3	3	2
Legend: Production Capabilities: 0 = No capability **or** no consensus; 1 = Limited; 2 = Some; 3 = Majority; 4 = All.							

Figure 10. Information Warfare Technologies.

What is not evident from the available data are China's capabilities to attack unprotected systems, such as power grids, civilian telephone systems, transportation networks, financial networks, and other increasingly information-and-computer-dependent sectors of civil society. Figure 11 provides a broader assessment of China's information capabilities and exposes an even wider set of limitations.

There is a wide swath of technologies involved in information systems (IS) simply because these technologies are applied over an extensive range of military applications. The applications include IS systems as part of "smart" and "brilliant" weapons, aircraft, ships, tanks, armored fighting vehicles, and communications systems and networks,

Technology Areas	CHINA	U.S.	RUSSIA	JAPAN	GERMANY	U.K	FRANCE
C^4I^2	1	4	2	3	3	4	4
CAD/CAM*	2	4	2	4	4	4	4
High Performance Computing	1	4	2	4	3	3	3
Human Systems Interface	1	4	1	4	3	3	3
Information Security	2	4	2	2	4	4	3
Intelligent Systems	1	4	2	4	2	3	1
Modeling & Simulation	0	4	0	4	3	4	3
Networks & Switching	2	4	2	4	4	4	4
Signal processing	1	4	2	3	3	3	3
Software	1	4	2	3	3	4	4
Transmission Systems	1	4	2	4	4	4	4

Legend:
Production Capabilities:
 0 = No capability **or** no consensus
 1 = Limited
 2 = Some
 3 = Majority
 4 = All.
*Computer-assisted design and manufacturing.

Figure 11. Information Systems Technologies.

including hand-held devices. Equally important is the human-systems interface with these technologies, as well as the ability to model and simulate the engineering and manufacturing processes. Human interface with the technologies is central to increasing reaction time in increasingly complex platforms, such as combat aircraft and attack helicopters, and in the ability of the operator and/or user to handle high levels of information and to make decisions in high-stress combat situations. Here again, China's deficiencies are extensive, and the speed with which its scientists and engineers can reach the level of advanced industrial and post-industrial states is difficult to predict.

Operational Implications.

The MCTL data are particularly important for their contribution to evaluating the military operational applications of the technologies assessed. Given that China's national military strategy has shifted from continental defense to peripheral defense and that maritime territories and claims are now of particular concern, we shall focus on technologies associated with naval and air power and with cruise and tactical ballistic missile capabilities. Because China's military analysts view future conflicts as potentially involving short-duration, high-intensity combat, the PLA's operational focus has shifted from defensive to offensive operations and the need to gain the initiative early in any engagement. Naval and air power is of particular importance in such operations. Thus, even within a military strategy designed to be defensive, force projection is a major concern of China's military planners.

Maritime Forces. As Figure 12 indicates, the MCTL assigns China low ratings in most of the technologies associated with naval warfare. To recognize the implications of these ratings, the analyst must consider and crosscheck more than one of the technology areas in order to translate MCTL evaluations into useful measures of operational capability in any area of naval technology. No weapon platform as complex as a modern surface or subsurface naval combatant is dependent upon a single set of technologies. Rather, to be effective, a warship is a "system of systems" and must integrate a number of different technologies into a single fighting system.

Submarine Technology. Evaluating the military utility of China's submarines demands attention to a number of related technology areas. For example, despite China's strength in nuclear systems, its weakness in related technology areas impedes the successful completion of a modern, quiet, nuclear submarine force. This assessment, together with the crudity of China's six nuclear-powered submarines (only four of which may be operational), indicates that China is not able to make operational use of its strong rankings in nuclear systems technology. Similar deficiencies impede development of a modern, conventionally-powered (diesel-electric) submarine force.

System	Rating
Nuclear Systems	
Fission Reactor	3
Materials Processing	4
Marine Systems	
Propulsion Systems	0
Survivability	1
Subsurface Vehicles	1
Signature Control	
Modeling	3
Materials-Design	2
Integration	1
Manufacturing	1
Logistics	1
Testing	1
Computer Codes	1
Guidance and Navigation	
Inertial	2
Sensors	
Radio & Data-Based	2
Active Sonar	2
Acoustic (Terrestrial)	0
Passive Sonar	2
Marine Platform	
Acoustic Sensors	2
Magnetic Materials	2
Manufacturing-Fabrication	
Advanced	2
Bearings	2
Production Equip.	2
Metrology	1
Inspection & Eval.	1
Robotics	1

Legend:
Production Capabilities:
0 = No capability **or** no consensus
1 = Limited
2 = Some
3 = Majority
4 = All

Figure 12. Naval Systems Technologies.

To be effective in the 1990s, let alone in the 21st century, a submarine must integrate a large number of advanced technologies, both to conceal its own presence and to detect its opponent's. Signature-control technology is crucial to designing a submarine with a low enough "signature" to avoid detection by opposing forces using submarine, ship, aircraft, space, and ocean-bottom systems keyed to sense and report audio, visual, magnetic, pressure, and infrared disturbances to the environment that would indicate the presence of a submarine. In sum, the less the submarine disturbs the ambient environment—the lower its signature—the more difficult it is to detect and the more effective it will be operationally. In these crucial areas, China receives a "3" in theoretical models technique, but only a "2" in materials and design concepts, and just "1s" in the other five sub-areas evaluated—not a strong showing. Furthermore, while minimizing its own signature, a submarine must also be able to detect opponents. Here China has a "0" rating in the crucial acoustic sensors area and "2s" in the active and passive sonar areas.

Guidance, navigation, and vehicle-control technologies directly affect a nation's ability to design and produce operationally effective submarines. This area includes the technologies on which are based inertial, radio, and databased-referenced navigation equipment, applicable both to the submarine's ability to navigate accurately and to fire cruise and ballistic missiles with precision. Here, China receives "2s" in inertial, radio, and databased-referenced navigation systems. In other words, the CMIC is unable to provide the most advanced navigational-locating systems, and the absence of these advanced systems limits submarine navigational accuracy and hence operational effectiveness. This shortfall can be partially alleviated by access to American global-positioning-system (GPS) satellites and the Russian Global Navigation Satellite System (GLONASS), but the GPS system would certainly be downgraded by the United States in the event of a military conflict.

Modern submarine construction involves the MCTL area classified as manufacturing and fabrication technology. Here China is evaluated with a capability of "2" in advanced fabrication and processing, bearings, and production equipment and of "1s" in both metrology and non-destructive inspection and evaluation. Without importing these technologies, China will be unable to construct an indigenous submarine force approaching those of the advanced industrial states.

China's purchase of *Kilo*-class diesel-electric submarines from Russia stems from these deficiencies. *Kilos* are advanced craft, more capable than the Chinese-built *Ming* and *Song* classes. The *Kilo* first went to sea in 1980 and remains one of the world's better conventionally-powered submarines. It is somewhat dated, since it does not have an Air Independent Propulsion system, but the *Kilo* still presents China with technological sophistication not available in the CMIC.

To increase its stealthiness for both offensive and defensive purposes, the *Kilo*'s hull is coated with anechoic tiles that reduce its susceptibility to sonar detection and diminish the noise created by its internal machinery. Submarines from China's yards, especially the nuclear-powered *Han* and *Xia* classes, lack such a coating and are relatively noisy and easy to detect. The *Kilo* also incorporates competent technologies for offensive operations, including acoustic sensors, electro-optical sensors, radar, lasers, and wire-guided torpedoes.

Clearly, by purchasing at least four and reportedly as many as 20 *Kilo* submarines in future years, Beijing is making a significant increase in submarine technologies available to the CMIC. Whether China will be able to utilize these technologies in a CMIC-designed submarine as a stepping stone to leap over the development, design, and implementation time represented by the 18 years of technological advances that went into the *Kilo* since it first sailed is open to question. It is more likely that the CMIC, after 10 years of laborious effort, will produce a submarine in 2008 that would have been state-of-the-art in 1988.

Surface Combatant Technology. China's newest surface warship is the *Luhu*-class guided missile destroyer (DDG), two of which have been placed in commission. Like most destroyers, the *Luhu* is designed as a multi-mission ship, capable of conducting naval warfare over, on, and beneath the sea. The world's most advanced destroyers are also designed to project power ashore. How well can the *Luhu* carry out these missions, all of which draw directly on the technologies surveyed in the MCTL?

In building the *Luhu*, China incorporated weapons, sensor, and propulsion systems from several foreign countries, including the United States, the USSR/Russia, France, the United Kingdom, Italy, and Spain. The most critical of these foreign components may be the propulsion system, a combined diesel-gas turbine (CODOG) arrangement built around U.S.-furnished LM-2500 gas turbine engines. Five of these engines, which the United States uses in several classes of warships and in the C-5 aircraft, were sold to China before 1989. Four are installed in the two *Luhus*.[31]

Of the MCTL technology area pertinent to marine propulsion, China is evaluated as having "no" capability in marine propulsion systems and "some" capability in gas turbine engines. The CMIC apparently has been unable to manufacture a viable maritime gas turbine engine, although this technology was developed in Germany in the late 1930s and went to sea in 1962 in a Soviet combatant. This CMIC shortcoming has presumably contributed to the hiatus in commissioning additional *Luhu*-class ships.[32]

Foreign designs also predominate in the *Luhu's* sensor-weapons suite. The guns and associated fire control directors are Soviet design, the torpedoes are Italian, and the missiles and associated fire control systems are French, as are the ship's two helicopters. Except for the guns and the surface-to-surface missiles, all were beyond CMIC's capability.

China's reliance on foreign systems in the *Luhu's* electronic warfare and radar systems is reflected in the MCTL's evaluations of "1" and "2" for the six sub-areas in electronics technology.[33] These technology areas include sonar, in which the *Luhu's* medium frequency system reflects the MCTL's evaluation of China's capability in marine active, marine passive, and marine platform acoustic sensors as "2." China shows no better capability in technology areas related to radar development, earning a "2" in electro-optical sensors, lasers, and radar.

The *Luhu* also shows no apparent stealth characteristics, a judgment supported by the MCTL's signature-control technology area. Here, China is evaluated as possessing "some" (2) or "limited" (1) capability in seven of the eight sub-areas, with a "3" earned for theoretical modeling.

China's front-line warship, the *Luhu*-class DDG, is multi-mission capable, but with systems based on older technology and without the ability to project power ashore. As with the *Kilo*-class submarine, China is attempting to compensate for CMIC shortfalls by purchasing foreign ships. An agreement may have been reached with Russia for the purchase of at least two *Sovremenny*-class guided missile destroyers.[34] Much larger than the *Luhu,* displacing 7,300 tons to the *Luhu's* 4,200 tons, the *Sovremenny* has a much better sea-keeping ability and a larger engagement envelope.

The *Sovremenny* is a 1980s-era DDG, designed to fight as a unit in a coordinated task force against U.S. Navy aircraft carrier battle groups. These ships were designed specifically for an anti-surface ship role; their anti-air and anti-submarine warfare capabilities are limited. In Soviet naval doctrine, these DDGs would be operating in company with ships more capable of defending against air attacks and hostile submarines.[35] But China does not have the modern combatants to operate the *Sovremenny* as a unit in a multi-capability task force. Instead, they would likely be employed as raiders or as part of a task group made up of the PLAN's best ships, *Luda* and *Luhu* destroyers and *Jiangwei* guided missile frigates. None of these ships, however, are any more capable than the *Sovremenny* at combating modern air and submarine threats. Hence, the PLAN would have to operate the *Sovremennys* very conservatively until it either modified them or acquired other maritime means to operate more capably in a multi-threat environment.

These ships, however, represent a significant advance in many capabilities for the PLAN. Most newsworthy is the *Sovremenny's* anti-ship missile, the SS-N-22, or SUNBURN in North Atlantic Treaty Organization (NATO) parlance. This is an extremely capable missile, with a flight profile that includes flying altitudes of less than 100 feet over the ocean's surface, speeds in excess of Mach 2, a range for the most advanced model of over 65 miles, and possibly intricate terminal flight maneuvers designed to foil defensive systems.[36]

Air Forces.[37]

China's multiple weaknesses in the projection of air power are widely recognized. Despite China's long-standing efforts to acquire the necessary capabilities, a central weakness remains the People's Liberation Army Air Force's (PLAAF) and People's Liberation Army Naval Air Force's (PLANAF) lack of operational aerial refueling capabilities and airborne warning and control system (AWACS) aircraft. These two deficiencies alone limit both the range of China's airpower to the unrefueled distance from land bases and its effectiveness in a variety of critical combat missions. We shall not go over this well-trodden ground in this chapter.[38] Rather, we will focus on the production capabilities of China's combat aircraft industries. Figure 13 provides the MCTL's overall assessment of these technologies. Although there is a strong crossover between

191

Systems	Rating
Aeronautics Systems:	
Aircraft Fixed Wing	2
Gas Turbines	2
Conventional Ammunition	1
Electronics:	
Materials	2
G.P. Equipment	2
Micro-Electronics	2
Components	1
Opto-Electronics	1
Guidance, Navigation	2
Manufacturing-Fabrication:	
Advanced Fabrication	2
Bearings	2
Production Equip.	2
Metrology	1
Inspection-Eval.	1
Robotics	1
Materials (Airframes)	3
Sensors	2
Signature Control:	
Modeling	3
Materials	2
Design	2
Testing	2
Integration	1
Manufacturing	1
Logistics	1
Computer Codes	1

Legend:
Production Capabilities:
1 = Limited
2 = Some
3 = Majority

Figure 13. Air Power Technologies.

military and commercial air-systems technologies, the MCTL focuses on military-specific technologies representing "the key means to rapidly project fire power against an adversary in the air and on land and sea."[39]

Using the MCTL as an indicator of China's relative status in these broad technology areas requires a narrowing of scope. Of the technologies that pertain to modern air power, China is evaluated as possessing "a majority" of the applicable technology in just two sub-areas (airframes and modeling for signature control), as possessing "some" of the technology in 13 sub-areas, and as having "limited" capability in 10 other areas.

The CMIC's inability to design and build modern combat airframes and power plants is compounded by China's deficiencies in essentially all other technology areas central to modern air forces. In electronics, guidance, navigation, and vehicle control, and sensors and signature control technology, China is evaluated as possessing no more than "some" of the required technologies.

Finally, in the technology area of armaments and energetic materials, which refers to a nation's ability "to develop and produce in quantity safe, affordable, storable, and effective conventional munitions and weapons systems," China is assessed as having only a "limited" capability.[40] For the purposes of air power, these include ammunition, bombs, fusing, and missiles.

Although Beijing's Soviet-derived combat aircraft from the 1950s and early 1960s, such as the MiG-19/J-6 and MiG-21/J-7, have all benefited over the past 20 years from the adaptation of Western military technologies, China's indigenous programs are best typified by the J-8 interceptor's long and difficult development history. This aircraft began development in 1964, was first flight-tested in 1969, and entered service in the early 1980s. Even after the aircraft's 20-year gestation period, the PLAAF still found the J-8 unsatisfactory and, as late as 1989, dubbed it an "operational test aircraft." PLAAF and PLANAF dissatisfaction with the J-8 spanned a range of requirements from a new fire control system to a more powerful engine. China's aircraft industry was unable to satisfy these demands and turned for assistance to Western suppliers, including the United States. Ultimately, "improved" J-8-2s began service with the naval air arm in 1992. This is a total of almost a 30-year development period for what remains a below-par combat aircraft—not yet the equivalent of a 1960s-era U.S. F-4 Phantom.[41]

Unable to design and build modern combat aircraft and their power plants and facing technology restrictions from Western Europe and the United States, Beijing turned to Israel and Russia for assistance. Israel is providing design and technology support for the J-10 multiple-role fighter program. Russia became the source of military aircraft and power plants, complementing its role as the principal supplier of advanced naval combatants. Russia's assistance includes provision for a manufacturing facility in China capable of assembling 10 to 15 Su-27s a year, with a final inventory goal of 275.[42]

The Su-27SK model that China is fielding is a very capable dual-mission aircraft, designed for both air superiority and ground attack. There is no evidence that the Chinese have improved their ability to absorb and replicate modern aircraft, however. Additionally, all of these aircraft reportedly are still returned to Russia for all but the most routine maintenance.[43] Although basically a late 1970s aircraft, the Su-27 embodies technology and manufacturing techniques beyond the CMIC's capabilities.

When its air power capabilities and characteristics are matched against MCTL technology areas, Russia earns a "4" in fixed-wing aircraft, China a "2." Russia also has higher ratings in gas turbine engine technology, electronic systems "hardening" against electro-magnetic pulses (EMP), human (crew) interface, and navigation and control systems. By the time China is capable of producing Su-27s without Russian assistance, it is likely that Harlan Jencks' assessment, made in the late 1970s, that the China's J-6/MiG-19 was "the most highly perfected obsolescent combat aircraft in the world" will yet again apply.[44]

Cruise and Tactical Ballistic Missiles.

The CMIC is credited with achieving a "pocket of excellence" in missile technology.[45] It is generally assumed that a key objective of China's defense establishment is to achieve a long-range reconnaissance/strike capability. The significance of long-range precision strike was amply demonstrated to the Chinese defense establishment during the Gulf War, especially the U.S. Navy's Tomahawk land attack cruise missile successes. It is probable this demonstration contributed to Beijing's decision to employ cruise and ballistic missiles in the Taiwan Strait military exercises of 1995 and 1996. These weapons are difficult to defend against, and their targets, beyond ships and aircraft, include those critical to coordinating and sustaining high-intensive combat: command and control nodes, air defense systems, and air, naval, and logistic bases. With sufficient accuracy, tactical missiles can replace manned aircraft for precision strike on all of these targets. Figure 14 provides the MCTL's evaluations of China's capabilities in 14 applicable technologies that apply equally to cruise and tactical ballistic missiles.

Cruise Missiles. Cruise missiles have a long history, going back to Germany's use of the V-1 in the closing year of World War II. As originally fielded by the United States and the Soviet Union in the early 1950s, cruise missiles were little more than pilotless aircraft. Since those early years, this weapon has gained in accuracy and range and now provides a relatively small, relatively inexpensive, fast "fire and forget" weapon that can be difficult to detect and shoot down. Cruise missiles do, however, have drawbacks that include limited warhead size, dependence on reliable target positioning data in OTH operational situations, the need for mid-course guidance, and the requirement for precision manufacturing and careful maintenance.

China makes extensive use of cruise missiles, and as with essentially all other areas of military technology, the CMIC's cruise missile developments originate in Soviet

System	Rating
Warheads	2
Fusing	1
Fabrication Materials	2
Radar	2
Inertial Navigation Systems	2
Radio & Data-based Referenced Navigation Systems	2
Gravity Meters	1
Control Systems	2
Microelectronics	2
Electronic Components	1
Electronic Materials	2
Electro-optical Sensors	2
Opto-electronics	1

Legend:
Production Capabilities:
1 = Limited
2 = Some

Figure 14. Tactical Missile Technologies.

technology transfers. China's programs[46] are grouped into two families: the *Hai Ying* (HY - Sea Eagle) and *Ying Ji* (YJ - Eagle Strike) series. Both families are given the letter "C" as a prefix before the number in export versions, as in C-201. China's first success was with the HY-1 series weapons derived from the Soviet *Styx*. Attempts to improve on this missile began in 1974. Typically, gestation was long and the new version was not "type qualified" until December 1983. "Poor system integration and quality control" have been blamed for at least part of the extensive development time.[47]

These and additional improved versions are potentially effective weapons, with the HY-2A (C-201) carrying a 1,129-pound warhead at sub-sonic speed (Mach .9) over medium range (59 miles) using an infra-red homing sensor. This missile is deployed on the *Luda* DDG and *Jianghu* guided missile frigate (FFG). The air-launched version of the HY-2A (C-601) has a range of 68 miles and is deployed on PLAN H-6D bombers. An extended-range version of the

HY-2 can reach out 84 miles, cruising at Mach .8 using active radar guidance and carrying a 1,100-pound warhead. This system can be launched from both air and ground.

The PLA's only known supersonic cruise missiles are the C-101 and HY-3/C-301 anti-ship missile. The C-101 has a range of 31 miles, while the ground-launched HY-3 carries a 1,126-pound warhead 81 miles using active radar guidance.

China's follow-on generation of cruise missiles, the YJ series, is based on the French *Exocet*. The YJ-1/C-801 entered service in 1985 and is smaller and lighter than China's earlier systems. Although limited in range (25 miles), it introduced a new capability by being deployed on the *Han*-class nuclear attack submarine, but a *Han* must come to the surface to fire the missile. The YJ-2/C-802 uses active radar guidance and cruises at Mach .9 with a range of 75 miles carrying a 363-pound warhead. The most recently deployed in this series is the air-, land- and sea-launched YJ-8A with a range of about 80 miles at an altitude of 20 meters.

These are capable weapons, but they do not match the sophistication of the Soviet-produced SS-N-22 to be supplied with the *Sovremenny*. The SS-N-22 incorporates several technology areas evaluated by the MCTL that are more advanced than CMIC capabilities. In energetic materials, crucial to warhead construction, Russia is credited with possessing a "majority" of the requisite technologies, while China is viewed as possessing only "some." In the areas of guidance, navigation, and vehicle control, the missile incorporates Russia's evaluations of "3" and "4" against China's assessed "2s" in these technology areas. The MCTL data offer strong indicators that in acquiring the *Sovremenny*'s SS-N-22 missiles, China is obtaining a weapon significantly more advanced than the CMIC is able to design, build, and place into serial production.

The extent to which China can both upgrade these capabilities and link them to the space and other remote sensors that will provide the reconnaissance/strike package the PLA desires is one of Beijing's most significant development dilemmas. That China is seeking to achieve this capability cannot be questioned. Indeed, the PLA has reportedly sought acceleration of the YJ-8A ground-launched land attack missile's development program. This weapon is believed to be the first in which China is seeking to incorporate GPS/GLONASS and a domestically developed Digital Scene Matching Area Correlation (DSMAC) guidance.[48]

Tactical Ballistic Missiles. As with cruise missiles, Germany's V-2 flown in 1944 was the first ballistic missile used in warfare. China's ballistic missile development originates in Soviet technology transfers in the years 1954-59. The PLA's tactical missile capability was highlighted by the use of these systems in its military exercises off Taiwan in 1995 and 1996. The tactical ballistic missiles deployed by the 2nd Artillery Corps are the M-series family of surface-to-surface solid-fueled systems. The "M" designation is provided to export models, with "DF" (*Dong Feng* - East Wind) designating systems deployed by the PLA. The DF-15/M-9, with a range of 370-plus miles carrying a 1,100-pound warhead, is believed to have an accuracy in the realm of 300 meters circular error probable (CEP).[49] Accuracy for the 180-mile range DF-11/M-11 carrying the same warhead is likely similar.

Tactical ballistic missiles with conventional warheads have limitations similar to cruise missiles: limited warhead size; dependence on reliable target positioning data and terminal guidance; and the requirement for precision manufacturing and maintenance. Once again, China's limited capabilities in all of these technologies, combined with remote sensor weaknesses, make progress toward a long-range reconnaissance/strike force a difficult task. The most likely source for improving China's capabilities in these technology areas is Russia, but the extent to which Moscow is willing to provide Beijing the extensive support that the CMIC requires is an open question.

The militarily critical factors for the employment of both cruise and tactical ballistic missiles are target location and missile guidance. Real-time location is essential for moving targets and must be determined by either space or other remote sensing systems. Of the two space-based systems available to China, a commercial receiver using GPS can determine its position within 100 meters. U.S. military receivers receive encrypted signals that can determine their position within 21 meters. This system can be augmented by Differential GPS (DGPS), providing an accuracy of less than one meter. It is possible for China to use GPS/GLONASS commercial positioning data to adjust a cruise missile's flight to the target.

Both cruise and ballistic missiles can use terminal guidance to identify a specific point in a target area. Terminal guidance can use a variety of technologies, including radar, imaging infrared, electro-optical, laser, and DSMAC when the precise location of a fixed target is known and, for DSMAC, when satellite imaging assets are available to provide the necessary scenes.[50]

The extent to which the CMIC has mastered these technologies is questionable, given that MCTL assessments grant China only "limited" or "some" capabilities in these technology areas (see Figure 14). Nonetheless, GPS/GLONASS-assisted guidance is almost certainly within China's capabilities and is one of the technology areas the CMIC is attempting to apply to its missile development programs.

"Walking on Two Legs": Future Strategy and Operational Concepts.

China's strategists recognize that achieving their current military security objectives in the next century will require continuing technological innovation, reorganization of the PLA's force structure, and continual assessment and development of doctrine and concepts of operations. Unless Beijing is willing to dramatically increase its defense expenditures, the CMIC's extensive deficiencies cannot be quickly overcome, but only partially alleviated. Assuming no dramatic improvements in overall PLA capabilities over the next decade, how is China planning to employ the PLA in the early part of the 21st century?

Beijing's shift in strategic scenarios from continental defense to limited high-technology wars on China's periphery is unlikely to change. Therefore the PLAN and the PLAAF will continue their current focus on establishing and maintaining control of Beijing's maritime territories and claims, including the air space above them, and on the ability to project power into these areas, denying them to adversaries. The primary objective will be to overcome what China's analysts refer to as the PLA's "short arms and slow legs."

Organizationally, the PLA will continue following two complementary paths: (1) cuts in manpower and equipment and (2) modifications of force structure essential to conduct joint operations. Reducing manpower and equipment stocks will cut the cost of sustaining what is now a bloated personnel base and obsolete arms. The force structure that emerges over the next decade will be "leaner and meaner." It will also reflect a more appropriate balance among the services because China's strategic planners recognize the value of joint operations. PLAN and PLAAF manpower may not increase, but their status within the PLA will be enhanced and their share of the budget will increase as their training and armaments bridge the transition from defensive operations, supporting continental defense, to missions critical in the force-projection capabilities required by China's revised military strategy.

Operationally, to use a phrase from Mao's years, China's strategists appear to be "walking on two legs" by following paths set by two distinctly different potential scenarios. Beijing's most politically sensitive territorial claims—Taiwan and the South China Sea—require China to field a PLA able to achieve its military objectives in the face of possible U.S. opposition. The other scenario embodies conflicts where the United States would not necessarily be directly involved, such as potential confrontations with Vietnam, India, or even in Central Asia. These possible conflict scenarios create two diverse, but complementary, approaches to military operations.

For conflicts not likely to involve the United States, Beijing will not hesitate to employ a force-on-force strategy. For such scenarios, the PLA places great emphasis on speed, mobility, and lethality in joint offensive operations. Here, many of the technologies associated with the RMA come into play, especially battle-space transparency, command and control, long-range precision strike, and information warfare. Without direct U.S. involvement in a military confrontation, China's probable technological advances over the next decade or so, combined with a revised force structure and improved training, will make the PLA a close match or superior to any potential single Asian adversary not under the American defense umbrella. Japan is in the secure position of being both superior to China in advanced military technologies and allied with the United States.

The PLA and Asymmetric Warfare. In conflicts potentially involving the United States, PLA analysts draw upon one of their strongest doctrinal traditions when delving into the dilemmas of defeating an adversary that is superior in arms and technology. They warn against the PLA developing technophobia as it faces the challenges of 21st century warfare. In particular, they concentrate on the potential frailties of advanced-technology weapons and equipment and on the extent to which China's armed forces are capable of offsetting the technological advantages of potential adversaries. The U.S. term-of-art for this approach to the conduct of war is "asymmetric strategy."

Intriguing as analyzing and predicting the consequences of asymmetric strategy may be, all competent armed forces seek to develop capabilities, strategy, and military operations to offset an adversary's strengths. Thus, asymmetric warfare is not a magic formula known to only a few or unique to China's military culture. Asymmetry in the conduct of war spans the history of military conflict and has been applied by armed forces across the technology spectrum. Surely the most dramatic asymmetric operation of recent wars was the United States' use of atomic bombs to destroy Hiroshima and Nagasaki, ending World War II. In this case, the United States exploited its unique possession of atomic weapons. The reverse of technology-dependent asymmetry is Mao Zedong's strategy of "people's war" and the strategy conducted by the Democratic Republic of Vietnam against French colonial forces and later against the armed forces of the Republic of Vietnam and the United States.

Asymmetry in warfare, therefore, falls into a pattern where technologically inferior forces base their asymmetric strategy on the exploitation of low-technology principles, and technologically advanced forces base their asymmetry on technological advantage. Those equal in technology seek to enhance or develop specific technologies that an adversary has not cultivated and to introduce more effective methods of applying these technologies through new concepts of operations and organization. American and Japanese development of offensive aircraft carrier operations and Germany's refinement of tank technology and the development of *Blitzkrieg* operations in the interwar period are but two examples.

Similarly, military-technical transformation in the conduct of war is a central component of warfare's history.[51] The possibility that a new technological transformation will create another revolution in military affairs has attracted the attention of most major military powers because of the implications for the future conduct of war. The United States, as the world's richest, most powerful, and technologically advanced state, has moved the furthest forward in developing and evaluating these technologies for their military utility. The USSR initiated inquiry into the potential for a military-technical revolution in the 1980s and was the first guidepost for PLA analysts. Since the Soviet demise and the Persian Gulf War, China's military researchers have looked to the United States for concepts on applying these emerging technologies to strategy and operations.

Precisely what capabilities do PLA analysts seek to neutralize, and what technologies and methods do they seek to employ? Beijing's security analysts have been declaring for more than a decade that any war in which China is likely to be engaged will not be total, but instead it will be a conflict limited in geographical scope and political objective. Beijing's advanced-technology focus appears to be on those technologies that will hinder an adversary's ability to project and sustain military power in areas of high political and security value to China, even if only for a limited period of time. The implications of this focus are that, in facing a technologically superior adversary in a limited war, the PLA will seek to:

1. hinder an adversary's capability to dominate the battle-space with superior detection, location, and command and control technologies; and

2. deny any navy freedom of movement in waters where naval forces can threaten China—a sea-denial strategy that includes the airspace above the oceans.

If the PLA could accomplish these goals, it would serve as a deterrent should a potential adversary not hold political objectives important enough to warrant the risk of military conflict with China.

The potential adversary of most concern to PLA analysts is the United States, either alone or in coalition with its allies. The most likely military confrontation with the United States would occur over Taiwan or the South China Sea. In both cases, the PLA would confront the joint operational capabilities of U.S. naval and air power. Given the seemingly overwhelming technological advantage held by American armed forces, an advantage the United States is intent on sustaining, what options are available to the Chinese armed forces over the next decade?

It is extremely unlikely that Beijing would once again contemplate a bolt-out-of-the-blue assault on unprepared American forces. First, U.S. reconnaissance capabilities now make a repeat of China's undetected entrance in the Korean War extremely difficult to prepare and undertake. Second, the consequences for China of such an act of war could be devastating. Given that a surprise attack is unlikely, our assessment will assume the usual high level of alertness sustained by Chinese and American forces operating in a high-threat environment, even if not directly engaged in hostilities.

Choosing submarine warfare as a primary instrument would immediately face U.S. Navy undersea warfare (USW) conducted by ships, aircraft, and submarines. Even with the *Kilo's* advantages, China's submarine warfare capabilities now and over the next decade will be unable to match or defeat those of the United States. Should the PLAN assemble a threatening task group of surface and submarine combatants, it simply could not survive in the face of U.S. detection, location, and engagement capabilities.

Similarly, references to saturating an American carrier battle group (CVBG) with a massive missile assault [52] do not appear to recognize that the threatening PLAN surface and submarine combatants could not survive to launch their cruise missiles. U.S. space-based, airborne, and shipborne detection and location sensors would identify their targets long before any PLAN combatants could come within engagement range to make use of their missiles. If a ship did survive, it would fire only once, because the missiles' launch and flight signatures would provide immediate targeting data to U.S. naval and air forces.

Should the PLAN or PLAAF seek to engage within the range of land-based aircraft, these aircraft would be detected, targeted, and destroyed by the U.S. Navy's aircraft and long-range air defense missiles before they could approach the effective range of their stand-off cruise missiles. Similarly, land-based tactical ballistic missiles would have great difficulty detecting and locating a CVBG with sufficient accuracy, because the battle group would be operating at speed with evasive maneuvers.

What assets does China plan to develop and deploy to offset U.S. detection, location, and command and control capabilities that provide so much of the American advantage? Destroying or simply eroding U.S. space-based reconnaissance and communications systems is one potential option. MCTL assessments indicate, however, that China does not have the supporting technologies that would allow either directed or kinetic energy systems to locate, track, and engage the proper target and to assess the damage done.

Anti-satellite space systems (ASAT) face similar problems, which is why China terminated its ASAT program in the 1980s, although more recent literature indicates it is still under consideration.[53] Once again, and despite access to GPS/GLONASS systems, the combined technologies involved in successful detection, location, engagement, and damage assessment required to successfully attack U.S. space-based assets are not present in the CMIC, and these technologies will not be present for many years without significant foreign assistance.

Information warfare (IW) is the darling of evidently an entire school of Chinese military analysts. Is IW the "killer" asymmetry—the magic weapon of a future "people's war"? Here again, the MCTL working groups found only extremely limited Chinese capabilities in both IW and information systems (IS) technologies. Furthermore, IW damage assessment is an extremely difficult undertaking. A decade from now, American capability to defend against an IW attack and the ability of the United States to use its own capabilities in such areas as command and control warfare will almost certainly continue to exceed those of the PLA. Engaging USN/USAF forces under the *assumption* that IW has significantly eroded their detection, location, and engagement capabilities would be an extremely risky endeavor, especially for the PLA, which would then be required to attack and defend against forces far more capable in all aspects of warfare.

Conclusions.

Operation DESERT STORM increased the PLA leadership's appreciation of the extent to which China's armed forces had fallen behind when compared to the capabilities of the world's most advanced industrial powers in both military technology and the operational art. Operation DESERT STORM also presented the distinct possibility that a revolution in military affairs was well under way. Had Beijing's national military strategy remained focused on continental defense, these developments may not have been viewed as so consequential for China's armed forces. But the revision of China's national military strategy 6 years before the Gulf War had already highlighted the PLA's operational deficiencies, especially the speed, mobility, and lethality required for the offensive military operations deemed essential to support the new strategy, particularly in force projection.

Lacking both the technological underpinnings and the operational skills essential for joint warfare in the latter part of the 20th century, PLA analysts and senior officers perceive their armed forces as woefully unprepared for 21st century warfare and the potential maturation of a revolution in military affairs. Nor is there much confidence that China's defense-industrial complex will be capable of providing the technology base that military analysts and leaders believe the PLA requires, evidenced by the creation of the newly created General Armaments Department and COSTIND's reorganization.

Even accepting the analytic difficulties presented by Beijing's lack of transparency, MCTL assessments portray a pattern of technological deficiencies that contribute to the PLA's concerns. Although the data do indicate that China possesses a broad sweep of those technologies necessary to generate effective operational military power in submarines, surface combatants, aircraft and missiles, in none of these areas does the CMIC appear able to design, develop, and manufacture the systems necessary for the PLA to achieve robust, reconstitutable modern status in any of the conventional military environments. Those areas where the CMIC will improve are, and will remain, heavily dependent on foreign technologies.

Even more striking is the CMIC's still rudimentary level of capability in the crucial 21st century "theaters" of space and information warfare. Of particular importance are information systems technologies, for they provide the link between contemporary warfare and 21st century warfare. IS technologies furnish the critical components for both command and control and for detection, location, and engagement, whether they are used for "hard" or "soft" attack. Here again, as in their examination of joint operations, Chinese analysts, who are investigating the implications of these technologies for the conduct of war, primarily repeat what they have gleaned from U.S. sources.[54] China's own capabilities are always viewed as future developments.[55] In this, they reflect the same future-oriented pattern as those focused on high-technology conventional arms and equipment, as when a 1997 *Liberation Army Daily* essay declared,

> The strong momentum of the world's military development undoubtedly represents a grim challenge for our units' quality building and military preparations against war.[56]

This sense of urgency is compounded by the connotation in most of the essays by military authors that there is no consensus within the PLA on the priorities for what is viewed as a new era in combat. General Fu Quanyu, the

PLA Chief of General Staff, raised this specific complaint as late as April 1998 in the Communist Party's principal journal, *Qiushi*.[57] General Fu's frustration can be seen in his plea that the CMIC concentrate its human, technological, and financial resources on "coming up with several 'killer weapons' that can effectively stifle the enemy."[58]

Fu Quanyu's dissatisfaction reflects a dilemma arising from the CMIC's extensive inadequacies. While the technology priorities of the PLA clearly include improving its battlespace reconnaissance; command and control; long-range precision strike munitions; and the capability to deny information dominance to any adversary, the CMIC is also directed to satisfy PLA requirements across the spectrum of modern warfare. Satisfying the PLA's demands across such an extensive range of requirements is beyond the CMIC's capabilities, and the necessity to purchase foreign technologies for essentially all air and naval combatants, including command and control and logistical support, creates a budgetary burden that Beijing's present national priorities will not sustain. Thus, China's military leadership is caught between the pressures of current and near-term needs and the high-technology demands of future warfare. Certainly priorities can be established and enforced, as China's past focus on nuclear weapons and propulsion plants demonstrates. It is not yet evident whether a similar decision has been made about establishing technological priorities designed to prepare the PLA for future warfare.

Consequently, whereas the PLA's ambitions are clear, the gap between ambition and capability could well be growing with the continuing advances in military technologies. Although it is critical not to underestimate the CMIC's future capabilities, it is equally important not to exaggerate its strengths and raise the specter of an emerging military superpower. Even accepting the difficulties inherent in MCTL assessments, these evaluations, when joined with analyses of the CMIC's problematic past and at least near-term future problems, offer very limited support for observers who suggest that China is technologically ten feet tall or about to leap into the nether reaches of information warfare.[59] Rather, the evaluations tend to support the apprehension reflected in China's military journals and in the speeches and essays by senior PLA officials. If the recent past is any indicator, what should be anticipated is a slow and sometimes erratic expansion of CMIC capabilities in technologies applicable to the areas viewed as critical in future warfare.

ENDNOTES - CHAPTER 4

1. See, for example, Lieutenant General Chen Bingde, Commander of the Nanjing Military Region, "Intensify Study of Military Theory To Ensure Quality Army Building," *Zhongguo Junshi Kexue*, No. 3, March 6, 1998, in *Foreign Broadcasting Information Service-China* (henceforth *FBIS-CHI*), March 10, 1998.

2. Alastair I. Johnston, "Prospects for Chinese Nuclear Force Modernization: Limited Deterrence versus Multilateral Arms Control," in David S. Shambaugh and Richard H. Yang, eds., *China's Military in Transition*, Oxford: Clarendon Press, 1997, pp. 284-312.

3. For a classic statement of this strategy see, "Nieh Jung-chen's, Nie Rongzhen August 4 Speech at the National Militia Conference," *FBIS-CHI*, August 9, 1979, pp. E1-10.

4. For analyses of this revised national military strategy, see Nan Li, "The PLA's Evolving Warfighting Doctrine, Strategy, and Tactics, 1985-95: A Chinese View," and Paul H. B. Godwin, "From Continent to Periphery: PLA Doctrine Strategy and Capabilities Towards 2000," both in Shambaugh and Yang, eds., pp. 179-223.

5. John W. Garver, "China's Push to the South China Sea, *The China Quarterly*, December 1992, pp. 999-1026.

6. In his August 6, 1993, *Jiefangjun Bao* essay, "Unswervingly March Along the Road of Building a Modern Army With Chinese Characteristics," General Liu Huaqing, China's then senior serving officer, specifically measured the PLA's capabilities with those of the U.S. armed forces demonstrated in the Gulf War. General Liu's assessment was that the PLA weaknesses went far beyond those associated with arms and equipment, but were equally evident in

operational doctrine, joint warfare, training, and in the comprehension of modern warfare. In *FBIS-CHI*, August 18, 1993.

7. One of the most useful essays analyzing Chinese doctrinal shifts published in a U.S. journal was prepared by a researcher at the PLA Academy of Military Science: Yao Yunzhu, "The Evolution of Military Doctrine of the Chinese PLA from 1985 to 1995," *The Korean Journal of Defense Analysis*, Vol. VII, No. 2, Winter 1995, pp. 57-80.

8. See, for example, Huang Xing, "Holding the Initiative in Our Own Hands in Conducting Operations, Giving Full Play to Our Advantages to Defeat Our Enemy—A Study of the Core Idea of the Operational Doctrine of Our Army," *Zhongguo Junshi Kexue*, No. 4, November 20, 1996, in *FBIS-CHI*, November 20, 1996.

9. Mark A. Stokes, *China's Strategic Modernization: Implications for the United States*, Carlisle Barracks, PA: Strategic Studies Institute, U.S. Army War College, September, 1999.

10. John Frankenstein and Bates Gill, "Current and Future Challenges Facing Chinese Defense Industries," in Shambaugh and Yang, eds., p. 132.

11. John Frankenstein, "China's Defense Industry Conversion: A Strategic Overview," in Jorn Brommelhorster and John Frankenstein, eds., *Mixed Motives, Uncertain Outcomes: Defense Conversion in China* Boulder, CO: Lynne Rienner Publishers, 1997, pp. 14-15.

12. Frankenstein and Gill, p. 132.

13. Richard A. Bitzinger and Bates Gill, *Gearing Up For High-Tech Warfare? Chinese and Taiwanese Defense Modernization and the Implications For Military Confrontation Across the Taiwan Strait, 1995-2005*, Washington, DC: Center for Strategic and Budgetary Assessments, February 1996, p. 17; Frankenstein and Gill, pp. 134-143.

14. Ka Po Ng, "Defense Conversion in the Chinese Press," in Brommelhorster and Frankenstein, eds., pp. 92-93.

15. *Ibid.*, p. 92; Richard D. Latham, "A Business Perspective," in Brommelhorster and Frankenstein, eds., pp. 165-166.

16. These issues are raised by Jiang Wanjun, "Evaluation and Analysis of the International Competitiveness of China's Science and Technology," *Keji Ribao*, February 14, 1998, in *FBIS-CHI*, March 25, 1998. It should be noted that *Keji Ribao* is published jointly by the State Science and Technology Commission, the Chinese Academy of Sciences,

and the State Commission of Science, Technology and Industry for National Defense. See also, Bitzinger and Gill, p. 20; Frankenstein and Gill, pp. 154-155.

17. Frankenstein and Gill, p. 157.

18. The other three general departments are the General Staff and the Political and Logistics Departments.

19. Eric Arnett, "Military Technology: The Case of China," in *SIPRI Yearbook 1995*, Oxford: Oxford University Press, 1995, p. 395.

20. For a judicious analysis of Russian transfers, see Dennis J. Blasko, "Evaluating Chinese Military Procurement from Russia," *Joint Forces Quarterly*, Autumn-Winter 1997-98, pp. 91-96

21. For Part 1, *Weapon System Technologies*, the TWGs evaluated the 18 technology areas of Aeronautics Systems; Armaments and Energetic Materials; Chemical and Biological Systems; Directed and Kinetic Energy Systems; Electronics; Ground Systems, Guidance, Navigation, and Vehicle Control; Information Systems; Information Warfare; Manufacture and Fabrication; Materials; Marine Systems; Nuclear Systems; Power Systems; Sensors and Lasers; Signature Control; Space Systems; and Weapons Effects and Countermeasures. Each of these technology areas is further divided into specific technology groups, which total 84 subsets.

22. In the relatively simple technology of "obscurants" the United States is evaluated at level "3." China is assessed at level "4." *MCTL* Sensors and Lasers FTA Summary Figure 15.0-2 p. 15-2. The United States is evaluated at level "3" in the "optronics" group of Space Systems Technology. China is assessed at level "2." *MCTL* Space Systems FTA Summary, Figure 17.02, p. 17-2.

23. *MCTL*, pp. 17-5 and 17-11.

24. *Jane's Special Report, China's Aerospace Industry—The Industry and Its Products Assessed*, Coulsdon, Surrey, United Kingdom: Jane's Information Group, Inc., March 1997, pp. 135-136.

25. Chou Kuan-wu, "China's Reconnaissance Satellites," *Kuang Chiao Ching*, Hong Kong, No. 36, March 16, 1998, in *FBIS-CHI*, April 8, 1998. (*Kuang Chiao Ching* (Wide Angle) is reputed to have close ties with China's defense establishment.) *Jane's Space Directory*, 13th Edition., Phillip Clark, ed., Alexandria, VA: Jane's Information Group, Inc., 1997, p. 192. See also Jeffrey Richelson, *America's Space Sentinels:*

DSP Satellites and National Security, Lawrence, KS: University Press of Kansas, 1999.

26. Jeff Gerth, "Reports Show Chinese Military Used American-Made Satellites," *The New York Times*, June 13, 1998, pp. A1, A8.

27. Stokes, Appendix Four.

28. *MCTL*, p. 4-1.

29. *Ibid*. p. 4-5.

30. Over the past 5 years and more, there has been a flood of essays in Chinese military, industrial, and other professional journals analyzing the implications of information warfare. Most of these essays reflect the analyses found in U.S. military and academic publications. A more recent example is Dai Kouhu, "Accepting the Challenge: China's Defense Information Modernization," *Zhongguo Dianzi Bao*, China Electronics News, October 24, 1997, in *FBIS-CHI*, January 12, 1998.

31. The fifth LM-2500 is likely on a test stand for reverse-engineering purposes, used for shore-based training or a source of spare parts, or has been accidentally destroyed.

32. *Jane's The World's Warships 1997*, Vol. 1, London: Jane's Publishing Group, 1998, p. 520, reports that China is attempting to procure marine gas turbine engines from the Ukraine.

33. The material technology area is also pertinent to capability in weapon guidance systems, surveillance, sensors, and electronic warfare systems. In the six sub areas evaluated, the MCTL, p. 11-2, assesses China with four "3s" and two "2s."

34. *Jane's* identifies these as two ships laid down in 1989 and 1990 and scheduled for commissioning in 1997 and 1998. Availability of *Sovremennys* may take several different paths, however. The Chinese may be ordering completely new ships, which would be the most expensive path, but would give the PLAN the most control over the vessels' characteristics and quality. They may be purchasing ships built for the Soviet/Russian navy that have already served as fleet units; this would be the quickest and least expensive path for the PLAN to acquire *Sovremennys*, but it would also allow very little flexibility in customizing the ships, and PLAN would also be obtaining ships that are "used," having been subjected to unknown stresses, and therefore ones that may have incurred significant, but difficult to detect, material defects. Finally, China could, as reported by *Jane's*, buy ships that have

been under construction for the Soviet/Russian navy. This would be cheaper than building ships from the keel up and would allow flexibility in customizing the vessels, but would likely result in the PLAN receiving ships that have been lying idle on the building ways for several years, a factor which normally results in many defects.

35. The *Sovremenny's* role in this task force was to attack American capital ships using surface-to-surface missiles. The carrier was, of course, the most desirable target, but Aegis cruisers were also valuable, for their operational destruction would create a void in the battle group's air defenses, potentially exposing the carriers to "stream raids" by Soviet aircraft.

36. "Surface to Surface Missiles," *Jane's Naval Weapons Systems: 1997*, London: Jane's Publishing Group, 1998, p. 15, also mentions a version with "an extended range" beyond 65 nm. *Jane's* 1995-96 *Major Warships* gives this range as 88 nm, but this figure is not reported in later editions. Nor is *Jane's* 1995-96 claim that the SS-N-22 is capable of carrying a nuclear warhead reported in later volumes. See CRS Report for Congress, *China: Ballistic and Cruise Missiles*, Congressional Research Service, The Library of Congress, 97-391 F, March 21, 1997, p. CRS-11.

37. For a thorough analysis of China's air power history and development through the early 1990s, see Kenneth W. Allen, Glenn Krummel, and Jonathan D. Pollack, *China's Air Force Enters The 21st Century*, Santa Monica, CA: RAND, 1995.

38. *Ibid*.

39. *MCTL*, p. 1-1.

40. *Ibid.*, p. 2-1.

41. For details, see Allen, *et. al.*

42. *Jane's All the World's Aircraft, 1997-1998*, London: Jane's Information Group, 1998, p. 438; Joseph C. Anselmo, "China's Military Seeks Great Leap Forward," *Aviation Week & Space Technology*, May 12, 1997, p. 69. *Jane's Defense Weekly*, June 10, 1998, provides the 10-15 annual production figure, which seems a more likely number than the 50 reported by *Jane's All the World's Aircraft*, 1997-1998. When its air power capabilities and characteristics are matched against MCTL technology areas, Russia earns a "4" in fixed-wing aircraft, China a "2." Russia also has higher ratings in gas turbine technology, electronic

systems "hardening" against electro-magnetic pulses, EMP, human/crew interface, and navigation and control systems.

43. Kenneth W. Allen, "PLA Force Logistics: What has changed?", Unpublished manuscript.

44. Harlan Jencks quoted in Allen, *et. al.*, p. 148.

45. The term "pockets of excellence," characterizing China's selective approach to defense modernization, was used by Chong-pin Lin, "The Power Projection Capabilities of the People's Liberation Army," in C. Dennison Lane, Mark Weisenbloom, and Dimon Liu, eds., *Chinese Military Modernization*, London: Kegan Paul International, 1996, p. 110.

46. Unless otherwise noted, the data for these missiles are drawn from Shirley Kan and Robert Shuey, CRS Report for Congress, *China: Ballistic and Cruise Missiles*, Congressional Research Service, The Library of Congress, 97-391 F, March 21, 1997.

47. "China: Surface-to-Surface Missiles," *Jane's Naval and Weapon Systems*, Issue 21, 1997.

48. See Stokes, Part III, "Cruise Missiles."

49. *China's Aerospace Industry: The Industry and Its Products Assessed*, Jane's Information Group: Coulsdon, March 1997, p. 133.

50. Kan and Shuey, pp. CRS-14-CRS-15.

51. See, for example, William H. McNeill, "The Structure of Military-Technical Transformation," speech at the Sixteenth Military History Symposium of the United States Air Force Academy, The Harmon Memorial Lectures in Military History, No. 37, United States Air Force Academy, CO: 1994.

52. Sun Zian, "Strategies to Minimize High-Tech Edge of Enemy," *Xiandai Bingqi*, No. 8, August 8, 1995, in *FBIS-CHI*, February 22, 1996, pp. 29-30.

53. Stokes, pp. 10-11, 186.

54. This was frankly admitted in 1998 by Dai Kouhu, "Accepting the Challenge."

55. See, for example, Liang Zhengxing, "New Military Revolution, Information Warfare," *Zhongguo Dianzi Bao*, October 24, 1997, in *FBIS-CHI*, January 1, 1998.

56. "Implement Military Strategic Principle for the New Period, Vigorously Push Forward Army Quality Building," *Jiefangjun Bao*, April 1, 1997, in *FBIS-CHI*, April 4, 1997.

57. Fu Quanyu, "Aggressive Exploration and Deeper Reforms to Promote the Comprehensive Development of Military Work," *Qiushi*, No. 6, March 16, 1998, in *FBIS-CHI*, April 13, 1998.

58. *Ibid.*

59. Michael Pillsbury, for example, suggests that many, if not most, U.S. assessments of China's RMA capabilities are too skeptical. See his *China and the Revolution in Military Affairs*, prepared for the Office of Net Assessment, Department of Defense, n.d. ca. 1997, pp. 29-30.

CHAPTER 5
U.S.-CHINESE MILITARY RELATIONS IN THE 21st CENTURY

Larry M. Wortzel

The actions that the United States takes today are framing the boundaries of the nation's future relations around the world. One of the most significant challenges facing the United States is the shaping of an Asian strategy for the next 20 years. It is imperative to formulate and execute a long-range strategy that will enhance relationships in Asia while protecting U.S. national interests. There has been a major change in the balance of power in Asia. The implosion of the Soviet Union, the collapse of Russia, and the economic crises in Asia have fundamentally changed the strategic landscape in the region. Beijing now sees China as *the* central power in Asia that must be considered in a geo-political and military equation.

Given China's dominant location on the Asian continent, its size, population, economy, and permanent membership in the United Nations Security Council, this long-term strategy must consider the following key questions. Does Beijing seek to dominate the Asia-Pacific region? Is there a "strategic glue" in U.S.-China relations? Are American military leaders deluding themselves into thinking that they can change the strategic culture of China and draw the Chinese military into the community of cooperating friendly armed forces? Is the Chinese People's Liberation Army (PLA) studying American military strategy, doctrine, and tactics to prepare itself to more effectively fight the United States' armed forces should the Chinese leadership decide that a conflict is necessary? These are the fundamental questions that must be confronted. This chapter will address these questions and attempt to characterize how the United States and Chinese militaries will relate to each other in the next century.

One thing about the nature of U.S.-China relations in the 21st century can be counted upon, there will be competition, friction, and conflict.[1] One can safely predict that a country the size of China, with a different strategic culture than the West and with its own fiercely proud and independent foreign policies, will not always see eye-to-eye with the United States.[2] Conflict does not necessarily mean war, and PLA officers avoid public utterances that take the United States as an enemy. The leaders of the PLA tell us that they admire the United States and its armed forces. General after general in the PLA repeats the mantra that "the PLA has a lot to learn by studying the U.S. military." I suspect, however, that what they seek to learn is how to fight against American tactics and equipment, whether employed by Taiwan, any other nation, or the United States, and to adopt the U.S. way of war for the PLA. Notwithstanding the statements of peaceful intentions, the PLA is working very hard to prepare itself to fight the United States, if it must, under certain circumstances.[3] Senior leaders of the PLA General Staff Department and the General Political Department have threatened off-line, in sidebar conversation while traveling or at dinners, after a few drinks, that "China will not be 'embarrassed' again by the United States as it was during the 1996 Taiwan Straits exercises."[4]

If one takes the time to socialize with the commanders, deputy commanders, or chiefs of staff of the Nanjing or Guangzhou Military Regions, which face Taiwan, these leaders will say that they intend to be ready to sink American ships, if necessary, and to intercept and destroy U.S. reconnaissance aircraft. Some of this is posturing, but more of it is a serious statement of intent.[5] China does not want to fight the United States, but there are certain territorial imperatives that the PLA's military leaders will enforce.[6] When it looked as if North Korea might collapse, in 1997, the most senior leaders and military strategists of the

PLA privately warned that if the United States thinks it can approach the Yalu River, even in support of humanitarian operations in North Korea, "it could look like 1950 all over again."[7] They made it very clear that China must be involved in the resolution of security problems in North Korea. Thus, the Korean Peninsula becomes part of the strategic glue that binds the United States and China at the same time that, if problems on the peninsula are handled poorly, it could become one of the most serious flash points in the region.

The future looks a great deal like a combination of cooperation, confrontation, and conflict. All of this can be managed, if handled with care, and the U.S. military must participate in the management of relations with China. The most sensitive issues, such as technology transfer policy; the strength and scope of U.S. alliances in the world; participation in international organizations; types of confidence-building measures; interpretation of the Law of the Sea; sovereignty matters; and policies concerning weapons proliferation and arms sales are also part of the glue that binds the United States and China. But these issues are also the primary sources of U.S.-China conflict and confrontation. How that conflict is managed will depend on the way that the United States views China.

Scholars such as Michael Pillsbury, in his collection of monographs on warfare in the next century by PLA officers, imply that the PLA is carefully studying U.S. military doctrine in an attempt to devise ways to defeat the U.S. armed forces. The PLA officers writing these essays seem to assume that the two countries will come into conflict.[8] Indeed, the PLA is using the armed forces of the United States, their doctrine and strategic orientation, as its model for what constitutes a modern, power-projection military force in the next century.[9] Other scholars argue that the Chinese military is the "gang that can't shoot straight" and that the PLA is not only unable to grasp modern tactics and doctrine, but also cannot produce the necessary hardware to equip a modern military.[10] Another school of thought holds that, like the missionaries of the 19th century, if American military delegations embrace the Chinese armed forces in friendship and share with them our ways and our bibles (military doctrine and manuals), the PLA will accept the revealed truth, change, and become a responsible military in a civil society.[11] Finally, a school of thought about China, that must be considered, holds that for philosophical and historical reasons, in terms of intent and capability, China will neither seek to, nor be able to, dominate the Asia-Pacific through the year 2015.[12]

The simple fact is that by virtue of size, population, economic power, geography, differences in strategic culture, and the size of its forces, especially ground forces, China is the dominant power in Asia. It is dangerous for the United States to systematically minimize assessments of China's military capabilities. With the collapse of Russia and the economic crisis in Asia since summer 1997, Beijing sees itself as the benefactor of a major change in the balance of power in Asia and intends to exploit this change. Moreover, it is clear from their internal writings that China's strategists have at least grasped the intellectual and doctrinal side of building a modern military, even if the PLA lacks money and hardware.[13]

Although we have had only glimpses of the plans of the Chinese military for future equipment, it is clear that the war-fighting debate in China has focused on improving areas like reconnaissance and sensor systems, electronic warfare and jamming, the use of information warfare and "logic bombs" to destroy enemy command and control systems, amphibious assault, and the use of missiles as a deep-strike, strategic, and operational weapon.[14] At the 1998 Defense Electronics Exhibition in Beijing, the General Staff Department (GSD) of the PLA; the GSD Communications-Electronic Warfare Department; the Ministry of Electronics Industry; and the now-modified Commission of Science, Technology and Industry for National Defense orchestrated an effort to bring to China the most modern electronic warfare equipment Beijing could attract.[15] At the August 1997 displays in the Military Museum in Beijing, designed to commemorate the 70th anniversary of the PLA, China teased observers with a limited view of what combat and support systems it would like to produce in order to improve the lethality and force-projection capabilities of its military. On display was a combination of force-projection systems that, if mass-produced and fielded, would give the Chinese ground forces the ability to sustain forces away from bases of supply without relying on the old methods of "People's War," that is, using local militia to sustain the combat forces. Included in the displays at the exhibition were significantly improved field mess (kitchen) systems to feed and sustain deployed troops; forward-area refueling points for armored warfare and airmobile, or helicopter-borne forces; and the sort of sensor-to-shooter target acquisition systems that depend on remotely piloted vehicles linked to a sophisticated intelligence and communications architecture. Combined with global positioning satellites, these sensor-to-shooter systems would permit the PLA to target enemy forces in deeper battle space on a real-time basis with cruise missiles, ballistic missiles, or air strikes. There is a substantial gap between what Chinese military leaders are doing and the public utterances of senior PLA leaders about its ability to modernize.

PLA leaders want to develop a rapid reacting, information-based Army supported by sensor-to-shooter systems, precision weapons, and modern combat platforms. PLA leaders want a world-class, secure and reliable command, control, communications, computer and intelligence (C^4I) system.[16] PLA leaders want the logistics capability to support deployed forces, within or outside China, without relying on help from the local populace or foraging.

There has been some very serious thinking done on future warfare within the PLA. Li Qingshan, a researcher at the Academy of Military Science, for example, has published a book entitled *The New Military Revolution and High Technology Warfare.*[17] Based on a detailed study of U.S. and European militaries and the Gulf War, Li concludes that:

• Modern armies must reduce their size but increase the quality of personnel, organizations, weapons, and equipment. In the balance between quality and quantity, it is quality that is the more important in armed forces.[18]

• Recruitment and retention of personnel should focus on education and quality (*gao de wenhua shuiping*).[19]

• The use of specific weapon systems, such as ballistic missiles, anti-missile systems, and land-attack cruise missiles, has changed the nature of warfare. Successful armies must adopt and defend against these systems, which are important for specific targets.[20]

• Armies must focus on the importance of force projection, be prepared to get reaction forces to the combat zone quickly, and also assess the weak points of the rapid deployment of forces and headquarters by air.[21]

• The core target of warfare in the 1990s is the hub of the command and control system, whether of deployed combat forces or of a national command and control center. After that, economic targets, transportation systems, and combat troops are the target.[22]

• Reconnaissance-and-intelligence-gathering systems of an enemy must be attacked, especially airborne and space reconnaissance systems, as well as the information systems that make all coordination possible.[23]

This roadmap for future warfare, in combination with the nation's size and geographical position, promises to make China a major regional power in the future.

A REGIONAL HEGEMON?

Based on comments by defense and foreign ministry officials in Seoul, Hanoi, Singapore, and Kuala Lumpur, I would argue that China now exercises hegemony over a considerable portion of East Asia.[24] Strategists at institutes in Vietnam understand this fact quite clearly. They use the term "Chinese hegemony" and explain it to mean that because China is so much bigger than Vietnam, with such a large, powerful army and in a geographical position to control even the flow of water into their country, Hanoi's government can do nothing to anger Beijing.[25] The United States, however, seeks to maintain its power, leadership, and influence in the same region. This means that, so long as the Chinese state does not collapse and the United States does not withdraw from Asia, U.S.-Chinese relations will be characterized by tension and conflict. Although there are areas where the interests and objectives of the United States and China coincide, this tension and conflict will necessarily translate into difficulties that will manifest themselves in bilateral military ties. The respective military establishments of each country will initiate programs to support conflicting goals and to influence the other side. Internally, in Beijing and Washington, this will stimulate considerable debate over how to develop programs designed to meet national objectives. In this chapter, the author will first analyze the long-term objectives of both the United States and China, then assess the areas of conflict in goals and strategies, and, finally, offer some suggestions about how to translate these goals into military-to-military ties that will carry the United States into the next century.[26]

Conflicting Goals Over International Leadership.

Two policy documents from the U.S. Government, the *National Security Strategy* and the *National Military Strategy*, set forth the ways that the United States' national security establishment seeks to exercise leadership, power, and influence around the world in the next century.[27] The key to understanding these two strategy documents is the commitment by the United States to remain engaged in the world and to "use all appropriate instruments of national power to influence the actions of other states and non-state powers."[28] In short, the United States will pressure or persuade other countries through active engagement in the world. The strategy also calls for the United States to "promote democracy and human rights," as a means to "enlarge" the community of free market democracies in the world. The instruments of national power under discussion in the *National Security Strategy* include diplomatic, economic, military, informational (or psychological), technological, and industrial capabilities. To ensure that the goals of the United States are met, the strategy statements envision "shaping" the international environment to make the world a more secure place and to reduce threats to the United States. The means by which the United States intends to shape this world include the continuation and strengthening of alliances, strong diplomacy, forms of international assistance, arms-control measures, efforts at deterring the proliferation of weapons of mass destruction, and military activities that deter aggression and coercion directed against the United States.[29]

How should we understand what it means for a country or an international organization to exercise leadership, power, and influence? The U.S. national security strategy emphasizes "keeping America strong, secure and prosperous while encouraging a stable prosperous Asia-Pacific community built around open markets."[30] The level of emphasis on increasing human rights around the world as a component of U.S. defense and foreign policy may vary from administration to administration. Despite the fact that China, like other authoritarian and Communist regimes, may find these policies objectionable, it is safe to say that U.S. policies will continue to support basic American values in the next century.[31]

A major element of the American strategy to accomplish national security objectives is the presence overseas of forward deployed military forces, backed up by a robust ability to project decisive force from the United States.[32] The

United States relies on these deployed forces to do several things. First, based on the American experience at the hands of Japan at Pearl Harbor, forward deployed forces serve as a "trip-wire" designed to warn of and absorb, if necessary, any future attacks. Second, forward deployed forces are visible signs of the American commitment to the peace and stability of the region. These forces sit astride both historical and potential zones of conflict.[33] In Northeast Asia, U.S. forces are on the Korean Peninsula, the "dagger and bridge" that has been the crossroads for conflict among Russia, China, and Japan for nearly 1,000 years. In Japan, they provide a welcome "cork-in-the-bottle," reassuring the rest of Asia that the genie of militarism in Japan will not again be loose and calming those who fear Japan could again become an aggressive military power. The U.S. presence in Northeast Asia also inhibits China *vis-a-vis* Taiwan, contributing to the peace and stability of the region. In Southeast Asia, through access agreements, U.S. forces patrol and protect vital sea lines of communication that carry 67 percent of the energy supplies used by China and Japan. The U.S. armed forces in the Asia-Pacific region also extend American deterrence to allies, ensuring that no arms race will take place and preventing the proliferation of nuclear, biological, and chemical weapons among allies who otherwise have the capacity to develop such weapons. This combination of alliances with the overseas presence of U.S. forces has proven effective both during the Cold War, when the focus of American policy was to contain the Soviet Union and the expansion of Communism, and in the present day. Frankly speaking, Chinese military officers do not like these forces or alliances.[34] Chinese officers resent the U.S. presence. Nonetheless, they realize that without a U.S. presence, China would need to devote significantly more resources to a potentially hostile Japan.

The People's Republic of China (PRC), on July 27, 1998, published its second White Paper, *China's National Defense*.[35] This long-awaited complement to the first White

Paper on arms control and disarmament, published in 1995, set forth China's national security goals and policies for the new century and provides Beijing's views of the international and regional security environments. Much of the second White Paper contains language that should comfort the United States and Asian nations. China proclaimed that its defense policy will subordinate "national defense construction to economic construction, and strengthen international and regional security cooperation."[36] China seeks to develop confidence-building measures (CBMs) with the Association of Southeast Asian Nations (ASEAN) and will cooperate with the ASEAN Regional Forum (ARF) to reduce conflict. However, there are qualifications to this cooperation. Although China tried to counter the "China threat theory" in the White Paper, Beijing made no compromises with respect to what it claims as its own territory or its willingness to use force in that territory.[37] The PLA is charged with maintaining the capability to defend all of Beijing's claims in the South China Sea and the Gulf of Tonkin, and Beijing continues to expand its presence in the Spratly Islands, despite claims of its peaceful intentions.[38] There is no room for discussion regarding the status of Taiwan. China's refusal to foreswear the use of force against Taiwan and the reinforcement of its expansive territorial claims in the South China Sea leave open the possibility of confrontation with the United States.

In the first paragraph of China's White Paper, Beijing stated clearly its own goals for leadership in the region: "it is the aspiration of the Chinese government and people to lead a peaceful, stable and prosperous world into the new century." The nations of the Asia-Pacific region, including the United States, should welcome this approach. Leadership is not a "zero-sum-game." There is plenty of room for leadership in Asia and the world, so long as that leadership is designed genuinely to promote peace and stability in consonance with international law and international norms.[39] Even the term "leadership," however, was the subject of some debate among Chinese strategists and military leaders. At the Academy of Military Science and among officers of the Military Intelligence Department, the term "leadership" (*lingdao*, or responsibility for leadership, *lingdao de zeren*) carries with it the sort of Leninist understanding in Chinese that connotes strong, authoritarian direction, as in "the leadership of the Chinese Communist Party." The Chinese strategists and military personnel who contributed to the White Paper preferred such terms as "special responsibility" (*teshude zeren*) to state the obligations of a great power to the region. Even after deciding on the concept of leadership in the more benign, Western sense for the White Paper, there was no such compromise by the Chinese in the understanding of peace and sovereignty. The White Paper seems to be a call for peace under specific terms, which include dominance over the territorial claims that China maintains in the South China Sea and over Taiwan.[40] This is a call for peace that asks other countries in the region to break their security ties with the United States. China seems to be focusing its own efforts on a program to reshape the strategic balance in Asia in its own favor in a way that diffuses American power and leadership in a "multi-polar world."[41]

For years Beijing was more comfortable with bilateralism. This approach gave it an advantage over weaker neighbors in disputes in the South China Sea and the Tonkin Gulf. Now, having been pulled into a multilateral approach by ASEAN, Beijing sees its utility. China's military leaders learned from their studies of the U.S. experience in the Gulf War that operating in a coalition forced the United States to compromise many of its own goals to maintain the coalition. U.S. authority and flexibility, therefore, was weakened in Beijing's eyes.

China emphasizes multilateral approaches to security because strategists in Beijing believe that China's international position is more central in the web of relationships that characterize the multilateral context. This is perhaps an explanation for the inter-linkages of "strategic partnerships" that Beijing has sought to forge with the Central Asian republics, Russia, Japan, Korea, the United States, and the European Union.[42] A web of "partnerships" around China conceptually places the "Middle Kingdom" at the center of the world, increasing China's influence and status.[43] Moreover, multilateralism works to undermine the U.S. bilateral alliances in Asia, one of Beijing's main foreign policy goals.[44] China has been frustrated in its goal of reuniting Taiwan with the mainland, and was embarrassed by the dispatch of two carrier battle groups from the U.S. 7th Fleet to the Taiwan Strait in March 1996. Beijing, therefore, wants to ensure that U.S. forces are restrained from responding to aggression against that island from bases in Korea or Japan. China was surprised by its inability to respond to U.S. carrier battle groups off Taiwan in 1996. PLA leaders were absolutely furious about the arrival of the *Independence* and the *Enterprise* battle groups. Generals in military region and central leadership positions made wild threats against U.S. forces, promising to seek naval battle groups with cruise missiles or ballistic missiles and to shoot U.S. aircraft out of the sky if the United States intervened in any conflict between the mainland and Taiwan.

Drawing on Classical Chinese Military Thought.

China has concluded that it cannot match U.S. military capabilities. Every PLA leader says this. But the U.S. armed forces do not have a clear picture of what the Chinese military forces can do. The PLA central leadership works very hard to conceal its own capabilities. The Air Defense Command Center shown to the U.S. Secretary of Defense in 1997 was a hollow shell of a local headquarters, not the equivalent of the U.S. National Military Command Center that Chinese leaders have seen.[45] When the Chairman of the Joint Chiefs of Staff, General John Shalikashvili, was given a demonstration of the "capabilities" of the 15th Airborne Army, it was pure comic opera.[46] High winds prevented an airborne jump, but what was demonstrated of troop capabilities was a "Keystone Cops-like" display of several motorcyclists jumping on a moving vehicle. This "exercise" was as scripted as a Jackie Chan (or Bruce Lee) movie in Hong Kong. It was polite to let the U.S. Air Force Chief of Staff fly a 30-year-old fighter when he visited China, but what does that tell the United States about how China intends to employ the Su-27s it has bought, along with the aerial refueling system it is developing and the airborne early warning radars it is putting together? Simply stated, we have never seen a real Chinese military exercise. We know that the PLA carries out real exercises at its own training grounds, much like those conducted at the U.S. National Training Center. But the most that U.S. military personnel have seen of the operational PLA in action was as it mobilized around Tiananmen Square and attacked into Beijing against its own people. During the Tiananmen Massacre, the U.S. military saw how the PLA can apply violence in the "complex terrain" of an urban area.

The PLA is methodically developing, however, into a force that can project itself internally and regionally. It is also experimenting with ways to respond militarily to U.S. forces should it need to do so, according to PLA officers. The improvements in force-projection capability, command and control, battlefield awareness, and simultaneity of operations shown at the exhibition in the Military Museum in Beijing to commemorate the 70th anniversary of the founding of the PLA gave foreign observers a glimpse of these improvements. I saw them the day the exhibition opened. Interestingly, 2 days later when the exhibition was formally opened by invitation to foreign observers and military attachés, the display had been changed significantly from its opening day. Many of the force-projection-related systems had been removed from public display.

China has taken a two-pronged approach to security relations. Notwithstanding the reactions to the bombing of the Chinese Embassy in Yugoslavia in May 1999, this approach can be expected to continue. On the diplomatic front with the United States, Beijing does the very minimum it must to avoid being perceived as an adversary and to gain access to U.S. doctrine and manuals. This is an extension of classical United Front operations by Communist armies.[47] Meanwhile, China is engaged in a diplomatic effort, designed to de-couple the United States from its allies, and in a military effort to build up a force of ballistics missiles it can use in the region. This is going on at the same time that the PLA is developing an over-the-horizon capability for cruise missiles that could attack American naval forces.[48]

Beijing has turned one of the maxims of *Sunzi* into a 21st century security strategy. China is "attacking the enemy's strategy" (*gu shang bing fa mou*) by portraying the U.S. policy of engagement as a new form of "containment," putting Washington and the Defense Department on the defensive in policy discussions.[49] Then Beijing is "attacking the enemy's alliances" (*qi ci fa jiao*) by seeking to undermine the system of alliances and long-standing friendships nurtured in Asia by the United States.[50] Beijing argues that these alliances are "relics of the cold war" that are not appropriate for the 21st century.[51] At the same time, China is also preparing to respond to the U.S. forces, if necessary, by developing the capacity to control sea lines of communication, project regional force, and deter the United States and other potential adversaries in creative ways without matching forces (*qi ci fa bing*). Recognizing its own weaknesses, however, the PLA wants to avoid a direct confrontation. If the United States and China have only achieved a minimum level in mutual transparency in defense policies, both have laid out reasonably clearly their strategic plans and goals. Even in these formal policy utterances, however, we see the basis for confrontation and conflict.

International Leadership, or Regional Hegemony?

For the United States, leadership means to actively pursue a world of expanded democratic values and free markets, using the military as one of the tools to shape the future. This necessarily translates into a highly ideological goal to Beijing, quite different from China's own stated objective of "non-interference in the internal affairs of other countries," a phrase taken from the Five Principles of Peaceful Coexistence espoused at the Bandung Conference. For China, leadership seems to mean an effort to dismantle or transform the alliances built by the United States after World War II. Beijing's preference for a "multi-polar world" is another way of saying that China seeks to create a world that is able to reject the particular type of values-based leadership exercised by the United States. Beijing seeks to shape a world in which the U.S. position is much weaker and U.S. policy is changed to take into account the other poles of power. One key phrase in the Chinese White Paper, in fact, is Beijing's attacks on "hegemonism." This is a code term used by Beijing to characterize its objections to American leadership in Asia. In an article commemorating the 71st anniversary of the PLA, Minister of Defense General Chi Haotian emphasized that "hegemonism and power politics are still the main roots to the threat to world peace and stability . . . including the reliance of other countries on military alliances."[52]

The concept of hegemony as a concrete description of international power, rather than as a pejorative term, is helpful in understanding what I believe will be central sources of tension between China and the United States in the next century.[53] Hegemony as a tenet of American foreign policy is discussed by Richard Haass in *The Reluctant Sheriff: The United States After the Cold War*. Haass paints a situation in which the United States may be the predominant power, but cannot dominate the whole world.[54] Therefore, Haass argues, when there are no clearly defined enemies, the best that the United States can hope to do is to work with other great powers within international institutions to regulate the world while it seeks to have its own way in certain regions. Of course, to understand this, one really must define "hegemony."

Edward Luttwak's description of "armed suasion" in his 1987 book, *Strategy: The Logic of War and Peace,* is a useful aid in understanding the meaning of the term hegemony. According to Luttwak, at the level of grand strategy, there may be no visible clash of arms, but a clash of power that derives from military strength.[55] This "armed suasion" both dissuades adversaries from challenging another power and persuades friends to persist in that friendship. David Shambaugh's exploration of the concept of hegemony in *The Korean Journal of Defense Analysis* is also useful as a working aid in understanding how the United States and China will come into conflict in the 21st century. Shambaugh adopts a definition from *Webster's New International Dictionary*—"Leadership; or a preponderant influence or authority, especially of a government or a state."[56] *Webster's Third New International Dictionary* retains essentially the same definition, leaving out the term leadership.[57] Quoting a study by Robert Keohane, David Shambaugh adds that a state must be powerful enough to maintain the rules for interstate relations and be willing to do so.[58] I argue in this chapter that the United States and China really are in conflict for hegemony in Asia, as the term is used in *Webster's Third*, and that the conflict will necessarily influence military-to-military relations between the two countries in the coming century.[59]

China's Dilemma: A U.S. Presence Is Still Useful.

China is in a difficult position in the near term. Beijing is working hard to undermine U.S. security relationships in the Asia-Pacific region, perhaps even the world. Beijing seeks to weaken or diffuse U.S. power.[60] As part of a diplomatic strategy to weaken alliances or put other countries on the defensive, Beijing accuses Australia,

Japan, and Korea of being mere vassals of the United States. At every available forum, China's government leaders work to convince the representatives of those countries that the world is no longer bipolar, that the relationships built up with the United States are relics of the Cold War, and that mutual defense treaties are a thing of the past.[61] This rhetoric, however, does little to resolve China's deeper concerns. Beijing realizes that the U.S. presence in Asia is a stabilizing factor. China's principal security concern today is the potential for a remilitarization of Japan.[62] When a new movie opened in Tokyo in April 1998, portraying World War II Prime Minister of Japan General Hideki Tojo as a war hero and a victim of U.S. persecution at the War Crimes tribunal, the "feelings of 1.2 billion Chinese people were really hurt."[63] Beijing has never been pleased that, unlike Germany, which as a nation has examined and apologized for its role in World War II, Japan seems to have trouble accepting responsibility as the aggressor. My colleagues in the PLA have complained that, in a nation where the transportation minister will apologize to all of the people for a collapsed bridge and where the finance minister will appear on television offering a tearful, humble apology for a collapsed bank, Japan's people and leaders have yet to directly acknowledge the role Japan played in that war.[64] In fact, despite the fact that the Japanese Army admitted in 1992 that it ran a system of brothels to "comfort troops," the Tokyo district court rejected the claims of 46 Filipino women forced into sexual slavery.[65] This continually piques Chinese leaders. The reaction in Beijing to this reexamination of Japanese history, even in popular film, is not just a sense of outrage on China's part. It is the reminder of a genuine fear that Japan will once more rearm and attack China, perhaps through Korea, as it did in 1894 and in 1931.

Although loath to admit it, China really is comforted by the presence of U.S. forces in Japan and Korea because these forces help to maintain the *status quo*. Beijing's leaders may complain about the American presence in Asia, but they realize that U.S. extended nuclear deterrence under the defense treaties with Tokyo and Seoul inhibits Japan and the Republic of Korea (ROK) from becoming nuclear powers, keeps a division on the Korean Peninsula, giving China a buffer state in North Korea, and inhibits Japan from rebuilding its military. Nonetheless, China will work to weaken Japan's security relationships with the United States. Beijing's actions are an attempt to put Tokyo and Washington on the defensive in their relations with China. First, this is an especially effective way to make the U.S. military more willing to meet China's terms in bilateral contacts and negotiations. Secondly, Beijing wants to inhibit Japan from allowing the United States to use Japanese soil as a platform from which to project forces in the event of China's use of armed force against Taiwan. During President Jiang Zemin's December 1998 trip to Japan, Prime Minister Keizo Obuchi took a strong stand on Taiwan. Unlike the embrace of Jiang during President William Clinton's visit to China, Obuchi stiffed Jiang on weakening the U.S.-Japanese defense guidelines.[66]

With regard to Korea, even in the event of an eventual peaceful reunification of the peninsula, the United States will probably seek to retain its alliance with Korea in some form and to retain an overseas presence on the Korean Peninsula. Beijing would prefer to keep a non-aligned buffer state between China and Japan, keeping the *status quo* on the peninsula with a North Korean state that depends on China. PLA senior leaders have told U.S. officials several times that China will not simply stand by and let North Korea collapse. More seriously, in several dialogues about security in Northeast Asia, PLA leaders have strongly hinted that if leaders in Washington or Seoul believe that their forces can simply march up north in the event of a North Korean collapse, even for humanitarian reasons, they are wrong. According to these PLA officers, even a near approach to the Yalu River could trigger the same sort of reaction from China that was seen in 1950.

In short, China insists on being a part of the resolution of the question of North Korea. In the event of an implosion, where humanitarian assistance is required from U.S. and ROK forces, the senior Chinese leaders with whom I have spoken say that both South Korea and the United States should leave the area around the Sino-North Korean border to the PLA. Although they do not expect the North to attack the South, the Chinese officers bluntly reminded me of what they termed "MacArthur's mistake of ignoring China." These senior military officers have laid down some clear warnings that Beijing wants a buffer state on the Korean Peninsula.[67]

These are two of the most serious areas where China and the United States differ over their approaches to the future security environment in Northeast Asia. In geopolitical terms, the United States wants to keep its overseas forces as far forward as possible, while China seeks to keep those forces away from what it considers to be its traditional client states and buffer states. The primary of these is Korea.

Turning toward Taiwan, even if one posits some form of political reconciliation or reunification of Taiwan with the mainland in the next 20 or 30 years, there is still a lot of room for conflict and tension between the United States and China. Strategic thinkers in Beijing may propose some form of "confederation" as a solution for resolving the division of the Korean Peninsula, but they adamantly reject confederation and insist on reunification between Taiwan and the mainland. An accommodation by China allowing for a political reunification would probably maintain a separate government on Taiwan, one that is very independent. If Hong Kong is a model, then Beijing would seek to place some military forces on Taiwan or on the outer islands. It is very unlikely that the majority party leading Taiwan, the Kuomintang (*Guomindang*), would accede to this and even less likely that the other major democratic parties on Taiwan, the Democratic Progressive Party or the New Party, would accept such a resolution.

Should this situation reverse itself, integration of the militaries of Taiwan and China would prove an even greater dilemma for the United States. Most seriously, the Chinese navy would be well-positioned astride major sea lines of communication in the western Pacific. But U.S. security considerations on the sale of military equipment would also be affected. Today, the United States has been quite liberal about approving the sale of advanced military technologies and weapon systems for Taiwan. One reason for this is that the U.S. defense establishment is reasonably comfortable with the fact that it is very unlikely that Taiwan would transfer the advanced technologies to a potential enemy.

The United States cannot be assured that China will seek to resolve territorial disputes peacefully. Despite Beijing's claims that it has only peaceful, defensive intentions, China refuses to renounce the use of force to settle territorial disputes and has used force in the international arena on a number of occasions in the recent past. Beijing has clearly stated its right to use force inside whatever area it defines as its own territory, even if that territory is in dispute. This threat bears directly on China's maritime claims as well as on disputed river boundaries. We are all familiar with the sensitive, diplomatic approach that Beijing took with the Soviet Union over the disputed boundaries of the Ussuri River in 1969. As China begins to try to control the headwaters of the Mekong, Irrawaddy, Brahmaputra, and Red Rivers, it could find itself at odds with Vietnam, Thailand, Burma, Laos, Bangladesh, and India.[68] Since China reserves the right to act independently within the territory it claims, Beijing may well ignore the concerns of these other countries when it tries to control the water and divert it within China.[69]

As for maritime disputes, the 1988 naval engagements against Vietnam in the Spratly Islands come to mind, as do the 1974 seizure of the Paracel Islands and the 1979 attack on Vietnam. Of course, Beijing has always been careful to couch its actions in terms of a "defensive counterattack" or an action to regain territory that it claims.[70] More recently,

236

China seized and occupied Mischief Reef, claimed by the Philippines, and demonstrated massive force against Taiwan as a way to express its dissatisfaction with what Chinese Communist Party leaders believed was a trend toward independence on that island. China is mercurial and given to what Iain Johnston has described as "parabellum" behavior, choosing to escalate rapidly to high levels of force early in any conflict or disagreement as a strategy to dissuade an adversary early and avoid a deeper confrontation.[71] In short, while President Clinton and Communist Party Chairman and President Jiang Zemin proclaimed that a new "strategic partnership exists between the two countries," China is not an ally of the United States. China is a fellow power with a seat on the Permanent Five of the United Nations Security Council. That said, China may someday be an enemy, not because of U.S. policy, but because of China's own policies and actions.

The United States encourages China to seek its place in the region as a great power and hopes that China does so peacefully.[72] But we should be wary. The United States would not like to see any of the advanced systems it has transferred to Taiwan, or to allied countries in Asia, fall into Beijing's hands, as did the transferred aircraft carrier *Minsk*, which went from Russia, to South Korea, to China (for scrap?).[73] Nor should Washington sell arms or advanced military technologies to the Chinese. China has a very poor record on the retransfer of defense systems and has exported items it reverse engineered to countries with which the United States could come into serious conflict. Among these defense systems are the C-802 system, reverse engineered from the French *Exocet* cruise missile and exported to Iran. Beijing has also worked with Iran to adapt the C-802 to strike aircraft that pose a serious threat to U.S. naval forces in the Persian Gulf. If China develops an airborne early warning aircraft with Russian, British, and Israeli assistance, it would probably transfer that system to Iran as well.

These sorts of transfers constitute a special problem for the United States. For Beijing they represent a way to further stretch already overworked American military forces and weaken the U.S. capabilities in East Asia. A deputy Military Region commander in Guangzhou pointed out to me that any U.S. carrier deployed to the Indian Ocean is not available to be used in the Taiwan Strait. In a period of shrinking American defense assets, when U.S. forces are already pushed to the limits of their operational tempo, China is quite willing to accommodate such countries as Iran as a means of weakening the U.S. presence in areas that are close to China's borders. Beijing does this because, in the event of another contingency where the United States could get involved around Taiwan or in Korea, the PLA does not want to be embarrassed again by two powerful naval carrier battle groups off its waters. At the more practical level, a C-802 missile fired from a Chinese aircraft or ship that can use a data link from an Su-30 or an airborne early warning aircraft becomes an over-the-horizon missile that can really hurt U.S. forces.

The urgency of these problems does not end if there is a change in the form of government in China. Whether a Communist regime or some other form of socialist or authoritarian regime is in control of China, U.S. and Chinese interests will differ. In fact, as the Communist Party seeks to retain its legitimacy, it has capitalized on a wave of nationalism that it helped to create. The staged demonstrations against the United States in Beijing in May 1999 underscore how Beijing seeks to use nationalism as a prop to support the Communist Party. Within the PLA, among the junior and middle grade officers (lieutenant through colonel) who will lead the Army in the next century, nationalist feelings are especially strong. They were fueled first by the U.S. response to China's missile-firings off Taiwan in 1996 and increased in fervor by the recovery of Hong Kong in 1997. Nationalism in China today is built on what the Chinese education system has emphasized, the "humiliation of China at the hands of foreign powers from the Opium War to the establishment of the PRC."

The Outline for the Future of the Presidential Summit.

When President Clinton and President Jiang met in Beijing in June 1998, they agreed to a series of confidence-building steps and measures designed to "increase and deepen cooperation between the two countries."[74] Principal among these was the confirmation of what is termed a common goal to halt the spread of weapons of mass destruction. Since 1989, when Deng Xiaoping told President George Bush that "China was not exporting anything called an M-11 missile to Pakistan and if such a missile existed it would not violate the Missile Technology Control Regime (MTCR)," the U.S. Government has ignored evidence that China armed Pakistan with these missiles.[75] Of course, this was done for reasons of expedience and geopolitics that supported a broader trade policy and other objectives. Later, despite evidence that China was assisting Pakistan in developing a nuclear program, the U.S. Government worked hard to minimize any sanctions against China, again to keep open avenues for expanding trade and commerce. This trade had the very positive effect of helping to improve the livelihood of a large number of Chinese people, developing a middle class that is still growing, and opening China to Western ideas and commerce. Ignoring these transfers, however, undermined the centerpiece of the U.S. national strategy, the non-proliferation policy. One might argue, in fact, that India was encouraged by this history to detonate its own nuclear bomb, believing that the United States would soon soften any sanctions.

First, one wonders why Beijing can be believed today when it says that it will cease to export the technology and systems to develop and employ weapons of mass destruction. The PLA and the Chinese defense industry establishment have not lived up to the promises of China's leaders in the past. This represents one of the most serious matters that will affect U.S.-China military-to-military relations in the coming century. Can China be believed when it says it will no longer export technologies, chemical precursors, and MTCR-controlled materials? The record of the past says that Beijing will work secretly to circumvent its promises and U.S. surveillance, especially when the reasons that the United States chose to ignore previous transfers are still valid—trade and cooperation on the Korean Peninsula. China's leaders say that they cannot keep track of all of the companies and business deals in China. In August 1998, I was in China with two U.S. generals, an historian, and a strategist, and in one city we had 14 Chinese security people following us. Beijing can track down and arrest a single literate person who writes a letter to the editor of a newspaper. I had dozens of security people following me around Beijing when I lived there. Perhaps if some of these security officers were used to track illegal exports, Beijing could live up to its promises.

The same doubts hold true of Beijing's promise not to target nuclear weapons against the United States. Is there a bilateral surveillance regime to verify this promise? A second reason that Beijing might choose to secretly circumvent its agreements is that proliferation undermines U.S. leadership.[76] When India and Pakistan exploded nuclear weapons in 1998, the moral authority of the United States was weakened, as was U.S. leadership. After all, the centerpiece of U.S. security policy was shown to have failed. Indeed, the world became more multipolar, reinforcing Beijing's own goals. India was probably reasonably certain that the United States would react meekly, which it did, because the United States selectively ignored China's exports to Pakistan and weakened its sanctions. So military relations with China will continue to be problematic because of China's propensity to ignore its own agreements. This will affect American technology transfer policies. The U.S. defense and intelligence establishments will probably remain reluctant to approve the transfer of militarily critical technologies to China.

The Maritime Consultative Agreement between the United States and China, designed to "promote air and naval operations and to avoid incidents at sea," may also prove a source of more tension than agreement. If Beijing has not renounced the use of force against Taiwan or in the South China Sea, one must question the rationale for letting Chinese observe joint exercises that involve war fighting or power projection. In fact, while the United States may take part in or observe a search-and-rescue exercise, on visits to the United States China will see naval combat and air operations. The first such exercise on search-and-rescue in Hong Kong in December 1995 was quite positive, according to the *South China Morning Post* of December 5, 1998. The debate in the United States over the wisdom of the implementation of this agreement will be carried out in the media and in the Congress, putting the U.S. military under considerable scrutiny and creating more room for tension and confrontation.[77]

Conclusions.

There is a great deal of mutual mistrust between the United States and China, particularly at the senior levels of the two armed forces. American generals are polite, but they are neither blind nor stupid. They know they are seeing very little of the real PLA. These generals see the intelligence on the real PLA exercises, they know what is going on in the information warfare realm, and they know Beijing is cheating on its statements with regard to proliferation. Chen Jian, a Chinese researcher at the U.S. Institute for Peace—like Deputy Chief of the General Staff Department (DCOGS) Lieutenant General Xiong Guangkai, DCOGS General Kui Fulin, Minister of Defense General Chi Haotian, and Chief of the General Staff Department General Fu Quanyou—tells us that it is up to the United States to exercise patience, assist China in its modernization programs, and treat the Chinese as equals.[78] But the military leaders of China, privately, tell us that they are quite ready to sacrifice modernization and development if they believe that core issues like Taiwan independence require conflict. Lieutenant General Li Jijun tells us that both countries must work together so that the United States does not create 1.2 billion enemies. Looking back at the Korean War, his veiled threat is that, if the United States does not engage in cooperative behavior, the price will be very high.[79] But person-to-person, he notes that he had "hundreds of American bombs dropped on him every day with no effect," disparaging U.S. air and naval power, but reposing supreme confidence in the power of artillery and infantry.

Cultural factors weigh heavily in the attempts to improve military-to-military relations between the two countries. Communication is useful, but it is not direct. The internal writings of Chinese military leaders portray the United States as an aggressive power out to undermine China and contain the nation. Movies and briefings prepared for internal use portray the United States as a potential enemy that must be placated in the near term. The private utterances of PLA leaders are also not optimistic. Beijing must realize that while it threatens war against Taiwan, while it uses its army as a main tool to repress the populace, as it did during Tiananmen, and while China refuses to renounce the use of force in the South China Sea, the United States is not very likely to assist in military or high-technology modernization. The United States should gauge its military cooperation with China by simple standards: do nothing to improve the ability of the PLA to wage war against its neighbors or Taiwan; do nothing to improve the PLA's capability to project force; do nothing to improve the PLA's (or the People's Armed Police's) ability to repress the Chinese population.

To quote Lieutenant General Li Jijun, "it is better for soldiers to talk and toast each other than to fight." U.S.-China military-to-military contacts build mutual understanding and personal relationships that can defuse a crisis. The bilateral security dialogue and American confidence-building agreements are useful. But as my Chinese colleagues say, "deeds must match words."

ENDNOTES - CHAPTER 5

1. It is important to remember that conflict can take many forms, diplomatic, economic, and social. But neither conflict nor competition necessarily means war. U.S.-China conflict does not have to be armed conflict. Many have interpreted the book by Richard Bernstein and Ross Munro to mean that China and the United States are future enemies. The two-volume set published in China, *E Zhi Zhongguo* (Containing China), is an example of how the Bernstein and Munro book was interpreted in the Chinese intellectual community. See Richard Bernstein and Ross H. Munro, *The Coming Conflict with China*, New York: A.A. Knopf, 1997. The conflict must be armed conflict.

2. Some of the factors over which there will be conflict are outlined in Yan Xuetong, ed., *Zhongguo Guojia Liyi Fenxi* (*An Analysis of China's National Interest*), Tianjin: Tianjin Renmin Chubanshe, 1997; and Yan Xuetong, ed., *Zhongguo Chuqi: Guojin Huanjing Pinggu* (*The International Environment for China's Rise*), Tianjin: Tianjin Renmin Chubanshe, 1998. Yan and his colleagues conclude that the international environment at the end of the Cold-War era is most conducive to stability in the Asia-Pacific region, creating the necessary conditions for China's rise as a power. On differences in China's strategic view see Zhu Mingquan, *Meiguo Guojia Anquan Zhengce*(*U.S. National Security Policy*), Tianjin: Renmin Chubanshe, 1996. Zhu assesses American security policy as a threat-based combination of realist and idealist theory that is still adjusting to a changed world. Even a capabilities-based strategy, such as the one adopted by the United States in the early 1990s, is still essentially a Cold-War, threat-based strategy, according to Yan Xuetong. At the November 4-6, 1998, "Conference on Strategy and Security in the Asia-Pacific," Monterey, CA, Yan argued that China bases its own strategy on perceptions of the *intent* of another nations, not on potential threat. Lieutenant General Li Jijun, of the PLA Academy of Military Science, argues that China has a security policy and strategy based on a tradition of fighting "just wars" (*yizhan*) from a defensive mentality that takes into consideration the ancient strategic texts of China (*Sunzi Bingfa*) and the *Romance of the Three Kingdoms*(*San Guo Yan Yi*). See Li Jijun, *Junshi zhanlue siwei* (*Strategic Thought*), Beijing: Junshi Kexue Chubanshe, 1996, pp. 50-81; Chen Liheng, *et.al.*, *Junshi yuce xue* (*Military Forecasting*), Beijing: Junshi Kexue Chubanshe, 1993; and

Pan Shiying, ed., *Dangdai zhongguo junshi sixiang jingyao* (*The Essence of Contemporary Military Thinking*), Beijing: Junshi Kexue Chubanshe, 1992.

3. Yue Shuiyu, *Sunzi Bingfa yu Gao Jishu Zhanzheng* (*Sunzi's Military Thought and High Technology Warfare*), Beijing: National Defense University Press, 1998; Xu Yongzhe, *Gao Jishu Zhanzheng Huoqin Baozhang* (*Guaranteeing Logistics in High Technology Warfare*), Beijing: Military Science Press, 1995; Zhu Youwen, *Gao Jishu Tiaojian Xia de Xinxi Zhan* (*Information Warfare Under High Technology Conditions*), Beijing: Military Science Press, 1998.

4. The PLA conducted major exercises in the military districts opposite Taiwan in 1995 and March 1996. In July and August 1995, the PLA conducted a missile exercise in the Taiwan Strait area. In October and November 1995, the PLA conducted a naval demonstration of force followed by an amphibious exercise in the Taiwan Strait. Then between March 8 and 25, 1996, the PLA conducted a series of live-fire exercises, amphibious and airborne exercises, and short-range ballistic missile firings in the Strait area. These exercises were designed to intimidate Taiwan by demonstrating Beijing's ability to strike Taiwan with short-range ballistic missiles, maintain air superiority and sea control in the Strait, and conduct an amphibious invasion of Taiwan. The United States responded by monitoring this activity with the Aegis guided missile cruiser USS *Bunker Hill*, reconnaissance aircraft, and two carrier battle groups, led by the aircraft carriers USS *Independence* and USS *Nimitz*. Office of Naval Intelligence, *Chinese Exercise Strait 961: 8-25 March 1996,* Office of Naval Intelligence: Washington, DC, May 1996.

5. Vivien Pik-Kwan Chan, "Beijing Defends 'Right' to Attack Taiwan," *South China Morning Post,* July 28, 1998.

6. Liu Huaqiu, *Shanghai Jiefang Ribao,* November 3, 1997, p. 5.

7. Larry M. Wortzel, *China's Military Potential,* Carlisle Barracks, PA: U.S. Army War College, Strategic Studies Institute, 1998, pp. 10-11, and 29.

8. Michael Pillsbury, ed., *Chinese Views of Future Warfare,* Washington, DC: National Defense University Press, 1997; Michael Pillsbury, *China's Assessment of the Future Security Environment,* Washington, DC: Office of Net Assessment, Department of Defense, forthcoming 1999.

9. Edward A. Robinson, "China's Spies Target Corporate America," March 30, 1998, *http://www.pathfinder.com/fortune/1998/980330 Chi.html*; Duncan L. Clarke, "Selling U.S. Weapons to China," *Christian Science Monitor*, July 22, 1998, p. 15; "High-Tech Arms Stressed for China's Army," *New York Times*, March 16, 1998, p. A6; Zhu Youwen, *Gao Jishu xia de Xinxi Zhan*(*Information Warfare Under High Technology Conditions*).

10. Kenneth Allen, *et.al.*, *China's Air Force Enters the 21st Century*, Santa Monica: RAND Corporation, 1995.

11. Eric A. McVadon, "China: An Opportunity or a Challenge," *Naval War College Review*, Autumn 1996, pp. 75-92.

12. David Shambaugh, "Chinese Hegemony Over East Asia by 2015?" *The Korean Journal of Defense Analysis*, Summer 1997, pp. 7-28.

13. See Pillsbury, *Chinese Views of Future Warfare*, and Li Jijun, *Junshi zhanlue siwei*. For a series of translations accessible to those who do not read Chinese, see Michael Pillsbury, ed., *Chinese Views of Future Warfare*. For a detailed treatment in Chinese, see Li Jijun, *Junshi Zhanlue Siwei* (*Strategic Thought*); Chen Liheng, *et.al.*, *Junshi Yuce Xue* (*Military Forecasting*); Yue Shuiyu, *Sunzi Bingfa yu Gao Jishu Zhanzheng* (*Sunzi's Military Thought and High Technology Warfare*); Xu Yongzhe, *Gao Jishu Zhanzheng Houqin Baozheng* (*Guaranteeing Logistics in High Technology Warfare*); Zhu Youwen, *Gao Jishu Tiaojian xia de Xinxi Zhan* (*Information Warfare Under High Technology Conditions*).

14. See Wortzel, *China's Military Potential*, pp. 11-14.

15. Work on this exhibition started in 1995, but internal bureaucratic wrangling for primacy and profits among the industries delayed the event. Originally the General Equipment Department of the PLA and the Commission of Science, Technology and Industry for National Defense (COSTIND) ran a press conference for commercial and military attaches in Beijing, announcing the conference in 1996. It was not held until 1998. Soon after the conference the new "fourth department" of the PLA, the General Armaments Department, was created out of COSTIND, and the civilian research component of COSTIND was renamed "State COSTIND."

16. David Reeths, William Edgar, David Roessner, Michael Salomone, "National Technological Competitiveness and the Revolution in Military Affairs," a paper presented at the conference of

the International Security Studies Symposium, Monterey, CA, November 1998.

17. Li Qingshan, *Xin Junshi Geming Yu Gao Jishu Zhanzheng (The New Military Revolution and High Technology Warfare)* Beijing: Junshi Kexue Chubanshe, 1995.

18. *Ibid.*, p. 35. See also Li Jijun, *Junshi Zhanlue Siwei (Strategic Thought*), pp. 180-186.

19. Li Qingshan, p. 41.

20. *Ibid.*, pp. 73-74.

21. *Ibid.*, pp. 79-81.

22. *Ibid.*, p. 91.

23. *Ibid.*, pp. 94-95, 146.

24. In the second quarter of 1998, I visited Hanoi, Seoul, and Beijing for meetings with strategists associated with military and defense policies where the question of Chinese hegemony was acknowledged. A colleague in the Department of National Security and Strategy of the U.S. Army War College, Dr. John Garofano, found the same attitudes in Singapore, Seoul, and Malaysia during the summer 1998.

25. Discussions with officials at the Military Strategy Institute of the Defense Ministry of Vietnam, the Central Committee of the Vietnam Communist Party, and the Academy of Social Science, Hanoi, June 27-July 1, 1998.

26. I will stay away from the mechanical side of the execution of these policies. By this I mean that the paper will avoid "getting down into the weeds" to discuss the "four pillars of the relationship." So long as the United States has a coherent, comprehensive strategy, it is not particularly important whether it is carried out through high-level contacts, functional exchanges, ship visits, or exercises. Regardless of the form or level of contact, the substance of the contact must support, not undermine, the basic policy.

27. *A National Security Strategy for a New Century,* Washington, DC: The White House, October 1998, referred to hereafter as *National Security Strategy; National Military Strategy of the United States of America—Shape, Respond, Prepare Now: A Military Strategy for a New Era,* Washington, DC: Joint Chiefs of Staff, 1997, referred to hereafter as *National Military Strategy.* See also *The United States Security*

Strategy for the East Asia-Pacific Region, Washington, DC: The Secretary of Defense, 1998.

28. *National Security Strategy,* p. 2.

29. *Ibid.,* pp. 6-9.

30. *Ibid.,* pp. i-iii.

31. China has signed the U.N. International Covenant on Civil and Political Rights. Like many countries, however, Beijing has defined its view of human rights differently from the United States. China takes a "basic needs" approach to human rights, arguing that before such "luxuries" as freedom of speech, freedom of the press, and the freedom to assemble can be granted to a people, the basic needs like food and shelter must be met. This position has been most powerfully argued by Singapore. See Goh Chok Tong, "Social Values, Singapore Style," *Current History,* December 1994, pp. 417-442; Melanie Chew, "Human Rights in Singapore: Perceptions and Problems," *Asian Survey,* Vol. XXXIV, No. 11, November 1994, pp. 933-948; also see Meredith Woo-Commings, "The 'New Authoritarianism' in East Asia," *Current History,* December 1994, pp. 413-416. President Clinton explained the U.S. position at Beijing University on June 29, 1998. A full text of his speech may be found at *http://www.china.com/clinton/english/news/speech/speech/06290002.html.* President Jiang Zemin's comments on free speech and the arrest of dissidents are at *http://www.china.com/clinton/english/news/speech/speech/06270004.html.*

32. *National Military Strategy,* pp. 3-5.

33. The Commander in Chief of the U.S. Pacific Command reinforced these points during a December 1998 visit to Australia. *Australian Financial Review,* December 8, 1998, p. 9.

34. This dislike, even distrust, of alliances was heightened by the accidental bombing of the Chinese Embassy in Yugoslavia by the United States, acting as part of NATO. See *The Washington Post,* June 11, 1999, p. A16.

35. Information Office of the State Council of the People's Republic of China, *China's National Defense,* Beijing, July 27, 1998. According to my discussions with some of the drafters of the White Paper, like the first White Paper on arms control published in 1995, this was a product of an interagency writing and coordination process involving the

Central Military Commission, the General Staff Department of the PLA, the Ministry of Foreign Affairs and the Ministry of State Security.

36. *Ibid.*, p. 1.

37. Li Haibo, "Imaginary Threat," *Beijing Review*, March 24-30, 1999, p. 4.

38. The PLA Navy is building piers and barracks on Mischief Reef, claimed by the Philippines, in what Philippine Defense Secretary Orlando Mercado characterized as "a creeping invasion." "Regional Briefing," *Review: Far Eastern Economic Review*, November 19, 1998; *http://www.feer.com.*

39. Zhu Mingquan makes the point that a cooperative approach to international policies becomes a "positive-sum-game," which emphasizes global and collective security organizations. Zhu Mingquan, *Meiguo Guojia Anquan Zhengce (U.S. Naitonal Security Policy)*, pp. 17-27, 110-129.

40. "Beijing Defends 'Right' to Attack Taiwan," *South China Morning Post*, July 28, 1998, p. 1; "China Can't Steal What is Already China's," *International Herald Tribune*," December 4, 1998, p. 8; Julian Baum and Susan Lawrence, "Breaking the Ice," *Review: Far Eastern Economic Review*, October 15, 1998, *http://www/feer/com.*

41. See Du Gong, ed., *Zhuanhuan zhong de shiji geju* (The World Structure in Transformation), Beijing: Shijie Zhishi Chubanshe, 1992.

42. On the strategic partnerships China has established, see Wany Yi, "Sino-French Relations More Mature and Stable," *Beijing Review*, Vol. 40, No. 21, May 26-June 1, 1997, pp. 8-11; *Beijing Review*, Vol. 40, No. 22, June 2-8, 1997, pp. 7-9; *The Korea Times*, November 11, 1995, p. 1; *China Daily*, October 12, 1998, p. 1; Ministry of Foreign Affairs and Japan, "Japan-China Joint Declaration on Building a Partnership of Friendship and Cooperation for Peace and Development," November 29, 1998; *Beijing Review*, Vol. 41, No. 1, January 5-11, 1998, p. 10-11 (ASEAN); *The Washington Post*, April 26, 1997, p. A27 (Russia); *Beijing Review*, Vol. 41, No. 10, March 9-15, 1998, p. 7 (European Union); The White House, "Fact Sheet: Accomplishments of the U.S.-China Summit," October 29, 1997.

43. *Shanghai Liefang Ribao*, November 3, 1997, p. 5; *The United States Security Strategy for the East Asia-Pacific Region*, Washington, DC: The Secretary of Defense, 1998, p. 34; *China's National Defense*, Beijing: State Council of the PRC, 1998.

44. *Review: Far Eastern Economic Review,* December 10, 1989, p. 21; *International Herald Tribune,* November 30, 1998, p. 8; Office of Naval Intelligence, Chinese Exercise Strait 961, pp. 1,7.

45. *New York Times,* January 20, 1998, p. 8. The center that Secretary Cohen saw was a local control and monitoring center, not a national command center.

46. General Shalikashvili spoke at the People's Liberation Army National Defense University in mid-May 1997, after which he visited the 15th Group Army. *Chicago Tribune,* May 15, 1997, p. 7.

47. On United Front theory and temporary alliances with potential main adversaries, see Benjamin Schwartz, *Chinese Communism and the Rise of Mao,* Cambridge: Harvard University Press, 1951; Edmund O. Clubb, *Twentieth Century China,* New York: Columbia University Press, 1964; Mao Zedong, "On the International United Front Against Fascism" *Selected Works,* Vol. III, Beijing: Foreign Language Press, 1967.

48. Wortzel, *China's Military Potential,* pp. 16-17.

49. The two-volume set published in China, *E zhi zhongguo (Containing China)* is an example of this.

50. See Roger Ames, trans., *Sun-Tzu: The Art of Warfare,* New York: Ballantine Books, 1993, pp. 93, 110-111. See also Wu Zhoulong, *et.al., Sunzi Jiaoshi (Explaining Sunzi),* Beijing: Junshi Kexue Chubanshe, 1996; Yue Shuiyu, *Sun Zi Bingfa yu Gao Jishu Zhanzheng (Sunzi's Military Thought and High Technology Warfare)*; Xu Yongzhe, *Gao Jishu Zhanzheng Houqin Baozhang(Guaranteeing Logistics in High Technology Warfare)*; Zhu Youwen, *Gao Jishu Taiojian xia de Xinxi Zhan (Information Warfare under High Technology Conditions).*

51. Liu Huaqiu, *Shanghai Jiefang Ribao,* November 3, 1997, p. 5; Li Qingsong, "Current International Military Security Situation," *Guoji Zhanlue Yanjiu (International Strategic Studies)* No. 1, Ser. 47, January 1998, pp. 9-15; *China's National Defense,* pp. 3-7.

52. Chi Haotian, "Da Li Jiaqiang Guofang he Jundui Xiandaihua Jianshe" ("Exert Great Effort to Strengthen National Defense and Military Building and Modernization"), *Qiu Shi,* No. 15, 1998, p. 15.

53. I ask the reader to distinguish here between the concept of hegemony as it is described in this chapter and the concept internal to Marxism-Leninism of the doctrine of hegemony espoused by the former Soviet Union and defined by the Chinese critique of that concept. The

Chinese Communist Party critique of "socialist-imperial hegemony" as a policy for expansion and neo-colonialism is based on the then-Soviet Union's claims of "limited sovereignty" for states in the "socialist camp; the international division of labor; and the leadership of the 'socialist camp' by the Soviet Union." See the critique of this doctrine in *Hong Qi*, No. 5, 1970, pp. 13-15.

54. Haass makes this point in a few places in his book, but he discusses the thesis in the most detail in Chapter Three, "A Doctrine of Regulation," pp. 49-77. See Richard N. Haass, *The Reluctant Sheriff: The United States After the Cold War*, Washington, DC: Council on Foreign Relations, 1997. For a discussion of Haass' ideas see Brian Urquhart, "Looking for the Sheriff," *The New York Review of Books*, July 16, 1998, pp. 48-53.

55. Edward N. Luttwak, *Strategy: The Logic of War and Peace*, Cambridge: The Belknap Press, 1987., pp. 190-207.

56. Shambaugh, p. 11.

57. *Webster's Third International Dictionary*, 1971 edition.

58. Shambaugh, p.11; Robert Keohane, *After Hegemony: Cooperation and Discord in the World Political Situation* Princeton: Princeton University Press, 1984. Shambaugh's point is that there are different definitions of the term, "coercive, benign, and benevolent," and one must be careful how the term is used.

59. As mentioned in endnote 1, it is important to understand that conflict does not necessarily mean war. I argue that conflict will be a major factor in bilateral relations between the United States and China as well as in multilateral relations in Asia because both countries are vying for dominance, but that there are only a few ways that we could see armed conflict.

60. For instance, see China's presentation at the ASEAN Regional Forum Intersessional Meeting on Confidence Building Measures, held in Beijing March 6-8, 1997, entitled "China's Defense Policy Statement."

61. *China's National Defense*, pp. 3, 21-22; Liu Huaqing.

62. Peter Landers and Susan V. Lawrence, "Sorry, No Apology," *Far Eastern Economic Review*, December 10, 1998, p. 21; Nicholas D. Kristof, "Jiang Trips Over the Issue of Japanese Apology," *International Herald Tribune*, November 30, 1998, p. 1.

63. This phrase is often used by PRC government publications to express outrage at some act of a foreign country. See *The Japan Times*, June 6, 1998, p. 3; *The Daily Herald*, Everett, WA, April 7, 1998, p. 3A; *Asia Magazine*, May 25, 1998. "Japanese 'Tojo' Movie Top-Grossing Film in First Half of 1998," *Bloomberg News Service*, Tokyo, June 12, 1998; *The Straits Times Interactive*, May 11, 1998, http://web3.asia1.comm.sg/archive/st/4/pages/stea4.html.

64. Prime Minister Hashimoto's 1997 visit to Manchuria and the site of the chemical and biological experiments was not really accepted in Tokyo and disavowed by some cabinet members.

65. *Associated Press*, "Court Rejects Claims of WWII Sex Slaves," *The Sentinel*, October 9, 1998, p. A7.

66. *The Washington Post*, December 6, 1998, p. C7.

67. I have been told this by several senior active duty and retired general officers in the PLA, some of whom fought in the Korean War. Some of these officers are Central Committee members. The PLA is quite serious about this point and wants to ensure that this message is not ignored, as it was in 1950.

68. The potential for serious disputes in this area was pointed out to me by Professor Sen-Dao Chang (Zhang Chengde), Geography Department, University of Hawaii-Manda. Dr. Chang reminded me of just how sensitive China can be to disputed river boundaries by reminding me of the way that the Zhenbao (Damansky) Island incident was handled by the PLA in 1969.

69. See Sen-Dao Chang, "Qianyi Zhongguo Shui Ziyuan Texu Kaifa he Liyong," ("A Preliminary Discussion of the Special Connections of the Development and Use of China's Water Resources"), University of Hawaii, Summer 1998.

70. "China Tells Vietnam Leave the Spratlys," *Washington Times*, September 11, 1998, p. 19.

71. See Alistair Iain Johnston, *Cultural Realism: Strategic Culture and Grand Strategy in Chinese History*, Princeton: Princeton University Press, 1995. See also Allen Whiting, *The Chinese Calculus of Deterrence*, Ann Arbor: University of Michigan Press, 1975.

72. Larry M. Wortzel, "China Seeks Traditional Great Power Status," *Orbis*, Spring 1994; Larry M. Wortzel, "China's Military Potential in the 21st Century," *Asia Pacific Magazine*, Australian National University, September 1998.

73. *European Stars and Stripes,* September 3, 1998, p. 16; Bruce Gilley, "Scrap Value," *Far Eastern Economic Review,* April 9, 1998, *http://www.feer.com.*

74. Fact Sheet, "Achievements of U.S.-China Summit," Office of the Press Secretary, The White House, June 27, 1998.

75. Bill Gertz, "Beijing Continued Arms Sales to Pakistan, Iran Last Year," *Washington Times,* July 22, 1998, p. 1; Bill Gertz, "White House Plays Down Test of Rocket Motor by Chinese," *Washington Times,* July 23, 1998, p. 16; Bill Gertz, "U.S. Protests Chinese Technology Sent to Iran," *Washington Times,* December 7, 1998, p. 1.

76. "U.S., China Sign Military Agreement," *Washington Times,* September 16, 1998, p. 5.

77. "Pentagon Inquiry Faults Missile Maker's China Aid," *New York Times,* December 9, 1998, p. 1; "The Trail of Dealings with China's Rocket Gear," *New York Times,* December 9, 1998, p. 14; "White House Confirms Protest to China," *New York Times,* December 8, 1998, p. 4.

78. Chen Jian, "The China Challenge for the Twenty-First Century," Washington, DC: U.S. Institute for Peace, June 1998.

79. Li Jijun, *Traditional Military Thinking and the Defensive Strategy of China,* Carlisle Barracks, PA: U.S. Army War College, Strategic Studies Institute, 1997.

CHAPTER 6
TAIWAN'S MILITARY IN THE 21st CENTURY: REDEFINITION AND REORGANIZATION

Arthur Shu-fan Ding
and
Alexander Chieh-cheng Huang

A giant wave is rising. The party flag is flying. This is the revolutionary Huangpu (Military Academy). Ideology should be carried out. Discipline should be kept. Prepare to be the spearhead of the struggle. We are fighting to open a road with our blood and to lead our suppressed countrymen, hand-in-hand, marching forward...

Song of the Chinese Military Academy

Every morning the cadets of the Chinese Military Academy in Kaohsiung, Taiwan, sing the same song to remind themselves of the goals of the National Revolutionary Army (*guomin gemingjun*) (hereafter referred to as the Taiwan military) set forth by Dr. Sun Yat-sen when he established the Academy in Huangpu, Guangdong, in 1924. Sadly, despite its lofty goals, the Taiwan military was soundly defeated by the Communists in 1949. Nevertheless, since retreating to Taiwan, the Taiwan military has abandoned its Bolshevik-inspired ideology and now proudly declares itself to be the ultimate defender of a young democracy. What were the reasons that led to such a change? How does the Taiwan military plan to transform itself in the future? What are the problems associated with the transformation? This chapter aims to discuss the changing political and strategic environment experienced by the Taiwan military, to examine the policies the Taiwan military adopted to cope with those changes, and to identify the challenges that the Taiwan military is likely to face in the near future.

TWO TRANSFORMATIONS: MILITARY DEVELOPMENT IN A CHANGING ENVIRONMENT

Some observers have argued that the People's Republic of China's (PRC) unsuccessful war against Vietnam in 1979 served as the first wake-up call for the PRC's defense modernization efforts. In the same year, Washington's de-recognition of the Republic of China (ROC) also evoked in Taiwan an urgent desire to maintain a strong and self-reliant defense capability.[1] In the nearly 2 decades since 1979, the Taiwan military has instituted significant modernization programs concentrating largely on weapons systems acquisition. However, the real transformation of Taiwan's military—including changes in its strategic concepts, defense policies, and relationship with civilian authorities—has come only in the last 10 years, primarily in response to two factors: democratization and Taiwan's strategic reorientation.

Democratization: From Party-Led Army to National Army.

Constitutional Reform. Following the steps taken by late-President Chiang Ching-kuo to relax political control of the society in Taiwan, President Lee Teng-hui in 1991 terminated the "Period of Mobilization against Communist Rebellion" and began a multi-year constitutional reform. One major reform has been the switch from indirect to direct presidential elections, which strengthened the power base of the president. In addition, the appointment of the premier as the highest official of the Executive branch no longer requires the confirmation of the Legislative branch, making the premier the president's proxy in carrying out policy. The effect of these changes has been to alter the previous separation between the "military administration system" (*junzheng xitong*) and the "military command system" (*junling xitong*), paving the way for stronger presidential control over military affairs.

The Rise of Political Opposition. The lifting of martial law and the legalization of political opposition have brought an end to the political dominance of the *Kuomintang* (KMT or Nationalist Party). Over the past 10 years, opposition parties, particularly the Democratic Progressive Party (DPP), have been increasingly able to expand their popular support and to attract voters. Advocating Taiwan's independence is no longer a political taboo, and the development of a civil society has forced KMT organs to retreat from military institutions. The military, under such circumstances, has had no choice but to transform itself from an anti-Taiwan independence force to a guardian of democracy and the constitution.

Strategic Reorientation: From Offense to Defense.

Redefinition of Military Strategy. After the termination of martial law, the ROC officially recognized that the PRC exercises effective control over mainland China and abandoned the unrealistic ambition of reunifying China by force. Taiwan's military strategy has since shifted from a focus on retaking the mainland by force (*fangong dalu*) to an emphasis on integrated defensive and offensive capabilities (*gongshou yiti*) to a purely defensive strategy (*shoushi fangyu*). This new strategic posture rendered obsolete the old forms of resource allocation, force deployment, and command and personnel structures.

Changing Military Technologies. Advances in military technology and the modernization of the People's Liberation army (PLA) have changed the nature of the threat to Taiwan's security. Improvements in weaponry and the increase of the PLA's force-projection capability have made the heavily fortified offshore islands of Quemoy and Matsu irrelevant to Taiwan's defense. The PLA's medium-range ballistic missile force has left the main island of Taiwan virtually defenseless against a missile threat. At the same time, advances in military technology have also allowed Taiwan to improve its own firepower and force mobility, while reducing manpower and adjusting military investment.

Beyond these great changes in Taiwan's political and strategic environment, the social and economic situation in Taiwan has forced a shift in military policy.

Strained Financial Resources. Two factors, the increasing cost of social welfare programs and the need for infrastructure investment, have forced a reduction in the share of the defense budget as a part of Taiwan's total government budget from 24.28 percent in fiscal year (FY) 1994 to 22.43 percent in FY 1998. The defense budget measured as a percentage of Gross Domestic Product (GDP) has also declined from 4.22 percent in FY 1994 to 3.26 percent in FY 1998.[2] Another financial reason behind the streamlining of the armed forces is the huge personnel costs in relation to operational costs and military investments. In the fiscal 1999 budget proposal submitted to the Legislative Yuan, the three major sections in the defense budget are: 50.05 percent for personnel costs, 19.09 percent for operational costs, and 30.86 percent for military investment.[3] Given that personnel costs take up about half of the total defense budget, it was no accident that Chief of the General Staff General Tang Fei complained that, without a streamlining of military personnel, the Taiwan military will not be able to pay its electricity bill by 2006.[4]

Decline in Available Draftees. Taiwan maintains a primarily conscript military force. The Taiwan military has also encountered manpower problems at the basic unit level. Fewer young people of talent are interested in serving in the military when they can be better off, at least financially, by working in the private sector. Another relatively long-term problem is the decline in net population growth. The 1998 *ROC National Defense Report* predicts that the numbers of eligible recruits will continue to decrease in the next 5 years from about 161,000 in 1998 to 148,000 in 2002.[5] Such factors as the graying of Taiwan's population, the out-flow of population due to increased crime rates, and the fact that more parents are sending their children to study abroad have contributed to the decline of available draftees.

The factors above have created a disturbing, if not alarming, situation. If the Taiwan military does not redefine and reorganize itself, it cannot meet the security challenges posed by the PRC and may not survive the rapid domestic political changes. In the next two sections, the authors discuss major measures adopted by the Taiwan military to adapt to the changing environment.

ENHANCING CIVILIAN CONTROL: THE MAKING OF NATIONAL DEFENSE LAW

Evolution of National Security Organizations.

During World War II, the national defense organization of the ROC was firmly placed under the control of the KMT. The Supreme Defense Council (*guofang zuigao weiyuanhui*) was the highest defense policymaking body, with the chairman of the KMT as its chairman.[6] After the promulgation of the ROC Constitution in 1947, the Supreme Defense Council was replaced by the National Defense Council (*guofang huiyi*) headed by the president of the republic. However, the swift defeat of the KMT government on the mainland in 1949 kept the National Defense Council from serving any substantial functions. After the ROC government retreated to Taiwan, Chiang Kai-shek established a National Security Council (NSC) (*guojia anquan huiyi*) following the American model.[7] However, after the lifting of martial law and the termination of the Temporary Provisions during the Period of Mobilization against Communist Rebellion, the legal basis for the NSC was put in question. In response to the new political and security conditions, the National Assembly amended the ROC Constitution in April 1991, establishing a new legal basis for the NSC.

In fact, the ROC government had begun contemplating drafting a new law on national defense as early as 1950 and submitted a draft of National Defense Organization Law (*guofang zuzhifa*) to the Legislative Yuan twice for review, in 1951 and 1954. Unfortunately, the Executive Yuan withdrew the drafts in 1971 without any substantial progress.[8] Instead, the ROC government promulgated a Ministry of National Defense Organizational Law (*guofangbu zuzhifa*) in 1970 and a Ministry of National Defense General Staff Organization Law (*guofangbu canmoubenbu zuzhifa*) in 1978. According to these two laws, which remain in effect, Taiwan's national defense organization was divided into two parallel systems: the military administration system and military command system. In the military administration system, military policies are carried out through a chain comprising the president, the premier, the minister of national defense (MND), and the chief of the General Staff. However, in the military command system, the president directly commands the armed forces through the chief of the General Staff. (See Figure 1.)

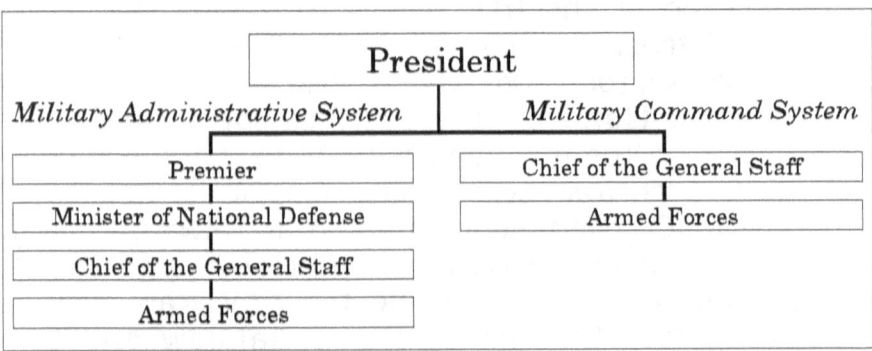

Figure 1. National Command Structure of the ROC. (Current)

The need for formulating a basic law on national defense was revived in 1993. No significant action was taken, however, until the National Assembly finished amending the ROC Constitution in July 1997. In September 1997, based on the amended constitution, the MND submitted a draft National Defense Organization Law to the Executive Yuan. The proposed law contained two versions: one maintaining the current two-track system and another suggesting the convergence of the two tracks. It is reported that the Executive Yuan preferred the second version, but that several generals privately appealed to President Lee against the convergence. The generals are said to have argued that the current system enables the president to exercise his power as commander in chief more effectively and that uniting the two systems would infringe on the president's power. The Executive Yuan felt the matter was too sensitive and sent both versions to the Office of the President for advice. Ultimately, President Lee supported the convergence and insisted that military affairs be subject to parliamentary supervision. That decision untied the most difficult knot in the making of the new law.[9] In addition, President Lee told Defense Minister Chiang Chung-ling that the function of a national defense organization is not merely an organizational issue, but rather it is to build appropriate defense systems and capabilities. Accordingly, Lee directed the MND to drop the term "organization" and to rename the draft "National Defense Law" on December 30, 1997.[10]

In a parallel effort, confirming Lee's directive to the Minister of Defense, the KMT's Central Policy Commission (*zhongyang zhengcehui*) on April 23, 1998, responded to a directive from Lee Teng-hui, acting in his capacity as KMT chairman, and concluded that the Ministry of National Defense should aim to achieve the "convergence of the military administration system and the military command system" (*junzheng junling yiyuanhua*) in drafting the new defense law. Accordingly, the MND submitted drafts of a National Defense Law (*guofang fa*) and the Amendments to the Ministry of National Defense Organizational Law (*guofangbu zuzhifa*) to the Executive Yuan on April 30, 1998.[11] The Executive Yuan formally approved both drafts on May 21, 1998.[12] The drafts were submitted to the

Legislative Yuan for review in the session that began in September 1998.

Unique Characteristics of the New Law.

The draft of the National Defense Law is divided into seven chapters and 36 articles.[13] It defines the goals and missions of the Taiwan military and the roles and functions of key players in the national command structure. In addition to those elements that are generic to similar laws of other nations, the National Defense Law contains two elements unique to the old defense structure: first, the creation of a National Military Council (NMC) (*guofang junshi huiyi*), and second, the convergence of the military administration system and the military command system. (See Figure 2.)

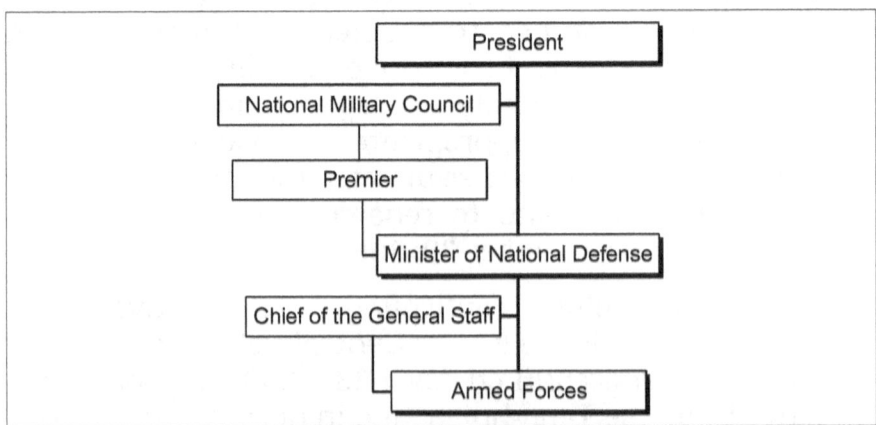

Figure 2. National Command Structure of the ROC. (Proposed in National Defense Law)

The Creation of a National Military Council. Reportedly, as it redefined the national command structure, the MND always considered the NSC to be the highest defense decision-making body. However, according to the NSC Organization Law promulgated following the last round of constitutional amendments, the NSC is a consultative agency with no decision-making power. Consequently, the MND adopted a concept similar to that used by the U.S.

Government and suggested the establishment of the NMC as the highest defense decision-making organization.[14]

- **Article 8**: As the commander in chief, the president commands the army, navy and air force. In exercising the power of commander in chief and in making military decisions, the president **shall** convene the National Military Council.

- **Article 9**: The president chairs the National Military Council and enjoys final decision power. The members of the National Military Council are the vice president, premier, secretary-general of the President's Office, secretary-general of the National Security Council, minister of national defense, chief of the General Staff and other participants appointed by the president.

According to defense officials, the NMC is not intended to be a permanent, standing organization, but to meet *ad hoc*. The president would convene meetings of the NMC only when there is a major defense decision to make. All other peacetime military decisions will be made during routine "military talks" (*junshi huitan*) between the president and military leaders.[15]

System convergence. Under the current system of military relations in Taiwan, a system which has not changed in 50 years, the president and the chief of the General Staff have become the two most powerful government officials exempted from parliamentary supervision. The draft National Defense Law seeks to revise this. The parliament or Legislative Yuan can supervise the premier, who is the highest official in the executive branch, but the Legislative Yuan is not entitled to oversee the president. Nor does the parliament have any supervisory authority over the chief of the General Staff, because this supervision could also be seen as infringing upon the president's constitutional right as the commander in chief of the nation. Therefore, during the past 50 years, the chiefs of the General Staff have always been able to decline invitations from the Legislative Yuan to report on military affairs.

As Taiwan's democracy matured, the refusal by the chief of the General Staff to report to the Legislative Yuan has become more and more unacceptable to legislators as well as to the general public. At the formal request of 124 people, led by Legislator Ding Shou-chung (KMT), the Council of the Grand Justices issued its interpretation of current laws on July 24, 1998, and affirmed that the chief of the General Staff, as an official in the executive branch of the government, cannot refuse to report to committee meetings of the Legislative Yuan. However, since the chief of the General Staff is not a member of the cabinet, according to the constitution, he is not required to attend or answer questions at the plenary session of the Legislative Yuan.[16] After learning of the interpretation from the Council of the Grand Justices, current Chief of the General Staff General Tang Fei indicated that he is fully aware of the political trend towards greater legislative supervision of military affairs and expressed his willingness to go to the Legislative Yuan even before the Legislature reviews the draft of the new National Defense Law.[17] On September 30, 1998, General Tang became the first chief of the General Staff reporting to the Legislative Yuan and answering questions.[18]

The draft of the new National Defense Law redefines the national command structure and proposes the inclusion of the defense minister in the military chain of command. It also redefines the relationship between the defense minister and the chief of the General Staff.

• **Article 10**: In exercising power as the commander in chief, the president commands the armed forces through the minister of national defense.

• **Article 14**: The minister of national defense is a position for civilians. The minister manages defense affairs of the nation and is responsible for the matters of both military administration and the command of armed forces.

- **Article 15**: The Ministry of National Defense should set up the General Staff Office (*canmou benbu*) to function as both the military staff for the defense minister and the commanding organization for joint military operations. The Office should have a chief of the General Staff who acts as the military staff for the defense minister and commands military operations under the minister's instructions.

- **Article 16**: Directly under the Ministry of National Defense, there should be the general headquarters of the army, the navy, the air force, the Tri-service Joint Logistics, the Reserves Command, the Military Police Command, and other military organizations, military schools, and troops.

In the existing national command structure, the military administration system and military command system converge at the Office of the President. Under the proposed law, the chief of the General Staff, who is the highest ranking person in military uniform, will be subordinate to the minister of national defense, a civilian. The minister of national defense becomes the principal military adviser to the president and controls both the military administration system and military command system. Since the defense minister is required to be a civilian and is a member of the cabinet, the Legislative Yuan is therefore in a firm position to supervise all military affairs. The new structure, if the law is enacted, would create a system similar to that in the United States, including similar National Command Authorities.

Debates and Dissenting Views.

The *Premier's Role in the National Command Structure. The United Daily*, one of the largest newspapers in Taiwan, issued an editorial on January 9, 1998, arguing that,

> converging the systems of military administration and military command is intended to correct the shortcomings of the current system and restore the integrity of executive power. But, since the premier, according to the constitution, is the head of executive branch and is responsible to the

legislative branch, he should be head of national defense affairs, not the president. The establishment of the National Military Council is an expansion of the president's power and will infringe upon the premier's executive power. Thus, the draft National Defense Law, in effect creates legislation that would damage the Constitution.[19]

The MND was unable to give any convincing response to such questions, but only issued a rebuttal, stating that "In practice so far, the power of the commander in chief is independent from both the executive and the legislative powers."[20] In other words, according to the MND, even though the new draft law gives the Executive Yuan the responsibility to make defense policies,[21] it is justifiable that the premier is not included in the chain of command.

The Need for a New National Military Council. In addressing the need for a NMC, the MND argued that although the constitution does not regulate how the power of the commander in chief is to be used, major policy decisions in most democratic nations are made in a collective fashion, and Taiwan should not be an exception. Taiwan studied the National Command Authority of the United States as a model and, given the differences in government structure, borrowed the concept. Taking the national security structure of the United States as an example, the MND proposed the establishment of a NMC.[22] The MND justified the establishment of such a council by pointing out that the NSC has no decision-making power, but only consultative functions. However, the MND conceives the NMC as a high-level, decision-making mechanism with no permanent or fixed organization. The president, through the consultative mechanism of the NMC, would make his policy decisions and command the armed forces.[23] There are problems with the MND proposal that still must be thought through. First, if it is true that military policies are to be decided collectively, given the existing functions of the NSC, is it necessary to set up another homogeneous organization? Second, if, as the MND argued, the national command authority goes from the president to the defense minister and then directly to the armed forces, it is really not an important issue whether the NSC is a consultative agency or a decision-making body. (See Figure 3.)

NATIONAL SECURITY COUNCIL	NATIONAL MILTIARY COUNCIL
• President (Chairman)	• President (Chairman)
• Premier (Vice Chairman)	• Premier (Vice Chairman)
• Secretary-General, Office of the President	• Secretary-General, Office of the President
• Vice Premier	• Secretary-General, National Security Council
• Minister of the Interior	• Minister of National Defense
• Minister of Foreign Affairs	• Chief of the General Staff
• Minister of National Defense	• Participants appointed by the President
• Minister of Finance	
• Minister of Economic Affairs	
• Chairman of the Mainland Affairs Council	
• Chief of the General Staff	
• Secretary-General, National Security Council	
• Director-General, National Security Bureau	
• Participants appointed by the President	

Figure 3. Members of Taiwan's National Security Authority.

Relations between the Defense Minister and the Chief of the General Staff. In the existing system, chiefs of the General Staff have had the difficult task of balancing their roles as military advisers to the president (in the military command system) and advisers to the defense minister and the premier (in the military administration system). The proposed new law plans to converge the two systems by making the defense minister in charge of both the military administration system and the military command system. However, problems remain. People may argue that the draft law is merely shifting the difficulties from the chief of the General Staff to the defense minister, since the minister will still have dual responsibilities to both the president and the premier.[24] Further, drafting a new law is easy, but making it function well remains a big problem. In the existing system, the Office of Defense Minister has only very small staffs, which are responsible for manpower, materials, and mobilization works. The General Staff Office, on the other hand, has a huge staff. Therefore, without an expansion of the Office of the Minister of National Defense, the new system will almost certainly invite more problems. One must also ask whether there should be legislation that regulates the size and function of these staffs.

The Roles of the Chief of the General Staff. In the national command structure of the United States, military operations are carried out by the commanders in chief of the unified and/or specified commands under the direct order of the President and the Secretary of Defense. In Taiwan's proposed new law, the chief of the General Staff is both the top military adviser to the defense minister and the supreme commander of joint military operations. Even though Taiwan is not a global military power, some experts suspect that the dual role of the chief of the General Staff could cause problems. Defense Minister Chiang Chung-ling addressed this issue in a Military Work Review Conference (*guojun gongzuo jiantaohui or ziqiang huiyi*) held on June 9, 1998.[25] Chiang argued that the General Staff Office functions as both military staff and military commanding organization. Unlike the United States, Taiwan has only limited armed forces and operational space and is, in fact, only one integrated military operations zone (*zhanqu*). Therefore, it should be no problem for the chief of the General Staff to wear two hats, i.e., providing military advice to and commanding military operations on behalf of the defense minister and the president.[26] General Tang Fei, however, indicated that the dual functions of the chief of the General Staff needed to be further clarified. Nominally, he said, the chief of the General Staff should be purely a military adviser; however, it would be risky if the chief of the General Staff is granted the responsibility of commanding the military only at wartime. Therefore, General Tang suggested it would be better to give the chief of the General Staff another title such as Supreme Commander of the Armed Forces (*guofangjun zongsiling*), which would provide authority to oversee the military during peacetime and war.[27]

Views from the Legislative Yuan. The Legislative Yuan stayed actively involved in the lawmaking process. Since the time that the Executive Yuan approved the MND draft, members of the Legislative Yuan have proposed at least six different versions of the draft.[28] Although both branches of the government support the concept of unifying the military administrative and command systems, there are at least two major differences between the Legislative Yuan versions and the Executive Yuan version.

• Concerning the national command structure, almost all interested legislators oppose the idea of establishing a NMC. Chu Feng-chi (KMT), Lin Chou-shui (DPP), and Chai Ming-hsian (DPP) have argued that the NSC already has all the functions of the proposed NMC and that there is no need for duplication. Chu and Lin propose that any NSC decision related to military affairs should be sent to the Legislative Yuan for review. Chai wants the Chairman of the NSC, i.e., the president, to submit a report on national security strategy to the Legislative Yuan annually. Chen Shui-bian (DPP) advocates the establishment of a new national command structure by setting up a National Security Administration (*guojia anquan zongshu*) in the Presidential Office and a National Security Affairs Commission (*guojia anquan shiwu weiyuanhui*) under the premier.[29]

• On the scope of political activities within the military there are also major disagreements. The Executive Yuan version regulates the political activities of the military, in principle, by stating "The ROC armed forces should operate beyond personal connections, local origins, or political party affiliation, and maintain administrative neutrality according to laws."[30] Versions proposed by other legislators present much more detailed rules that are intended to maintain a separation between political parties and the military by restricting military personnel from participating in party organs and political activities. In addition, some members of the Legislative Yuan proposed more interesting rules. For example, Lin Chuo-shui (DPP) suggested that military personnel should not be allowed to manage or invest in any mass media, and Edward Chen (New Party) even proposed language saying that active duty military personnel should not be allowed to initiate or participate in military coups.[31]

STRENGTHENING MILITARY CAPABILITIES: THE *JING SHI* PROGRAM

The Evolution of Defense Reorganization Programs.

The MND began streamlining military structures and manpower as early as 1985. From 1985 to 1990, according to the General Staff Office, all services had taken steps to streamline their organizations.[32] The real, meaningful defense reorganization effort began when Admiral Liu Ho-chien was appointed chief of the General Staff. Under his auspices, the *Zhong Yuan* (central field) Program was instituted. As originally conceived, the *Zhong Yuan* Program was intended to relocate and consolidate the various command headquarters of the armed forces in order to facilitate future defense and force reorganizations.[33] Later the *Zhong Yuan* Program was gradually expanded into a comprehensive military restructuring program.

In August 1993, the MND issued its ROC Military Ten-Year Force Target Program (*guojun shinian bingli mubiao guihua*)[34] to describe its plans to fundamentally reform the armed forces in three stages. In the first stage of this program, the MND sought to rationalize and consolidate the structure and manpower ratios of the three services. In the second stage, the MND aimed to adjust staff systems and cut back overlapping units. In the third stage, the MND hoped to consolidate the General Staff, the general headquarters of each service, and the military academies.[35] The overall objective of the reforms was to shift the Taiwan military from an offensive orientation to a defensive one. Chief of the General Staff Admiral Liu also announced that Taiwan should reduce its total military force to fewer than 400,000 men, or to 1.7 percent of the total population; and reduce the number of generals and admirals to 400, a 45-percent reduction from the 1993 level. Other reorganization moves anticipated under the *Zhong Yuan* Program were even more radical. They included the following adjustments:

• dissolving the general headquarters of the army, navy and air force and dividing Taiwan into several unified commands directly under the chief of the General Staff;[36]

• making the commanders in chief of the various services vice chiefs of the General Staff (VCGS);

• downgrading the head of the General Political Warfare Department to one of the deputy chiefs of the General Staff (DCGS);

• integrating the DCGS for planning (J-5) into the DCGS for operations (J-3); and,

• creating a new Operations Command directly under the chief of the General Staff.[37] (See Figures 4 and 5.)

Some top generals reportedly warned that Admiral Liu's plan was a form of "shock therapy." They argued that the military had played a key role in maintaining Taiwan's peace and stability and has been loyal to President Lee, and therefore the government should be very careful when implementing large-scale organizational reform. Due to the lack of consensus among top military leaders as well as among the services, Chief of the General Staff Liu later pared down his plan.[38] Some of the strongest voices against the *Zhong Yuan* Program came from army generals. The ROC Army, which traditionally has been the dominant

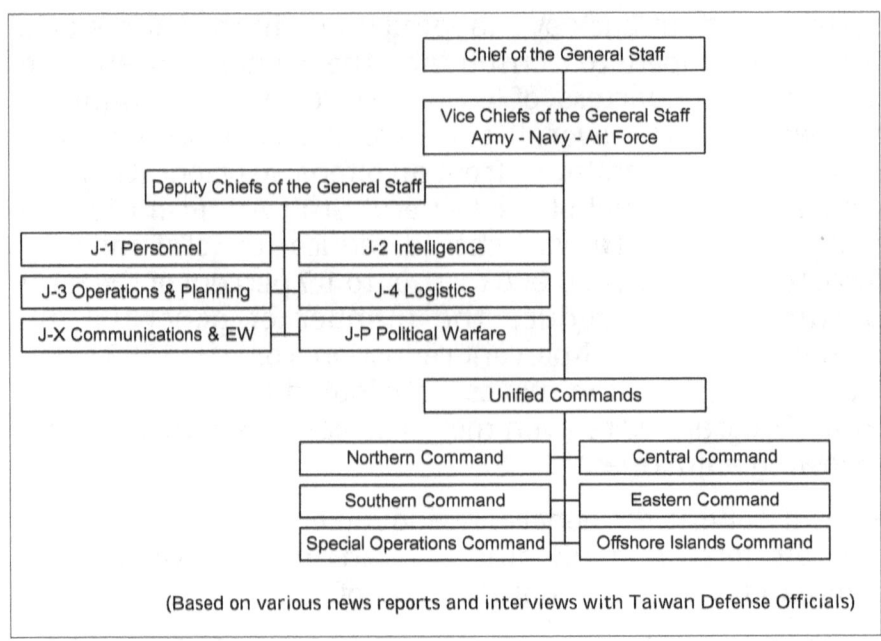

**Figure 4. The *Zhong Yuan* Program.
(Initial Concept)**

branch among the three services, worried that its share of the defense budget and its ability to shape military strategy would shrink substantially.[39] Officers in the political warfare system were likewise said to be worried about losing influence as a result of the reorganization program. Domestic political considerations also eroded the base of political support for the *Zhong Yuan* Program. President Lee, in his capacity as chairman of the KMT, was concerned about the possible loss of votes in several elections at that time, particularly those votes that could only be obtained by mobilizing the political warfare system. As a result, Admiral Liu's *Zhong Yuan* Program was put on hold. In mid-1995, General Lo Pen-li succeeded Admiral Liu as chief of the General Staff. General Lo and Defense Minister Chiang, both senior generals from the army, jointly modified the military reorganization plan and brought to an end the *Zhong Yuan* Program.

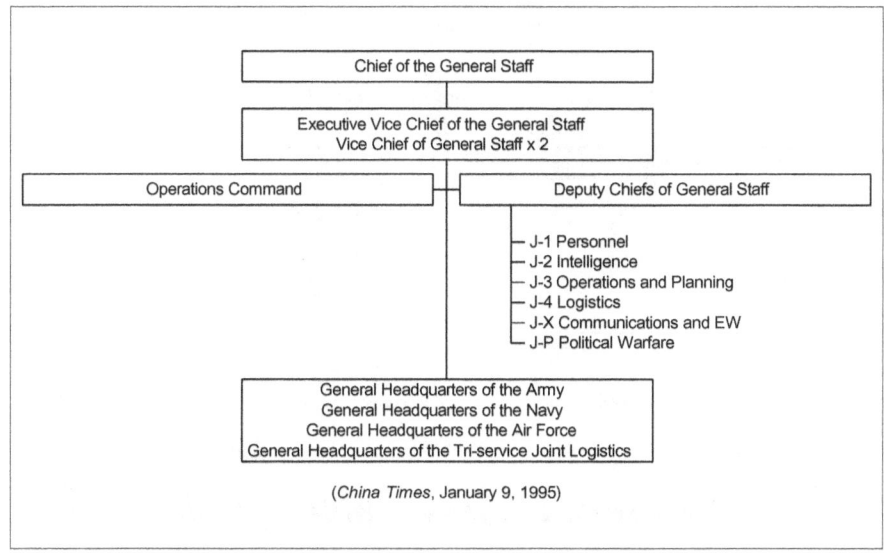

Figure 5. The *Zhong Yuan* Program. (Modified)

Under the leadership of Minister Chiang and General Lo, the Ten-Year Force Restructuring Guideline, issued in 1993, was changed to the ROC Military Organization and Force Restructuring Program (*guojun junshi zuzhi ji bingli tiaozheng guihua*), or in short, the Streamlining and Consolidation (*Jing Shi*) Program.[40] According to the Defense Ministry, the objective of the *Jing Shi* Program is to streamline the command (higher) levels and consolidate the field (lower) levels of the military structure. The *Jing Shi* Program is also designed to reduce manpower by raising the emphasis on firepower and mobility and creating a military force that is elite (*zhi jing*), small (*liang xiao*), and lethal (*zhanli qiang*).[41] (See Figure 6.)

Major Components of the *Jing Shi* Program.

Force Cuts. The *Jing Shi* Program was approved by President Lee in December 1996[42] and took effect in July 1997.[43] The target date for the completion is set for June 2001, 2 years earlier than the estimated completion date of the previous ROC Military Ten-Year Force Target

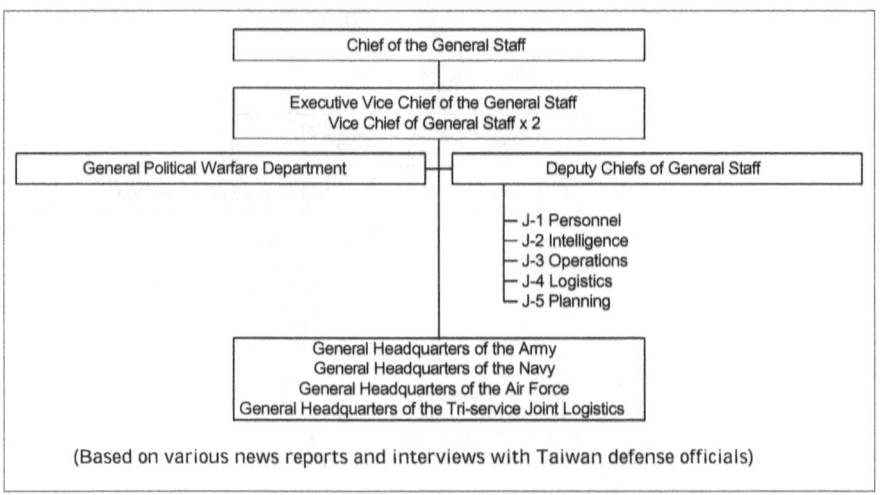

Figure 6. The *Jing Shi* Program.

Program.[44] Upon the completion of the *Jing Shi* Program, the Taiwan military's total manpower will be trimmed from 453,000 to 400,000, nearly a 10 percent cut. The army will remain the largest service in terms of manpower, with 200,000 men in total, while the navy and the air force each will have 56,000 men. The remaining personnel will be allocated among the Military Police Command, the Tri-Service Joint Logistics Command Headquarters and various reserve units. As for officers, the manpower cuts will be around 25 percent in the army, 20 percent in the navy, and 10 percent in the air force.[45] Mobilization capabilities will be dramatically improved, and it is expected that upon completion of the program, the Taiwan military will be able, in case of an emergency, to mobilize 290,000 men from the total reserve force in 1 day.[46]

General Staff Cut. Senior staffs have also been targeted for reduction. The manpower of the General Staff Office is to be cut by one-third of the 1997 level. A new Bureau of Communications, Electronic and Information Warfare (*tongxin dianzi zixun ju*) will be established by merging the Bureau of Communication and Electronics of the Ministry of National Defense (*tongxin dianzi ju*) and the Management Information Center under the J-5 of the

General Staff Office (*guanli zixun zhongxin*).⁴⁷ The Bureau of General Affairs (*zongwu ju*), the Bureau of Military History and Translation (*shizheng bianyi ju*), and the Office of the Chief of the General Staff (*canmou zongzhang bangongshi*) will be merged into a Bureau of Military Affairs (*junwu ju*). In the end, the present 25 departments under the five deputy chiefs of the General Staff will be reduced to 16 in number.⁴⁸

Major changes will take place in the General Political Warfare Department (*zong zhengzhi zuozhan bu*). In addition to downsizing its staff, the staff in charge of political indoctrination and civil-military relations (P-2), the military welfare staff (P-5), and the spokesman's office will be reportedly merged into a new division. However, personnel staff in the political warfare system (P-1), the anti-corruption staff (P-3), and the counter-intelligence and internal security staff (P-4) will remain largely unchanged.⁴⁹

Military Education Reform. Under the reorganization program, several military schools will be merged, and the total number of military schools will be reduced from 31 to 20.⁵⁰ In the army, the Transportation School, the Defense Management College, and the Sanitation School will be merged into the Army Logistics College (*lujun houqing xueyuan*). The navy's Navigation, Engineering, Communication and Electronics, and Ordinance Schools will be merged into the Navy Navigation Technology College (*haijun hanghai jishu xueyuan*). In the air force, the Mechanical and the Communication and Electronics Schools will be merged into the Air Force Aviation Technology College (*kongjun feixin jishu xueyuan*). The Defense Language School will become part of the Military Intelligence School. The Chungcheng Institute of Technology and the Defense Management College will merge to become the Defense Science and Technology University (*guofang keji daxue*).⁵¹

General Lo has also instructed his staff to study the possibility of cutting back the time allocated for political indoctrination in the military and to change the format for such indoctrination. At a military-wide meeting on the reform of military education held in October 1997, General Lo reportedly said that, while making everybody a revolutionary fighter through political indoctrination is a fine ideal, what the Taiwan military needs most is a professional capability in various fields. He emphatically pointed out that an emphasis on political rectitude over professional capability has been the major obstacle to modernizing the Taiwan military.

Military Training Reform. A new National Military Training Center (*guojia junshi xunlian zhongxin*) will be set up in southern Taiwan to provide joint warfare training for ROC military units, focusing on the battalion level. In the training center, a mock PLA unit at battalion level will also be set up as an aggressor. The mock PLA is expected to be equipped with PLA weapons systems and to apply PLA tactics.[52]

Important new offices, the Education, Training, and Doctrine Development Commands (ETDDC)(*jiaoyu xunlian ji zhunze fazhan silingbu*) are set up under the general headquarters of all three services. The Army ETDDC is derived from the old army Operations Development Committee (*lujun zuozhan fazhan weiyuanhui*).[53] The Navy ETDDC replaces the Fleet Training Command (*jiandui xunlian silingbu*).[54] The Air Force ETDDC is transformed from Eastern Air Force Command (*kongjun dongbu zhihuibu*).[55] These efforts indicate that, in addition to introducing new weapon systems in recent years, high-ranking officials in Taiwan's military are beginning to emphasize doctrine development and campaign research.

Some other changes will also be made in the different services, depending on each branch's unique needs. The army, for instance, has merged the G-3 responsible for operations with the G-5 in charge of planning and budgeting.[56] Also, the army will merge the Airborne Paratroop and Special Operations Command, which is commanded by a lieutenant general, with the Army Aviation Command, which is currently headed by an army major general, to form a new organization tentatively named the Army Airborne and Special Operations Command (*lujun hangkong tezhan silingbu*).[57] In the navy, the Marine Corps will be downsized from two divisions to two brigades and several battalions.[58] A new department in each service is being set up to handle communications and information by merging information centers with communication and electronics departments.[59]

Logistics Reform. The Tri-Service Joint Logistics General Headquarters will also undergo some changes. The General Headquarters will expand its function to centralize responsibility for the common goods and services used by all three services *(tongyong houqin)*, such as military uniforms and staple food. Service logistics department will be responsible for meeting service-unique logistical needs (*zhuanye houqin*).[60]

Structural Changes. The biggest structural changes are being made in the army. The army will gradually replace its division-level units with combined arms brigades (CABs) (*lianhe bingzhong lyu* or *lianbing lyu*) that have adequate manpower, better mobility, and ample firepower.[61] This change in the army's force structure is related to Taiwan's specific geographical circumstances. First, Taiwan is close to its principal threat and within easy range of the PLA's power projection. Secondly, Taiwan's terrain is not favorable to large-scale maneuver operations. The structural changes also indicate a defensive problem for Taiwan, insufficient defensive depth. With limited forces available and a coastline which runs 400 kilometers from north to south, it is necessary to restructure combat units and to improve mobility and power.[62]

The PLA is rapidly modernizing. In recent years, especially since the Gulf War in 1991, the PLA has been preparing itself to fight a high-technology war, as illustrated by a changing military doctrine, procurement of foreign weapon systems, and training and education.[63] Applying the high-technology doctrine to reunify Taiwan, the PLA reportedly has been asked "to operationalize a Taiwan invasion scenario in a way they have not done in the past."[64] The PLA's rapid modernization has pressured Taiwan to respond with equal speed.

Combined Arms Brigades. The ROC army is expected to regroup its forces into five types of brigades that will form a strike force. At this stage, the composition of only two types of its brigades has been revealed. The armored infantry brigade (*zhuangbu lyu*), composed of 4,300 troops, M-41 tanks, M-113 APCs, the M-48H main battletank, and M-109 artillery, is responsible for countering a PLA airborne paratroop invasion and for rapid response.[65] The airborne cavalry brigade (*kongqi lyu*), administered by the newly organized Army Airborne Special Operations Command, will be equipped with AH-1s, OH-58s, UH-1Hs and B-234s helicopters. It will have a total of 2,000 troops and be responsible for repulsing armored attacks, riot control, countering an airborne invasion, and serving as a strategic reserve unit.[66] It is expected that three airborne cavalry

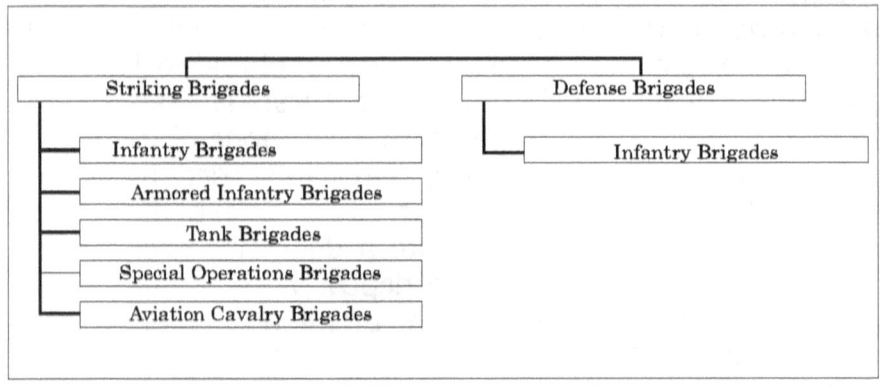

Figure 7. Combined Arms Brigade.

brigades will be located in the army's bases in northern, central, and southern Taiwan. The composition of the three other kinds of brigades, the motorized infantry brigade (*bubing lyu*), the special operations brigade (*tezhan lyu*), and the tank brigade (*zhuangjia lyu*) have not been revealed. (See Figure 7.)

The ROC Army has already set up the experimental formations (*shiyan bianzhuang*) for these five types of brigades. Public sources indicate that, as of late September 1997, the army had developed experimental formations at the battalion level for all five types of brigades. Experimentation at the brigade level will start in July 1998. By the year 2000, all five types of brigades should be operationalized.[67]

Taken together, these five types form the 12 main striking brigades (*dajilyu*), which will be backed up by 18 second-line defense brigades (*shoubeilyu*). The second-line brigades will be responsible for providing training to new conscripts and for educating mobilized reserve forces during peacetime. In case of war, the second-line brigades will be mobilized to perform combat duties.[68]

Problems and Debates.

Experiments and Uncertainties. Anyone who has interacted with high-level military officials in Taiwan in the past few years realizes that many leaders can neither describe nor predict the result of the *Jing Shi* Program. This lack of clarity has made the general public in Taiwan suspect that either the program is poorly defined or that it has not been clearly explained to the officer corps. The military restructuring program will fail if it is not based on a comprehensive assessment of future military threats and available defense resources. The MND claims to have conducted thorough studies about the force restructuring program. If that is so, the MND and senior military leaders owe the entire armed forces and the electorate a good explanation of the objectives and missions of the program.

Streamlining and Consolidation. According to the MND, the *Jing Shi* Program will streamline higher-level command structures and consolidate lower-level troop units, but how the program is to be implemented is unclear. At least three sets of hard questions should be asked. First, who decides which units are to be cut; does the MND have a convincing rationale behind those decisions; and will the reorganized military structure and operations chain of command meet the security challenges of the future? Second, does the military have concrete plans to recruit talented soldiers and noncommissioned officers to support its missions before carrying out the consolidation program at the troop level? How does the military consolidate its troops when conscript military service is fixed at a 2-year term in all three services? And, third, does the MND expect the armed forces to perform the same missions and workloads as before with the streamlined command structure and manpower? If not, what are the adjustments made so far and by what rationales and measures? If these questions can not be sufficiently answered, the *Jing Shi* Program runs the risk of "streamlining without consolidation."

Restructuring Logistics Support. Given Taiwan's unique geography, one of the reasons for the military restructuring program is to enable smaller tactical units to engage in independent operations. That is the reason that logistics support was moved from division level to brigade level. In addition to the emphasis on tri-service joint logistics (under the MND) and special logistics (under the service general headquarters) in the *Jing Shi* Program, a more realistic approach may be to establish regional depots for swift, forward logistics support. It has been rumored that an army attack helicopter, grounded in a remote area because of mechanical problems during a military training session, once had to wait a long time for the Army Aviation Command to send in a maintenance team to fix and fly it back to home base. It is said that the air force is experiencing similar maintenance problems with different types of fighter jets. Forward logistics support may resolve these problems.

Handling of Unneeded Weapons and Equipment. Presidential reviews of newly formed military units with brand new, advanced weapons are always media extravaganzas. Behind the scenes, however, phasing-out or decommissioning weapons and equipment afterwards is a major problem for the Taiwan military. The acquisition of new weapons systems and the streamlining of forces have accelerated the need to dispose of large quantities of old equipment. When the military reduces its force structures and establishes new units under the *Jing Shi* Program, often the old or unwanted equipment will be left behind. Commanders of new units will not know how to dispose of it. The army can keep small arms, such as rifles, in warehouses, in case of future mobilization, but the MND may have to spend more money than it saved from force streamlining just to dispose of unneeded tanks, armored amphibious vehicles, and heavy artillery pieces.

More Command Levels. The island of Taiwan is smaller than any of the PLA's military regions. As Defense Minister Chiang Chung-ling has argued, all of Taiwan should be seen as one integrated military operations zone. However, there are too many layers in the military chain of command for Taiwan's military to be an efficient fighting force. Under the new National Defense Law, the minister of national defense will be included in the national command structure, while the chief of the General Staff will continue to command joint military operations. Under the *Jing Shi* Program the divisions continue to be the command unit for several brigades during wartime. In structural terms, the *Jing Shi* Program increases the levels of command rather than reducing them. Thus, it remains to be seen how such a design will affect the combat effectiveness of Taiwan's military.

CHALLENGES AHEAD

As debate over the modernization of Taiwan's defense continues to unfold, defense officials and analysts in Taiwan should address the following issues.

Domestic Politics.

The Taiwan military has begun the process of transformation from a party-led army to a national army, and its support of democratization seems unquestionable. However, it remains to be seen how the military would react to the victory of an opposition candidate in a presidential election or what its position would be in case of a national referendum on Taiwan's independence. The formulation of the National Defense Law should be seen as the military's effort to place itself under civilian control and further de-politicize itself before the DPP comes to power. Regardless of the underlying motivations, the undeniable trend has been towards putting the military under civilian leadership. Consequently, the Taiwan military needs urgently to identify new allies and patrons from the civilian sector. Only by reaching out to the civilian elite can the military protect its institutional interests in the long run.

Cross-Strait Relations.

Since the Taiwan military considers the PLA its main threat, developments in relations between Taiwan and mainland China have a direct impact upon Taiwan's military strategy, missions, and equipment acquisitions. The Taiwan military is making every effort to prepare itself to cope with the military threat from the mainland, but it cannot rule out a possible relaxation in relations as dialogue between the two sides is expected to resume soon. The Taiwan military must consider what kind of impact an agreement to end the threat of hostilities between the two sides would have on Taiwan's foreign military procurement. It should also consider meeting and talking with the PLA, as cross-strait dialogue continues, in order to devise confidence-building measures.

National Defense Priority.

In Taiwan's *1998 National Defense Report*, the Ministry of National Defense defines "resolute defense" *(fangwei gushou)* and "effective deterrence" (*youxiao hezu*) as Taiwan's "strategic concept" (*zhanlue gouxiang*), which means the Taiwan military will try to build up a defense capable of deterring a PLA attack.[69] However, the means to this end remain the subject of many debates. The navy and the air force may believe that effective deterrence requires the ability to control the sea and air space between Taiwan and the Chinese mainland. The army tends to think that air superiority and sea denial cannot be sustained and therefore considers the ability to win a decisive ground battle on the western shores of Taiwan as the best deterrence.[70] It is interesting to note that in his first report to the Legislative Yuan, the Chief of the General Staff General Tang Fei gave specific emphasis on sea and air operations, and investment in command, control, communications, and intelligence (C^3I) and "software" integration, without even mentioning anti-amphibious operations. This raised some concerns from the army.[71] No matter what the result of that debate may be, how "effective deterrence" is conceived will define the priorities of defense operations, the direction of military investment, and the formation of force structure.

Joint Warfare Doctrine.

While the Taiwan military has long emphasized the importance of joint operations, the *Jing Shi* Program does not provide sufficient information on how the Taiwan military will advance its joint-warfare doctrines. A joint military doctrine will not necessarily be developed by putting the cadets of the army, navy, and air force academies under one roof. Even making the commanders in chief of the three services vice chiefs of the General Staff, as suggested in the *Zhong Yuan* Program, may not improve joint operations capability.[72] The military restructuring program now underway provides Taiwan's defense leaders an excellent opportunity to inject or incorporate the concept of joint-warfare into the program. If the Taiwan military misses this chance, enhancing the military's joint warfare capabilities will be even more difficult once the force restructuring is complete.

Revolution in Military Affairs.

In the *1998 National Defense Report*, estimates of the military capabilities of both the Taiwan military and the PLA were solely based on conventional warfare scenarios. Despite several years of intense discussion and debate over the concept of the revolution in military affairs (RMA) by major powers, Taiwan's military leaders seem reluctant to actively engage in related studies. Some officers even discount the concept of the RMA entirely, arguing that Taiwan is a democratic society and people hate any concept involving the word "revolution." Judging from available information, the directions of force restructuring in the *Jing Shi* Program are not designed to counter possible electronic and information warfare waged by the PLA.[73] The Taiwan military should actively examine the development of the new military thinking in the PLA when proceeding with its own defense modernization.

CONCLUSION

Looking through a telescope, the challenges to Taiwan's military modernization rest less on the acquisition of new hardware and more on such "software" issues as strategies, missions, doctrines, education, and training. The Taiwan military has spent the last decade making vast improvements in its arsenal, but the formation of the National Defense Law and the introduction of the defense reorganization program are only the first two steps in the beginning of Taiwan's effort to modernize its approaches to these "software" issues. The relative weight given to this latter effort will continue to be the focus of debate for interested people inside and outside of Taiwan's armed forces. If Taiwan's defense modernization objective is to build a better civilian-controlled, professional armed forces that is small, elite, joint, mobile, retaliation-capable, and alliance-ready, the painful process of redefinition and reorganization is at least as important as fulfilling the revolutionary goals of the Huangpu Military Academy.

Postscript.

This chapter was completed in September 1998. As indicated in the discussion, defense reform in Taiwan is an ongoing process, and several changes have been made. In a cabinet reshuffle in February 1999, General Tang Fei was appointed minister of national defense, a dramatic change of his role, if not position, in the reform of defense organization. The draft of National Defense Law was then withdrawn by Minister Tang to incorporate various views of legislators and defense specialists into the law. The new draft was approved by the Cabinet on August 26, 1999, and resubmitted to the Legislative Yuan. Among many important changes in the new draft, two stand out: (1) the concept of establishing a National Military Council was dropped, consolidating decision-making power in the National Security Council, and (2) the services general headquarters and armed forces will remain under the defense minister's command as proposed in the last draft. The role of the chief of General Staff is further clarified, and given operational command authority in both peacetime and war. Minister Tang has expressed his sincere hope that the Legislative Yuan will pass the new law soon enough to expedite the defense reform process. The authors are committed to watch these developments closely and continue vigorously their inquiry in the study of defense affairs.

ENDNOTES - CHAPTER 6

1. Robert Karniol, "Strong and Self-reliant," *Jane's Defense Weekly*, July 8, 1998, p. 23.

2. *Republic of China National Defense Report, 1998*, Chinese Edition, Taipei: Liming Publisher, March 1998, p. 111. The fiscal year in Taiwan is July 1 to June 30.

3. Ke Cheng-heng, "Examining the Budget Proposal for Fiscal Year 1999," *Wealth Magazine (Cai Xun Monthly)*, May 1998, pp. 134, 138.

4. See *China Times* (internet interactive edition), August 1, 1998, see http://www.chinatimes.com.tw/news/papers/ctimes/cpolitics 87080112.htm.

5. *Republic of China National Defense Report, 1998*, pp. 85-86.

6. Members of the Supreme National Defense Council included Standing Committee members of the KMT Central Committee, the presidents and vice presidents of the five (Executive, Legislative, Judiciary, Examination, and Control) Yuans, and members of the Military Council (*junshi weiyuanhui*). Please see Wego Chiang, *Introduction to National Defense Institutions (guofang tizhi gailun)*, Taipei: Central Publication Service, 1981, pp. 131, 168. Quoted from Tien Yue, "Study on Defense Strategy," *Chinese Strategy Quarterly* (*zhonghua zhanlue xuebao*), Taipei: Society of Strategic Studies, Spring 1998, p. 15.

7. *Ibid.*

8. *Republic of China National Defense Report, 1998*, p. 139.

9. See *China Times* (internet interactive edition), June 1, 1998, see http://www.chiantimes.com.tw/news/papers/ctimes/cpolitics/87060 107.htm.

10. *United Daily*, December 31, 1997. See also *Republic of China National Defense Report, 1998*, pp. 140-141.

11. *Liberty Times*, May 18, 1998.

12. *Central Daily*, May 22, 1998.

13. A member of the National Defense Committee of the Legislative Yuan provided the draft of National Defense Law. The Chapters of the Law are:

Chapter I: General Provisions

Chapter II: Authorities, Responsibilities, and Mechanism of National Defense

Chapter III: Authorities, Responsibilities, and Organization of the MND

Chapter IV: Rights and Obligations of Military Personnel

Chapter V: National Defense Preparedness

Chapter VI: Protection of National Defense Secrecy

Chapter VII: Supplemental Provisions

14. *China Times*, January 4, 1998.

15. *Ibid.*

16. Interpretation of the Council of the Grand Jutices – Number 461, issued on July 24 ,1998. See *China Times* (internet interactive edition), July 24, 1998, see *http://www.chiantimes.com.tw/news/papers/express/xfocus/87072403.htm*.

17. *Ibid.*

18. *China Times*, October 1, 1998, p. 4. In the National Defense Committee session, General Tang issued a report on "The Progress and Review of Military Modernization" (*guojun xiandaihua zhi cejin yu jiantao*) and answered questions from the committee members. The session was opened to the press.

19. "The Legislative Yuan should not pass the unconstitutional National Defense Law," *United Daily* editorial, January 9, 1998.

20. *Youth Daily*, January 14, 1998.

21. See Article 11 of the draft of the National Defense Law.

22. *Youth Daily*, January 14, 1998.

23. *Ibid.*

24. De-yun Lu, "Who's the Boss? Defense Minister or the Premier?" *United Daily*, May 22, 1998.

25. *Youth Daily*, June 10, 1998.

26. *Ibid.*

27. *China Times*, October 1, 1998, p. 4.

28. The six versions have been proposed by Ting Shou-chung (KMT), Chen Shui-pian (DPP), Chu Feng-chi (KMT), Lin Chou-shui (DPP), Edward Chen (CNP), and Chai Ming-hsian (DPP). See *China Times*, June 1, 1998, *http://www.chinatimes.com.tw/news/papers/ctimes/cpolitics/87060108.htm*.

29. Information provided by members of Legislative Yuan.

30. A member of the National Defense Committee of the Legislative Yuan provided the drafts of National Defense Law.

31. Information provided by members of Legislative Yuan.

32. The army cut the numbers of its light divisions, infantry divisions; the navy cut its amphibious warfare training center, landing craft command, 1st Marine Division, logistics command; the air force cut its training command, corps of engineers, and anti-air artillery group. See *Capital Morning News*, August 10, 1990.

33. *United Daily*, November 9, 1992.

34. The program was also called the "Ten-year Force Restructuring Guideline" (*shinian bingli zhengjian gangyao*).

35. *Independent Morning News*, November 4, 1993.

36. Author's interview with Taiwan military officials.

37. *China Times*, January 9, 1995.

38. *Ibid.*, January 3, 1995.

39. *Ibid.*, May 25, 1997.

40. *Republic of China National Defense Report, 1998*, p. 145. See also *Youth Daily*, December 26, 1996.

41. *Republic of China National Defense Report, 1998*, pp. 146, 148.

42. *China Times*, December 25, 1996.

43. *Republic of China National Defense Report, 1998*, p. 149.

44. The old 10-year plan was expected to be carried out from 1993-2003. See *Youth Daily*, June 21, 1996.

45. *United Daily,* March 28, 1997; and *China Times,* April 23, 1997.

46. *Central Daily,* June 9, 1997.

47. *Ibid.,* June 3, 1998.

48. *United Daily,* March 29, 1997; and *China Times,* December 25, 1996.

49. *Ibid.* Based on a interview with officials from the General Political Warfare Department in June 1998. However, nobody in the department really knows what the final result of this reorganization will be.

50. *Republic of China National Defense Report, 1998,* p. 166.

51. *Independent Morning News,* October 12, 1997.

52. *China Times,* June 29, 1997.

53. *Liberty Times,* June 17, 1998.

54. *Central Daily,* June 10, 1998.

55. *Liberty Times,* May 11, 1998.

56. *China Times,* April 27, 1997.

57. *Independent Morning News,* October 12, 1997.

58. *Liberty Times,* April 23, 1997.

59. *United Daily,* March 28, 1997.

60. *Central Daily,* March 6 and June 9, 1997.

61. Although the army division will be preserved in the army's command structure, it is no longer an integrated tactical command unit. The streamlined army division will not be given combat and logistics support duties. Its missions are confined to tactical command, with limited staff members and supporting troops. During wartime, each division will command one to three defense combined arms brigades and two to three striking combined arms brigades.

62. *Independent Morning News,* November 1 and November 2, 1997.

63. For the development trend, please see David Shambaugh and Richard Yang, eds., *China's Military in Transition*, Oxford: Clarendon Press, 1997; and Viacheslov A. Frolov, "China's Armed Forces Prepare for High-tech Warfare," *Defense and Foreign Affairs Strategic Policy*, January 1998, pp. 7-8.

64. Barton Gellman, "Reappraisal Led to New China Policy," *The Washington Post*, June 22, 1998, p. A16.

65. *Independent Morning News*, November 2, 1997.

66. *Central Daily*, October 31, 1997.

67. *Ibid.*, October 15, 1997.

68. *Independent Morning News*, November 1, 1997.

69. *Republic of China National Defense Report, 1998*, p. 52.

70. In fact, the MND once argued that the money saved by cutting back an entire army division could purchase only two F-16 fighter aircraft, strongly implying that it is more cost effective to buy divisions than to buy jets. See *United Daily*, October 16, 1990.

71. *China Times*, October 1, 1998, p. 4.

72. Informed resources revealed that the Taiwan military has begun stressing jointness in the areas of command, control, communication and intelligence, however, there is no publicly available information on these efforts.

73. In addition to the establishment of the Bureau of Communications, Electronic and Information Warfare in the General Staff Office, the air force will form an Electronic Warfare Group (*dianzhan dadui*) composed by a fleet of C-130HEs. (See *Central Daily*, June 10, 1998.) These efforts are examples of Taiwan's efforts in emphasizing electronic and information warfare capabilities. However, they cannot be interpreted as true awareness of the important role of the RMA in future warfare by the general officers corps in Taiwan military.

CHAPTER 7
TAIWAN'S MILITARY: A VIEW FROM AFAR

June Teufel Dreyer[1]

Introduction.

The Republic of China on Taiwan (ROC) has sought to cope with military and diplomatic pressures for unification from the People's Republic of China (PRC) by revamping a military that was made up of a disproportionate number of ground-force personnel into a smaller, better-coordinated force which emphasizes air and sea operations and by embarking on a naval modernization which aims at keeping the sea lanes surrounding Taiwan open, supplying the offshore islands under ROC administration, enhancing counter-blockade activities, and, in general, preventing the People's Liberation Army Navy (PLAN) from gaining sea control. At the same time, Taipei is enhancing the air force's ability to provide early warning of attack; to conduct all-weather air combat control; to assist the navy in counter-blockade endeavors, and, in general, to deny the People's Liberation Army Air Force (PLAAF) air superiority in the area surrounding Taiwan, while continuing modernization of ground-force equipment and improving missile and anti-missile systems.

Although significant advances have been made, a number of problems remain. These include difficulties in attracting a sufficient number of high-quality people into the military and retaining them; a series of accidents that have cast doubt on military safety procedures; and procurement scandals that dilute public support for defense budgets. Taipei also has weaknesses in equipment and difficulty remedying them due to the PRC's ability to dissuade third countries from selling military equipment and technology to the ROC. There are problems in coordination among the services and problems of conformity with weapons bought from several sources. Vulnerability to missile attacks on Taiwan from the mainland is a concern, requiring the creation of a consensus within the ROC on how best to defend itself against an attack.

The ROC government has also established channels for communication with Beijing, attempted to strengthen its ties with third countries, and sought solutions to coping with psychological pressures from the mainland. Its continuing ability to counteract these pressures from Beijing will be a major challenge for the Taipei government in the coming decade.

Background.

Relations across the Taiwan Strait in the 1990s showed tendencies toward both conciliation and confrontation. On the conciliation side, Taipei in 1991 established an "unofficial" organization, the Strait Exchange Foundation (SEF), which would hold talks with a mainland "unofficial" organization on the resolution of outstanding issues. A few months later, Beijing set up a counterpart organization, the Association for Relations Across the Taiwan Strait (ARATS). A well-publicized series of discussions between the SEF and the ARATS took place in Singapore in 1993; a second round of talks was scheduled for 1995. The volume of trade between the mainland and Taiwan has increased each year. ROC businesses also invested heavily on the mainland; by the end of 1997, these investments were estimated to have exceeded $30 billion.[2] A number of potentially inflammatory issues, such as the repatriation of illegal immigrants; crimes committed against Taiwan businesspeople and tourists; and the falling of a ROC artillery shell on a mainland coastal village, were settled with minimal rancor.

At the same time, however, each side watched the other with great wariness. Lee Teng-hui, a Taiwanese, had succeeded to the ROC presidency in 1988 and had accelerated the process of democratization begun by his predecessor, Chiang Ching-kuo. This simultaneously enhanced the power of the Taiwanese, very few of whom were in favor of unification with the mainland. In 1991, the ROC formally disavowed its claim to sovereignty over the mainland. Since it did not simultaneously endorse Beijing's right to sovereignty over Taiwan, this could be construed as a tacit move toward independence.

In response to the mainland's effort to reduce the number of countries that granted official diplomatic recognition to Taiwan and to push it out of international organizations, Lee actively sought to expand his country's global presence. Where pressure from Beijing made official relations impossible, Taipei devised various sorts of unofficial arrangements. One of these was "vacation diplomacy." For instance, Lee and other high-ranking officials, while on "private visits" to a country, would schedule a golf date with their opposite numbers. It may be assumed that more than golf was discussed. A Taipei official might also express a desire to see a famous museum abroad and dine with the country's dignitaries. The ROC's interest in financing worthy developmental projects could be raised at this time. The government, goaded by its political opposition, also applied for membership in the United Nations, despite feeling that the chances for success were slim. Beijing interpreted Lee's actions to mean that he was moving the island toward independence.

Meanwhile, the Beijing leadership was smarting from the international criticism it had received as a result of its brutal suppression of dissidents in Tiananmen Square and elsewhere in China in 1989. Always sensitive to matters touching on sovereignty, it became hypersensitive after the Tiananmen incident and increasingly nationalistic. In February 1992, the National People's Congress passed a law unilaterally declaring the PRC's sovereignty over all disputed areas, including Taiwan, and asserted the right to adopt all measures, including force, to back up its claims.

Denied U.S. military weapons as part of sanctions levied against it as a result of the Tiananmen incident, Beijing sought purchases from Russia. Facing serious financial difficulties, Russia, the inheritor of much of the arsenal of the recently disintegrated Union of Soviet Socialist Republics (USSR), was happy to sell. In August 1992, Washington announced that it would sell 150 F-16 fighter planes to Taiwan. Domestic factors were operative in the United States as well. With the Cold War ended, the U.S. defense industry was in recession, and aerospace industries were important voting blocs in Texas and California, considered crucial to incumbent President George Bush's hopes for re-election. In what may have been an *ex-post facto* rationalization,[3] the administration claimed that it had warned Beijing prior to the Chinese purchase of Su-27s that the sale would activate the provisions of the Taiwan Relations Act of 1979 to keep a balance in the Taiwan Strait. In any case, shortly after the F-16 sale was announced, France agreed to sell 60 *Mirage* 2000-5 planes and six *Lafayette*-class frigates to the ROC, causing Chinese leaders to worry that other countries might follow suit.

In Beijing, policy toward Taiwan continued to harden. Decisions relating to Taiwan after 1989 were believed to have been made by Deng Xiaoping and Yang Shangkun, the latter being head of the Taiwan Affairs Leading Small Group (TALSG) as well as president of China and secretary-general of the party and state central military commissions. At the Communist Party's 14th Party Congress held in autumn 1992, Yang was forced to resign due to factors relating to the struggle for succession to Deng Xiaoping. Some months before the congress, Yang began to be accused by rivals of planning to derail Deng's plans to have Jiang Zemin succeed him. Yang apparently lost Deng's confidence and resigned from all of his formal positions, allegedly because of his advanced age. Jiang Zemin became head of the TALSG. Shortly thereafter, Deng Xiaoping's health began to fail, and he withdrew from active participation. Military leaders who had been opposed to Yang asserted stronger opinions on Taiwan policy.[4]

In 1993, the same year that the SEF-ARATS talks began, the mainland's weapons procurement from the former USSR began to be directed to the Nanjing Military Region, opposite the ROC, and military training activities in and near the Taiwan Strait increased. This pattern has persisted, indicating that the ROC had become the focus of PRC military preparations.[5] In 1993 as well, the PLA adopted a new strategic doctrine: "local war under high-technology conditions." This was an update of a strategy of focusing on local, limited wars on China's periphery that had been adopted in 1985,[6] an update prompted by observation of high-technology weapons and accompanying tactics used by the United States during the Gulf War. However, it had obvious relevance with regard to possible PLA actions toward Taiwan.

In 1995, after Lee Teng-hui made a highly publicized trip to the United States, the PRC responded in July 1995 and March 1996 with a series of missile tests and training exercises in and near the Taiwan Strait. Official sources in Washington said that the number of troops and weapons involved in the PLA's exercises would have been inadequate for an invasion and that therefore no invasion had been intended. Instead, this was pressure by Beijing intended to moderate Taiwan's search for "international space." A more recent American statement, however, has said that China and the United States were closer to the brink of war at this time than they had been in 2 decades.[7] In any case, Washington dispatched two aircraft carrier battle groups to the area. China's military actions had forced the United States out of its preferred strategy of strategic ambiguity to one that a ranking American defense department official has described as "strategic clarity but tactical ambiguity." Washington, however, quietly warned Taipei that it had not given the island an unconditional guarantee of support and that it would be best for all concerned if the ROC government refrained from provocative actions in the future.

There is also ambiguity about what constitutes provocative actions. It is not normally considered provocative for a head of state—or even a province thereof—to visit another country. Almost any action that Taipei takes to counter the slow strangulation of its international persona, however, could be construed by Beijing as provocative.

Generally speaking, foreign military analysts were not impressed with the quality of the maneuvers they observed in the 1995-96 exercises. One of the missiles may have gone awry; a warship collided with a commercial ship leaving the harbor at the same time; some troops died of exposure on the beaches; and the air force's Su-27s made only a token appearance. The PLA had a difficult time carrying out exercises under stormy conditions, which are very common in the Taiwan Strait, and the exercises were halted early due to the weather. PLA senior leaders admitted these shortcomings, but added that, nonetheless, they had learned important lessons about the command and control of joint forces.

Recent Developments.

Exercises are, of course, designed to discover weaknesses so that they can be remedied. In recent years the PLA has been working in a number of areas with relevance to a Taiwan scenario. These include efforts in the following areas.

• Improving the range and guidance systems of its short-to-medium-range missiles.

• Acquiring additional Su-27 fighter planes. Already 50 planes have been received; a licensing agreement allows the PRC to co-produce 200 additional planes in China.[8]

• Acquiring four *Kilo*-class diesel-electric submarines, which are much quieter and therefore harder to detect than the PRC's older models. The *Kilos* are equipped with advanced sonar equipment, copies of which will be placed on the PRC's *Song*-class boats. In June 1998, Russia agreed to build ten submarines for the Chinese navy.[9]

- Purchasing two *Sovremenny*-class guided missile destroyers, equipped with sophisticated Sunburn anti-ship missile capabilities. According to a former naval attaché to Beijing, these represent technology an order of magnitude beyond those of Taiwan.[10]

- Adding approximately 20 principal surface combatants, including *Luhu*-class guided missile destroyers and *Jiangwei*-class guided missile frigates, to its naval forces.

- Announcing plans to expand the number of rapid reaction units (RRUs), highly-trained and mobile troops which would be important to an invasion of Taiwan.[11]

- Increasing attention to weapons, technical support, and logistics for the PLA. In spring 1998, at the same time as a massive downsizing and restructuring of the Chinese government (including the PLA) was announced, a Central Military Commission directive established a new department, the General Armaments Department (GAD) of the PLA. The GAD will oversee the military's weaponry and, reportedly, some of its logistics functions.[12]

- Increasing its satellite reconnaissance capabilities against the ROC. A Chinese source claimed that, although Taiwan's *Lafayette*-class frigates have good stealth capabilities when viewed from a horizontal position, they are fully exposed to the PRC's radar reconnaissance satellites from above.[13]

- Establishing offshore satellite stations, the latest of which to become public is in the South Pacific state of Kiribati. Although supposedly for civilian use, other sources have claimed that the station will allow the PLA to "know the exact location of U.S. aircraft carriers . . . as well as

Taiwanese [sic] destroyers and frigates . . . neither the U.S. nor the Taiwan naval forces could defend themselves."[14]

• Evincing intense interest in the revolution in military affairs (RMA). Though there is much discussion of the RMA and its implications in mainland military publications, the focus of attention—and progress—seems to be in the area of information warfare. Discussions seem optimistic that the PLA will be able to successfully render inoperative the command and control operations of a technologically superior enemy through such methods as inserting computer viruses.[15]

• Instituting a training class for top PLA officers on technology and its applications in modern warfare, with the expectation that the lessons learned will be incorporated into comprehensive military drills.[16]

• Exhibiting enhanced interest in psychological warfare and unconventional operations, including infiltration of troops for surprise attacks and/or ambushes.[17]

• Increasing discussions of the ROC's military holdings in official and semi-official sources, always denigrating the ROC's capabilities. For example, a Hong Kong magazine known to have close ties with the PLA noted that the island's military helicopter transport capability was weak and that its fleet of UH-1Hs had reached the end of its service life. In any case, the article continued, Taiwan's narrow eastern and western plains were both within range of the PLA's superior naval fire capabilities.[18]

Within the ROC, there is ongoing concern over the implications of this buildup. Key questions involve, first, what form an invasion, if it comes, is likely to take. A second, and related, question is what countermeasures should be taken to deal with the invasion. With regard to the first question, the ROC's Ministry of National Defense anticipates that an invasion would take one of four forms:

• a partial naval and air blockade of Taiwan's offshore islands or certain other areas;

• a comprehensive naval and air blockade of the waters and air space around Taiwan proper and its offshore islands;

• an attack on the offshore islands designed to force Taipei to negotiate; or

• a direct, coordinated amphibious, air, and airborne assault on the island of Taiwan that bypassed the offshore islands.[19]

While none of these would be welcome developments, it is generally believed that the second and fourth scenarios are not within the PLA's current capabilities. A failure in either of these two all-out attack scenarios would be viewed as an international humiliation for the PRC and its military. Political forces within Taiwan that favor a formal declaration of independence would be reinforced, and such a declaration might actually be made. It might well be backed by an international wave of sympathy for the victim-state.

Although the first and third scenarios could be attempted, and would have adverse consequences for the island in terms of lost trade, skittish stock markets, and public anxiety levels, their chances of success are marginal. A partial blockade could be circumvented: ROC sources many years ago announced plans to convoy ships into Taiwan ports on the east coast, where the PLA's ability to enforce a blockade would be weaker. A blockade is a protracted affair, and the areas around Taiwan are important waterways used by the commercial shipping of dozens of states. Since these countries' economic interests would be jeopardized, international pressure would be brought to bear on the PRC.

Seizing the offshore islands would be costly for the PLA, both in terms of equipment costs and human casualties. Occupying them cannot be assumed to force the Taipei government to the bargaining table. It could stiffen resolve *not* to negotiate, with the argument being advanced that this would be tantamount to appeasing aggressors. Other countries with territorial disputes with the PRC—and there is a long list, including Japan, Vietnam, the Philippines, and Malaysia—might be induced to stiffen their resolve or even discuss collective defense so as not to suffer similar treatment.

Indeed, apprehension over the implications of China's behavior toward Taiwan in 1995-96 was a major factor in Japan's willingness to enter into a stronger security relationship with the United States in April 1996 and to agree to provide help to the United States in case of a crisis in the Taiwan Strait. Beijing protested strongly and repeatedly after a Japanese cabinet minister seemingly offhandedly mentioned that contingencies involving Taiwan would be included in the Acquisitions and Cross-Servicing Agreement with the United States. The Japanese government responded that the area involved was situational, not geographic. Beijing demanded that the area be specified and that Taiwan not be included. Tokyo has not complied.[20]

For the moment, then, barring some unlikely occurrence, the PLA's military strategy must be to build up its strength sufficiently to be able to dominate Taiwan psychologically; to increase its capacity so that it can successfully carry out an invasion of Taiwan; or to make the island's successful defense against an invasion so unlikely that the Taipei government would be willing to concede. Chinese pronouncements assume that time is on their side, and certain Western analysts appear to agree.[21] Caveats to this prognosis are rare to nonexistent. Among the factors often ignored are:

• the dichotomy between China's announced plans to build a weapon or weapons system and its ability to serially produce the item or items, deploy them, and effectively use them. While it is possible that the PRC will master the integration of new levels of technology into its military, it is also possible that the mainland will continue to make halting and irregular progress, as it has in the past.[22]

• the effects, as yet unknown, of the Asian currency crisis on each side of the Taiwan Strait and the implications for defense readiness,

• the effect on the PRC's stability of growing forces such as democratization, population shifts, and, in the case of some ethnic minorities, separatism. For example, an exiled Uygur leader has threatened that, if the mainland were to invade Taiwan, there would be a mass uprising in the northwest province of Xinjiang in order to take advantage of the PLA's preoccupation with activities on the southeast coast,[23]

• the fact that, although Taiwan's only international antagonist is China, the PRC has many other potential enemies, one of whom—India—has justified its nuclear tests in terms of its being slighted by the international community in favor of China, and

• improvements in the ROC military.

The ROC's Response.

While the PLA has been making the above-mentioned improvements to enhance its capabilities against Taiwan, the ROC military has been modernizing as well. Its efforts have included a wide range of measures designed to make its military an effective counter to the mainland. The ROC military is addressing the mismatch between a military culture that derives from its past position as a continental force and the ROC's present strategic circumstances. This involves revamping a military that contained a disproportionate number of ground-force personnel and equipment into a smaller, better coordinated force that emphasizes air and sea operations. Specific measures taken by Taiwan include the following.

• In 1998, the ROC's Ministry of Defense announced that the country's military would be reduced in size from 450,000 to 400,000 by the end of June 2001. Most of the cuts will be from the ground forces.[24]

- Proportionally, the higher levels of command will bear the brunt of cuts: the number of generals is to be reduced by one-fourth and that of other officers by 11 to 20 percent.[25] A total of 1,700 higher-ranked personnel slots are being eliminated. The aim is to trim forces by 17 percent while raising combat capability by 13 percent.[26]

- A Warfare Headquarters has been established to monitor potential threats and the readiness levels of military units.

- A general restructuring is taking place which includes streamlining the chain of command and consolidation of basic structures.[27] The general staff has been reorganized, with the number of vice chiefs of staff being reduced from four to three. The Military Affairs Bureau has absorbed the General Staff Office, the General Affairs Bureau, and the History and Political Translation Bureau, to create unified management over organizations of a similar nature.[28]

- The services are being restructured into joint branch brigades, to include helicopter, tank, and motorized infantry assets, which can be mobilized immediately in response to a threat.[29]

Taiwan's military has also embarked on a naval modernization aimed at keeping the sea lanes surrounding Taiwan open, supplying the ROC's offshore islands, enhancing counter-blockade capabilities, and, in general, neutralizing the PLAN's efforts at sea control.

- The navy has taken delivery of six *Lafayette*-class frigates from France. The ships, designated the *Kang Ting*-class, have a 3,500-ton displacement and a 25-knot top speed; their outer hulls are coated with a special composite material to reduce radar detection. These frigates are being fitted with Phalanx air-defense systems; Sea Chaparral surface-to-air missiles; *Hsiung Feng* anti-ship missiles; and an anti-submarine warfare helicopter.

- Nine Knox (*Chih Yang*[30])-class frigates have been leased from the United States with options to purchase or lease additional ships. These displace 3,000 tons, have a speed of 27 knots, and are equipped with MK 15 Phalanx 20-millimeter guns and AN/SWG-1A Harpoon anti-ship missile launchers and decoy launching systems.[31] The sonar systems of these frigates provide the ROC navy with its most effective anti-submarine warfare capability. Since the *Chih Yang* frigates are not equipped with surface-to-air missiles, the Phalanxes serve as the sole air defense and cruise missile defense for the ships.[32]

• Seven Perry-class frigates have been produced in Taiwan with the help of technology acquired from the United States. Known as the *Cheng Kung*-class, these will also have anti-submarine warfare as their primary function.

• S-70 C anti-submarine helicopters acquired from the United States were equipped with low-frequency sonar to detect submarine activity in the waters near Taiwan.

• Taiwan has begun producing *Chin Chiang* coastal patrol boats. These will displace 500 tons and have a 25-knot speed. Their American-made fire control systems include laser distance measuring equipment and infra-red thermal imaging facility. The boats are also equipped with Danish-made radars. Eleven patrol boats are projected to enter the inventory, each to be armed with 20 mm. and 40 mm. guns and four *Hsiung-Feng* I anti-ship missiles.[33]

• The ROC will build four Aegis-class guided missile destroyers. Each of the Aegis-class vessels is expected to cost $NT 150 B, or US$ 4.4 billion, at current exchange rates of 34 NT to the U.S. dollar. The U.S. Arleigh Burke-class destroyer, which would presumably serve as the model for the ROC version, displaces 6,000 tons and is equipped with the advanced MK 41 vertical-launching mobile missile-launching station as well as intelligence and information-gathering systems.[34] Aegis-class ships are used in the United States military to vector attacks on enemy planes some distance from aircraft carriers, leading to the conclusion that the ROC military intends to intercept PLA aircraft earlier.[35]

Although it would seem logical to conclude that the ROC wanted Aegis-class destroyers to counter the *Sovremenny*-class destroyers being acquired by the PRC, Taiwan sources interepret PLAN's acquisition of *Sovremenny*-class destroyers as aimed primarily at deterring future U.S. deployments of carrier battle groups rather than at attacking ROC warships. They see the ROC navy's procurement of Aegis-class ships not in terms of countering the *Sovremennys*, but rather in the role of highly capable combat systems which can be used as air-and-surface command and control centers, as they were in the Gulf War. The Aegis ships could be modified to provide limited theater missile defense (TMD) capabilities as well.[34] The ROC has also announced the *Kwang Hua* Six project to construct a fleet of 30 150-200-ton fast-attack missile boats for use against enemy ships. The ships' surfaces are to be capable of absorbing or deflecting radar.[36] The first vessel will probably be built in a foreign country, with the remainder to be constructed in the ROC, as was the case with the Perry/*Cheng Kung*-class ships.

The ROC will improve its air capabilities as well. Plans call for enhancing the air force's ability for early warning of attack, its conduct of all-weather air combat patrol, assisting the navy in counter-blockade endeavors, and, in general, preventing the PLAAF from gaining air superiority in the area surrounding Taiwan. Specific programs include:

• producing up to 130 of the Indigenous Defense Fighter (IDF or *Ching-kuo*). One wing, comprising 70 planes, was commissioned in April 1997. The first squadron, 18 IDFs, of the second wing, was deployed in February 1998, and the wing as a whole, 60 planes, is to be commissioned in 1999.[37] The military-owned Chung Shan Institute for Science and Technology (CSIST) is currently working on a third-generation fighter with greater combat range and additional functions.[38]

• acquiring a total of 150 F-16s, of which 80 have been delivered and 60 commissioned. In June 1998, the United States sold 28 Pathfinder and Sharpshooter pods to the ROC to improve the F-16s capabilities for low-altitude and night flights, as well as the accuracy of the planes' weapons systems.[39]

• acquiring a total of 60 *Mirage* 2000-5 fighter planes, with delivery completed by the end of 1998. The *Mirages* are equipped with *Mica* intermediate-range air-to-air missiles, of which 960 have been purchased. The *Mica* has the ability to target and hit enemy planes beyond visual range, the so-called "fire and forget" capacity which is expected to be useful against the mainland's Su-27s.[40] Also acquired for the *Mirage* were 480 *Magic II* short-range air-to-air missiles, for a total purchase price, including auxiliary fuel tanks, ground maintenance support vehicles, tools, and monitoring equipment, of NT$167.6 billion (US$4.9).[41]

• purchasing four E-2 surveillance planes, the object being to keep one in the air all the time for air and surface surveillance of the mainland.

• procuring locally-developed remote control reconnaissance aircraft to boost information-gathering equipment. This unmanned aerial vehicle (UAV), developed by CSIST, has a combat radius of 50 kilometers and can fly from 6 to 8 hours. It is expected to bolster coastal defense work.[42]

The ROC's ground forces are also undergoing a modernization program to improve equipment. In June 1998, just prior to U.S. President William Clinton's visit to the mainland, the ROC took delivery of ten M-60-A-3 tanks and M-109 self-propelled 155 millimeter artillery.[43]

The RMA is transforming the ROC armed forces. On July 1, 1998, Taiwan established an electronic warfare unit in response to military maneuvers on the mainland in spring 1998 in which the PLA practiced introducing computer viruses into an opponent's command and control systems. Taiwan intends the unit to jam military communications and missile-firing signals. In addition, Taiwan has taken the following steps.

- The air force remodeled one of its two C-130H transport aircraft as an electronic warfare aircraft, renaming it *Tien Kan* ("Sky Interference") and fitted it with jamming equipment designed by CSIST. It hopes to acquire another C-130H for conversion at a later date.[44]

- The four Grumman E-2T Hawkeye early warning planes to be purchased are being more closely linked to military information networks.

- Ten F-16s are to be converted into reconnaissance aircraft.

- RF-104 Starfighter reconnaissance planes are to be replaced by more capable RF-5Es.[45]

- The United States is strengthening military software exchanges with Taiwan, including data link systems to facilitate communications among the ROC's F-16s, E-2T early warning/command aircraft, and its warships.[46]

The overwhelming missile advantage on the PRC's side is being addressed by making the following improvements in missile and anti-missile systems.

- Sky Bow IIs, based on the U.S. Patriot missile used in Israel and Saudi Arabia against Iraqi missiles but built by CSIST, are replacing the island's aging Nike Hercules missiles.[47]

- An improved *Hsiung Feng II* anti-ship missile has been developed that is similar to the U.S. Harpoon air-to-ship missile, though said to be slightly superior in reliability and range. It uses shipboard or airborne radars to acquire targets, the Global Positioning System for initial guidance, and then turns to radar guidance, radar homing infra-red, or image infra-red guidance in the final stage before reaching its target.[48]

- CSIST is developing an anti-tactical ballistic missile (ATBM) system, adapted from an improved version of the *Tien Kung II* air defense radar system. It is estimated that the new radar system will take 3 to 4 years to develop and that several radar systems will be constructed at a cost of just under U.S. $87 million each.[49]

- Three Patriot II anti-missile batteries have been purchased from the United States and installed near major population centers in the northern part of Taiwan.[50]

- A supersonic ship-to-ship missile, the *Hsiung Feng III*, was test-fired in April 1998.[51]

Problems remain for the ROC armed forces, especially in attracting qualified people into the military. Taiwan's economic prosperity has created many jobs that pay more and require less sacrifice than a military career. Some young men have physically abused themselves to obtain draft exemptions.[52] There have also been several cases of young recruits committing suicide due to the rigors of training. While these are few in number, they are well publicized and have a negative effect on the image of the military. Such prestigious sources as the Academia Sinica have suggested shortening the period of compulsory military service from the current 2 years. However, the military argues that this would be dangerous to national security, producing a force unable to master modern tactics and equipment. At the time the plan was suggested, PLA ground-force conscripts served for 3 years; naval and air force recruits for 4 years. The discrepancy in training time would quickly become apparent in time of war.[53] Subsequently, the PLA reduced the term of service to 2 years for all services. It now appears that a smaller number of ROC conscripts will serve the normal 2-year term. The remainder of young males of draft age will be absorbed into social service programs with terms 6 months to a year longer than military service; it is anticipated that the extra time that must be served for nonmilitary service will provide an incentive for young men to choose the military.[54]

The Ministry of National Defense has responded to declining interest in military careers by making special efforts to attract new people. It is reaching out to aborigines[55] and women; females now serve on *Chih Yang* (Knox)-class frigates.[56] A Reserve Officer Training Program was introduced in fall 1997, offering recruits the equivalent of U.S. $303 each month in tuition aid and living allowances; the trainees must serve in the military for 5 years after graduation. So far, the program has attracted few young people.[57]

A spate of accidents that call military safety procedures into question has hurt the military's efforts. Between February and April 1998, a T-38A Talon trainer crashed, killing one crewman;[58] a TH-55 training helicopter crashed, killing both pilots;[59] a Knox-class frigate sideswiped an anchored Perry-class frigate while maneuvering into its berth at Tsoying Naval Base;[60] a F-16 fighter disappeared while on a routine training flight;[61] and a *Mirage* was seriously damaged after apparently being hit by a pigeon near its base at Hsinchu.[62] On discovering that local people were avid pigeon-raisers, the air force appealed for cooperation. While no one was injured in the *Mirage* incident, the air force revealed that 22 of its officers had been killed in the line of duty since 1995 and promised an investigation.[63] The accidents, however, continued. In July, a missile speedboat hit a reef on the Penghu Islands,[64] and in September, the engine of an air force academy jet caught fire on the runway, slightly injuring the pilot.[65]

Procurement scandals have also hurt the military and its professional image. Following on the heels of bribes being paid to French officials as part of the purchase of the *Lafayette*-class frigates mentioned above, a major general, who was a department head at CSIST, was arrested in connection with receiving kickbacks from an unnamed foreign supplier.[66] In another incident, a major general, who was head of the Combined Service Force Engineering Department, was taken into custody and charged with taking bribes in connection with the awarding of a contract for the construction of an ammunition depot. The case came to light when the briber, who failed to win the contract, fire-bombed the general's home.[67]

Taiwan, of course, is democratized, and there is now public debate on the utility of military expenditures. These cases had the potential to undermine public support for the defense budget, with serious implications for the ROC's future. In a poll taken in mid-May 1998, 60 percent of the respondents expressed dissatisfaction with corruption and inefficiency in budget allocations, including but not confined to those involving the military.[68] The country's defense minister barely survived a vote of no confidence by the Legislative Yuan. The Procurement Bureau, which had previously reported to the General Staff, was placed directly under the Ministry of National Defense, and the Legislative Yuan was charged with supervising its budget-related operations.[69]

Despite all of these improvements, equipment weaknesses persist. The navy's S-70 anti-submarines helicopters are not capable of detecting the PRC's new *Kilo*-class submarines.[70] The ROC would like to buy more capable P-3 Orion anti-submarine planes with ultra-low frequency sonar that would permit the detection of quieter submarines such as the *Kilo*.[71] However, the United States has thus far declined to sell them.[72] Since its purchase of two submarines from the Netherlands more than a decade ago, the ROC has been unable to purchase additional boats. These would be useful in blockade interdiction and to torpedo enemy surface ships.

Coordination among the services must also be improved. For example, the three services purchased three different types of air-defense missiles.[73] Drills undertaken as part of the May 1998 *Han Kuang* 14 exercises revealed other problems of coordination.[74] Weapons bought from several different sources did not conform to uniform specifications. This is the result of mainland pressure on potential foreign suppliers and is difficult to remedy. For example, the navy originally intended to purchase the electronic warfare systems for the *Lafayette*-class frigates from Thomson of France, but it backed away because Thomson's bid was so high. The navy then approached Israel's Elisra company, which showed initial interest, but withdrew after remonstrations by Beijing. The navy then asked that an indigenous system be developed within a very short time frame. The problems are still being worked out.[75]

Beijing continues to increase its short-and medium-range ballistic missile inventory. This increases the island's continued vulnerability to missile attack from the mainland. As demonstrated in the 1996 Taiwan Strait exercises, one of Beijing's more effective military options against Taiwan would be to use conventionally-armed missiles to disrupt transportation, destroy logistics sites, and establish air superiority over the island. Hence, there have been calls for a ballistic-missile defense system with early-warning capabilities. The Theater Missile Defense system (TMD), now being developed by the United States, uses satellite technology to detect enemy missile firing locations and will be able to launch missiles from either land or sea to destroy incoming missiles. However, the PRC has put pressure on Washington not to sell the system. During President Clinton's visit to China in summer 1998, the United States reportedly told Beijing that it had "no plans" to transfer the technology. This, of course, would not preclude such action in the future. The PRC in turn announced that it had no plans to transfer missile technology to Iran.[76] Beijing thus created a linkage between the two issues, knowing that the Clinton administration attaches great importance to stopping the flow of missile technology to Teheran.

A leading Taiwan newspaper expressed skepticism about TMD, describing it as a "bottomless pit" of expense whose reliability was uncertain. In the newspaper's view, the development of medium- to long-range missiles so as to actively deter the enemy would be a better use of defense money.[77] Military sources argue that this line of reasoning stems from a widespread misconception that TMD is theater high-altitude air defense (THAAD), tests of which have resulted in several failures. They point out that there are other ways than THAAD to defend against short-range ballistic missiles (SRBMs) and that Taiwan cannot be without a defense against SRBMs. The PRC could fire a few hundred of these against ROC airfields, command and control centers, power plants, and early warning radar sites, thus grounding the ROC's F-16s and *Mirages*. This is similar to actions that the United States took against Iraq in the Gulf War, actions studied carefully by the PLA.[78]

North Korea's late August 1998 attempt to launch a satellite—initially perceived as being a missile—revived support for TMD in Japan as well as Taiwan.[79] A month later, the U.S. House of Representatives passed a resolution directing the Department of Defense to study the feasibility of including Taiwan, Japan, and South Korea in its TMD system.[80] Despite considerable debate, Taipei remains officially noncommittal about whether it wishes to participate. In October, the U.S. State Department described ROC interest in TMD as "primarily informational at this point."[81]

Domestic politics on Taiwan also pose problems for the military. A significant number of native Taiwanese perceive the higher ranks of the military as dominated by mainlanders who are members of the Kuomintang (KMT) and who express resentment over the size of defense budgets. At the same time, some members of the major opposition party, the Taiwanese-dominated Democratic Progressive Party (DPP), are given to issuing provocative statements with regard to the island's independence. So long as the DPP remained a minority party, there was little potential that such statements would escalate the threat to the ROC's security. However, should the DPP become the majority party, come to power, and enact constrained defense budgets while continuing its inflammatory rhetoric, the country's security could be jeopardized. It is, of course, possible that the responsibilities of actually governing could cause the DPP to modify its positions on these issues.

ROC defense analysts and politicians frequently posit a scenario in which mainland military threats to Taiwan cause the island's stock market to go into free fall and its population to flee the country by any means possible. Some go so far as to argue that the United States will in those situations be obliged to come to the ROC's defense. If there is an alternate scenario in which a citizenry, afraid of losing the political freedoms and economic prosperity it has achieved, vows to fight bravely to keep them, then those who hold this view have been curiously quiet. While the flee-rather-than-resist hypothesis is no doubt a truthful expression of the opinions of those who advance it, this must be good news to officials in Beijing because it tells them that the inhabitants of Taiwan are uninterested in fighting for their homeland. The same scenario is simultaneously bad news for the United States because it tells Americans that, although ROC citizens will flee the country rather than fight, they expect the United States to fight for them. In the absence of clear signals from the citizens of Taiwan that they consider their country worth fighting for, it is unimaginable that Americans will wish to do it for them. A better formula for defeat can scarcely be imagined. It is an issue that the ROC's major parties must address in order to arrive at a consensus.

Future Trends.

In the near term, the Taiwan and mainland militaries are capable of doing considerable damage to each other, with neither side able to be certain of victory. The PRC does not seem to be building enough amphibious landing craft—one of its major deficiencies in any invasion scenario with the ROC—to be able to land sufficient troops on the island. At present, Beijing seems to be aiming at destabilizing the island. In mid-July 1998, ROC security officials, citing a "mainland Chinese electronic magazine," reported that a decision had been made to undermine Taiwan so that it could be annexed without invasion.[82] The strategy was allegedly adopted by the Second Working Conference on Taiwan Affairs, held in Beijing in mid-May, and included infiltration, subversion, and sending a secret "fifth column" to the island to win the support of its people by new propaganda tactics. The same officials suggested that Beijing might have released the report for purposes of psychological warfare.[83] At the same time, the ROC justice ministry began a probe into suspected involvement of mainland Chinese capital in underground currency exchanges on the island. While granting that nothing more than flouting the rules for personal benefit may have been the motivation, the ministry pointed out that such activities could also have been consciously designed to destabilize the island's currency.[84]

Another, more transparent tactic is to demoralize the ROC's population by weakening the ties between the island and its major protector, the United States. Persuading President Clinton in late June 1998, during his visit to the PRC, to state the "three no's"—no support for Taiwan's independence; no support for "two Chinas" or "one China, one Taiwan"; and no support for Taiwan's entry into organizations composed of sovereign states—was a signal victory for Beijing. The ROC's foreign minister said that "unquestionably" the "three no's" had had an adverse psychological effect on the ROC.[85] Mainland propaganda quickly took advantage of the opportunity. The Beijing-based Central People's Radio broadcast to Taiwan said that Clinton had stated the "three no's" because, given the "compelling international situation," the United States had no other choice. Therefore, the broadcast continued, Taiwan had "no other option than to pursue a more positive mainland policy." The general tone may be summarized as "your position is deteriorating quickly. This is the best deal you can get; it had best be taken now before it is replaced with one less favorable to Taiwan."[86] A Hong Kong magazine reputed to have close ties with the PLA echoed the message, closing a lengthy analysis of the deficiencies of the ROC's anti-missiles capabilities with the warning that "peaceful negotiations between the two sides [are] the only way out."[87]

The ROC has its own counter-strategies. It has been pointed out by some that the United States said only that it would not *support* Taiwan independence, two Chinas, and entry into certain international organizations, not that it *opposed* them. In addition, it notes that America remains bound to support the sale of defensive arms to the island through the Taiwan Relations Act (TRA), and that both Houses of the U.S. Congress have reaffirmed their intention to observe the provisions of the TRA. Within the United States, Clinton was strongly criticized by both Democrats and Republicans for his iteration of the "three no's," and Congress passed resolutions supporting Taiwan, adding to the ambiguity of the situation. All of these were heavily publicized by ROC media.

In late August 1998, Washington announced the sale of Stinger missiles to Taiwan for $180 million. Beijing denounced the sale as a violation of its sovereignty.[88] However, this announcement alleviated ROC anxieties that, during his visit to Beijing, Clinton had secretly promised to cut off future arms sales to Taiwan. Nonetheless, the development of strategies to counteract these and future pressures from Beijing will be a major challenge for the Taipei government in the coming decade. No less difficult will be coping with the internal problems of military reorganization, enhancing the attractiveness of a military career to its citizens, ending the procurement scandals which have weakened support for defense budgets, and developing domestic consensus on a strategy for cross-strait relations.

ENDNOTES - CHAPTER 7

1. The author wishes to thank Mr. Kenneth Allen, Stimson Center; Dr. Edward Dreyer, University of Miami; Mr. Patrick Tyler, *New York*

Times; Lieutenant Hsiao-pin Yu, ROC Navy; and several sources who requested anonymity for their comments on an earlier draft of this paper.

2. Not all of the money that is invested is reported.

3. Patrick Tyler, *New York Times*, interview by author, October 9, 1998. This is the conclusion reached by Mr. Tyler after interviews with relevant administration sources.

4. Tai Ming Cheung, "Chinese Military Preparations Against Taiwan Over the Next Ten Years," in James R. Lilley and Chuck Downs, eds., *Crisis in the Taiwan Strait*, Washington, DC: National Defense University Press, 1997, p. 46.

5. John Culver, "Defense Policy and Posture II," in Hans Binnendijk and Ronald N. Montaperto, eds., *Strategic Trends in China*, Washington, DC: National Defense University Press, 1998, p. 72.

6. Replacing a prior strategy of preparation for an "early, major, and nuclear" war with the Soviet Union, and reflecting the improvement in Sino-Soviet relations that had begun in the 1980s.

7. *Agence France Presse*, "U.S., Beijing On Brink Of War In 1996: Paper," *Hong Kong Standard*, June 22, 1998, quoted from *The Washington Post*, June 21, 1998.

8. According to a Moscow source, managers and engineers from an aviation plant in Shenyang completed a training program for production of the Su-27s in July 1998. The Shenyang plant expects to manufacture two planes by the end of 1998. By mid-summer 1998, China had received 48 Su-27s. Sergei Blagov, "Jet Team Finishes Training in Russia," *South China Morning Post*, July 17, 1998.

9. *Ibid*.

10. "Destroyers A Threat To Taiwan," *South China Morning Post*, April 8, 1998, quoting U.S. Rear Admiral (Retired) Eric McVadon. Admiral McVadon described the *Sovremenny's* SS-22 Sunburn missiles as skimming the water at 2.3 times the speed of sound and very difficult to detect.

11. Willy Wo-Lap Lam, "PLA Overhaul To Cut Troops, Add Mobility," *South China Morning Post*, April 8, 1998.

12. "'Crucial' Weapons Unit Set Up," *South China Morning Post*, April 6, 1998. The functions of the PLA's General Armaments

Department would thus appear to overlap with those of its General Logistics Department.

13. Chou Kuan-wu, "China's Reconnaissance Satellites Are Hallmark of China's Overall National Strength and a Security Tool," *Kuang Chiao Ching* (*Wide Angle Mirror*), Hong Kong, March 16, 1998, translated in U.S. Technical Information System, *Foreign Broadcast Information System-China* (henceforth *FBIS-CHI*)-98, April 8, 1998.

14. Bruce Gilley, "Pacific Outpost: China's Satellite Station in Kiribati Has Military Uses," *Far Eastern Economic Review*, April 30, 1998, pp. 26-27.

15. See, e.g, Fan Yinhua, "The Contemporary Military Revolution and New Thinking Modes," *Jiefangjun bao* (*Revolutionary Army Daily*), Beijing, March 24, 1998, p. 6, in *FBIS-CHI*-105, April 15, 1998; Zhang Deyong, Zhang Minghua, and Xu Kejian, "Information Attack," *Jiefangjun bao* (*Revolutionary Army Daily*), March 24, 1998, p. 6, in *FBIS-CHI*-104, April 14, 1998.

16. *Reuters*, "High Technology War Drills Begin," *South China Morning Post*, April 14, 1998.

17. Jia Fengshan, "Role of Special Warfare Is Undergoing a Change," *Jiefangjun bao* (*Revolutionary Army Daily*), April 7, 1998, p. 6, in *FBIS-CHI*-112, April 22, 1998.

18. Yuan Lin, "Cross-Strait Military Helicopter Contest," *Kuang Chiao Ching*,-307, April 16, 1998, pp. 24-29, in *FBIS-CHI*-127, May 7, 1998.

19. Lu Te-yun, "Taiwan Officials Assess PRC Electronic Warfare Capability," *Lien-ho pao* (Taipei), May 13, 1998, p. 3, in *FBIS-CHI*-141, May 21, 1998.

20. Akinori Uchida, "Japan's Support of U.S. Forces May Widen in Scope," *Yomiuri* (Tokyo), March 15, 1998.

21. These sentiments are expressed, e.g., in Tai Ming Cheung, "China's Military Agenda Toward Taiwan," p. 18; and Michael D. Swaine, "The Military Challenge to Taiwan," p. 22, conference papers, International Institute for Strategic Studies/Chinese Council for Advanced Policy Studies Conference, Washington, DC, July 1, 1998.

22. For skeptical views on China's ability to achieve such a breakthrough, see Bates Gill, "China and the Revolution in Military Affairs: Assessing Economic and Socio-Cultural Factors," and Lonnie

Henley, "China's Capacity for Achieving a Revolution in Military Affairs," in *China and the Revolution in Military Affairs* Carlisle Barracks, PA: U.S. Army War College, Strategic Studies Institute, May 20, 1996, pp. 1-41, 43-47, respectively; also Kenneth W. Allen, Glenn Krumel, and Jonathan D. Pollack, *China's Air Force Enters the 21st Century*, Santa Monica, CA: The RAND Corporation, 1995, pp. 122-125. John Culver expresses the view that, while the PLA may be able to become a modernized, potent fighting force, it is not a foregone conclusion.

23. "Uighurs Said Waiting for Opportunity To Rise Up in Xinjiang," *China News Agency*, June 6, 1998.

24. Sofia Wu, "Interior Ministry Unveils Conscription System Reform Plan," *China News Agency*, July 16, 1998.

25. *Agence France Presse*, "Lee Commands Military to Wage War On Graft," *Hong Kong Standard*, June 10, 1998.

26. See, e.g., Republic of China, *1998 National Defense Report* Taipei: Li Ming Cultural Enterprise Co. Ltd., 1998, pp. 164-165.

27. Deborah Kuo, "ROC Striving To Streamline Military," *China News Agency*, June 16, 1998.

28. "Taipei To Establish Military Affairs Bureau," *Chung-yang jih-pao (Central Daily News)* (Taipei), January 1, 1998, p. 4, in *FBIS-CHI*-007, January 7, 1998.

29. *Agence France Presse*, "Military Drill To Deter Threat From Mainland," *Hong Kong Standard*, June 17, 1998.

30. *The Military Balance 1997/98*, London: International Institute for Strategic Studies, 1997, p. 194, lists this as the *Chin Yang*-class.

31. "Taipei Awaits More U.S. Frigates," *South China Morning Post*, July 21, 1998.

32. Author's interviews, July 1998.

33. Lilian Wu, "Coastal Patrol Vessel Launched in Kaohsiung," *China News Agency*, June 18, 1998.

34. Lin Wen-fen, "CSC Shows Strong Interest in Building Aegis-Class Frigates," *China News Agency*, March 6, 1998.

35. Author's interviews, June 1998.

36. "Taipei Plans 'Stealth' Missile Boats," *Hong Kong Standard*, March 9, 1998; Lu Te-yung, "Taiwan Plans To Build New Patrol Boats," *Lien-ho pao*, September 6, 1998, in *FBIS-CHI*-256, September 13, 1998.

37. Sofia Wu, "First Squadron of Second IDF Wing Formed at Tainan Airbase," *China News Agency*, February 19, 1998.

38. Lin Chien-hua, "CSIST Develops Third-Generation Warplanes," *Tzu-li wan-pao* (*Independence Evening News*), Taipei, June 7, 1998, p. 3, in *FBIS-CHI*-187, July 6, 1997.

39. *Agence France Presse*, "U.S. Upgrades Taiwan's F-16 Weaponry," *Hong Kong Standard*, June 3, 1998.

40. Lu Chao-lung, "Taiwan Mirage Fighter Successfully Launches Mica Missile," *Chung-kuo shih-pao*, May 10, 1998, in *FBIS-CHI*-134, May 14, 1998.

41. "Taipei Asks France for Early Delivery of Mirage Fighters," *Lien-ho pao*, July 13, 1998, in *FBIS-CHI*-196, July 13, 1998.

42. Lu Chao-lung, "Chungshan Institute Builds Unmanned Reconnaissance Plane," *Chung-kuo shih-pao*, March 29, 1998, in *FBIS-CHI*-92, April 2, 1998; *Agence France Presse*, "Island-Built Pilotless Aircraft To Boost Reconnaissance Capability," *Hong Kong Standard*, March 30, 1998.

43. *Agence France Presse*, "Taiwan Gets Arms Ahead of U.S. Visit," *Hong Kong Standard*, June 22, 1998.

44. Sofia Wu, "ROCT Military Strengthening Electronic Warfare Capabilities," *China News Agency*, March 9, 1998; *Agence France Presse*, "Air Force in Attempt to Jam Rivals," *Hong Kong Standard*, June 15, 1998.

45. *Associated Press*, "Warning On PLA Electronic Ability," *South China Morning Post*, May 18, 1998.

46. Jay Chen and Sofia Wu, "U.S. Reinforcing Military Software Exchanges With Taiwan," *China News Agency*, May 24, 1998.

47. Wu Zhong, "Upgrade For Taipei Missiles," *Hong Kong Standard*, January 2, 1998.

48. *Associated Press*, "Military Develops Missile," *Hong Kong Standard*, July 12, 1998.

49. Sofia Wu, "MND Confirms Development of New Defensive Systems," *China News Agency*, July 21, 1998.

50. Julian Baum, "Defence Dilemma: Despite New Threats, Taiwan Leans On Old Strategies," *Far Eastern Economic Review*, May 28, 1998, p. 33.

51. *Agence France Presse*, "Anti-Ship Missile Test," *South China Morning Post*, April 6, 1998.

52. Juping Chang, "Social Service Work To Replace Conscripts' National Guard Duty," *Free China Journal* (Taipei), September 25, 1998, p. 6.

53. Sofia Wu, "Defense Ministry To Review Conscription System," *China News Agency*, July 18, 1998.

54. Juping Chang, p. 6.

55. Sofia Wu, "Army To Recruit More Aboriginal Youths," *China News Agency*, March 18, 1998.

56. Sofia Wu, "Female Naval Officers to Serve On Knox-Class Frigates," *China News Agency*, February 5, 1998.

57. Deborah Kuo, "ROTC Not Selling Well In Taiwan," *China News Agency*, May 27, 1998.

58. *Associated Press*, "Pilot Dies After New Air Force Accident," *South China Morning Post*, February 25, 1998.

59. Elizabeth Hsu, "Army Chopper Crashes, Two Killed," *China News Agency*, March 17, 1998.

60. Maubo Chang, "Navy Frigate Hits Anchored Warship In Tsoying Harbor," *China News Agency*, March 19, 1998.

61. "F-16 Fighter Disappears As Air Dramas Roll On," *South China Morning Post*, March 20, 1998.

62. Maubo Chang, "Mirage Fighter Damaged By Bird," *China News Agency*, April 7, 1998.

63. Elizabeth Hsu, "22 Air Officers Killed in 13 Crashes In Three Years," *China News Agency*, March 21, 1998.

64. "Taiwan Missile Boat Hits A Reef Near Penghu," *China News Agency*, July 12, 1998.

65. Victor Lai, "Pilot Injured As AT-3 Training Jet Catches Fire On Landing," *China News Agency*, September 4, 1998.

66. Jason Blatt, "Military Unit Chief Suspected of Bribery," *South China Morning Post*, April 6, 1998; *Associated Press*, "General Held Over Kickbacks," *Hong Kong Standard*, April 6, 1998.

67. Sofia Wu, "Defense Ministry Vows To Wipe Out Graft," *China News Agency*, March 16, 1998; Maubo Chang, "CSF Engineering Head Arrested In Graft Scandal," *China News Agency*, March 17, 1998.

68. Sofia Wu, "Poll Finds Wide Discontent With Budget Policy," *China News Agency*, May 24, 1998.

69. Premier Hsiao Wan-chang Vincent Siew, "Excerpts From Administrative Report to the Legislative Yuan," *Chung-yang jih-pao*, September 12, 1998, p. 7, in *FBIS-CHI*-262, September 19, 1998.

70. Sofia Wu, "Female Naval Officers."

71. However, the detection operation requires sophisticated coordination and is particularly difficult in the relatively shallow waters of the Taiwan Strait, due to problems of tropospheric scatter. The author thanks retired U.S. Naval Rear Admiral Eric McVadon and Mr. Nicholas Eftimiades, Defense Intelligence Agency, for these observations.

72. Sofia Wu, "Taipei to Maintain Bid For Submarine Purchase," *China News Agency*, April 21, 1998.

73. Lu Chao-lung, "Air Force Buys Sky Swords From Chungshan Institute," *Chung-kuo shih-pao*, March 26, 1998, in *FBIS-CHI*-90, March 31, 1998.

74. *Associated Press*, "Taiwan Military Drills 'Expose Weaknesses'," *South China Morning Post*, May 15, 1998.

75. "Navy Has A Blind Military Ace," *Hsin hsin-wen* (*The Journalist*) (Taipei), January 11, 1998, p. 29, in *FBIS-CHI*, April 9, 1998.

76. Sofia Wu, "Taiwan Said Excluded From Theater Missile Defense System," *China News Agency*, May 13, 1998; Susan V. Lawrence, "Sparring Partners," *Far Eastern Economic Review*, July 9, 1998, p. 14.

77. Lin Chien-hua, "What Equipment Should Taiwan Use To Defend Itself," *Tzu-li wan-pao*, November 9, 1997, p. 2, in *FBIS-CHI*-364, December 30, 1997.

78. Author's interviews, August 1998.

79. Peter Landers, Susan Lawrence, and Julian Baum, "Hard Target," *Far Eastern Economic Review*, September 24, 1998, pp. 20-21.

80. Sofia Wu, "ROC Welcomes U.S. Congress Concern For Taiwan's Security," *China News Agency*, September 30, 1998.

81. Jay Chen, "U.S. Reacts Cautiously To Call For Taiwan TMD Study," *China News Agency*, October 2, 1998.

82. "Beijing's Strategy To 'Undermine Taiwan From Within' Confirmed," *China News Agency*, July 11, 1998; and "Beijing Plans To Disintegrate Taiwan From Within: Report 2," *China News Agency*, July 13, 1998.

83. *Ibid.*

84. Sofia Wu, "MOJ Probing Suspected Inflow Of Mainland Capital," *China News Agency*, July 9, 1998.

85. Lin Chun-te, Wang Yuen-hua, and Hsieh Hsin-yin, "Exclusive Interview With Foreign Minister Hu Chih-chiang," *Chung-yang jih-pao*, July 5, 1998, p. 2, in *FBIS-CHI*-190, July 9, 1998.

86. "News Square" program, Chinese People's Radio to Taiwan, July 8, 1998, in *FBIS-CHI*, July 9, 1998.

87. Yuan Lin, "Probing Capability of Taiwan's ABMs," *Kuang-chiao ching*, No. 311, August 16, 1998, p. 61, in *FBIS-CHI*-252, September 9, 1998.

88. Vivien Pik-kwan Chan, "Arms Sales To Taipei 'Assault On Sovereignty'," *South China Morning Post*, August 29, 1998.

CHAPTER 8
CONCLUDING COMMENT:
THE POLITICAL ANGLE—NEW PHENOMENA IN PARTY-ARMY RELATIONS

Ellis Joffe

The uniformly illuminating papers presented at the conference looked at the People's Liberation Army (PLA), focusing on its policies and capabilities as it moves into the next century from several critical angles: technology, budget, concepts, external impact, and Taiwan's military. One angle not covered was politics—the state of party-army relations and their possible future directions. The purpose of this chapter is briefly to fill this gap.

The importance of this political angle derives from the changes that have occurred in the internal role of the Chinese military under President Jiang Zemin. These changes have not only turned the PLA into a pivotal player in Chinese leadership politics, but, as a result, have also affected its capabilities in most of the areas covered by the conference monographs.

Is China a pivotal political player? Some analysts make the opposite argument. They suggest that the role of the PLA in politics has diminished, and its influence has waned. They point to several reasons: the consolidation of Jiang's position as paramount leader, the absence of leaders in the PLA who possess the stature to stand up to Jiang, the growth of military professionalism, and the strengthening of China's economic bureaucracies.

The result, in their view, is that the civilian leadership has distanced the army chiefs from the political arena, reduced their capacity to shape national decisions, and brought them under tighter political control. The most striking demonstration of this assertiveness was Jiang's order to the military to get out of business activities, an order that these analysts say was not only peremptory but downright demeaning.

The core of this argument—the declining presence of the military in politics—is correct. However, the effects of this diminished presence, as well as its causes and implications, are debatable. The central theme of this chapter is that although the military has substantially disengaged from the political arena, its potential and capacity for political intervention and influence are greater than ever before. This theme is based on the assumption that each of the reasons held up as signs of the PLA's political decline has another side to it, one open to a different interpretation.

To start with the first reason, one of the big surprises of Chinese politics has indeed been the consolidation of Jiang's position as paramount leader. In the twilight of the Deng era, Jiang was viewed by many observers, in China and outside, as a political weakling, and he was not given much chance of longevity at the top on his own. However, he quickly proved his detractors wrong, a development for which there are several explanations.

The first is doubtless personal. Whatever really lies behind his seemingly easygoing exterior, Jiang is obviously endowed with considerable political skills. First of all, these skills have ensured his survival as Deng's successor in the jungle of Chinese politics, although Jiang does not have the outstanding charismatic qualities which had underpinned the personal authority of both Mao and Deng. In addition, Jiang has demonstrated his political skills in other ways, including getting rid of rivals such as the mayor of Beijing, forging a firm consensus among his colleagues, working out a beneficial relationship with the military, and reaping the domestic advantages of his efforts to improve relations with the President of the United States.

In strengthening his position, Jiang has utilized other resources. One is institutional—his posts as general secretary of the Communist Party, chairman of its Central

Military Commission, and president of the Republic give him immense power, much symbolic prestige, and extensive exposure. Most importantly, these posts give Jiang the unparalleled advantage of placing trusted officials in key posts, which he has done extensively in the party, the government, and the PLA. In addition, he has made major efforts to solidify PLA support by being exceptionally friendly to causes important to the PLA, especially in ardently advocating military modernization.

No one will dispute that Jiang's impressive performance in the political and military arenas has narrowed the gap between his symbolic and real power as paramount leader. This has also strengthened his position in relation to PLA commanders, and his position is further augmented by the commanders' ingrained inclination to support the leader in power as well as by their professionalism. The foregoing could lead to the conclusion that the military's support of Jiang is assured.

Such a conclusion suffers from a fundamental flaw. Put simply, it is this: whereas under Mao and Deng military support of the paramount leader was axiomatic and immutable, under Jiang it cannot be taken on trust and under certain conditions may be transferred to a rival.

This uncertainty exists because Jiang does not have the unique authority in the military enjoyed by both Mao and Deng, despite the differences between them. Derived from their political stature, Mao's and Deng's authority was buttressed by military background, revolutionary antecedents, and long-standing connections, and it was invulnerable. Although Jiang has neutralized some weaknesses—for example, by enhancing his stature on the political scene, manipulating rivalries between PLA leaders, and forming personal connections in the PLA—he is far from invulnerable.

To be sure, Jiang will get PLA support as long as things are going well from the vantage point of the PLA leaders—as long as, at the very least, the economic situation is stable enough to prevent social unrest, and the basic demands of the military for modernization and financial support are satisfied. However, if things go wrong, all bets will be off. In that event, Jiang will not be able to assume, as Mao and Deng could, that military support will be forthcoming. On the contrary, PLA leaders might withdraw it or back an opponent.

Those who disagree with this reasoning may claim that the military's conditional support is not more than an assumption and that Jiang is strong enough to ensure PLA support in all circumstances. The response is two-fold. First, this is indeed an assumption, but it is based on an assessment of the leader's position in the PLA relative to his predecessors. And this assessment suggests that Jiang does not have an implicit *carte blanche* from the military, as Mao and Deng did. He has to work for its support and his operational latitude is limited.

This conclusion is reinforced by Jiang's actions. First, he has given PLA chiefs unprecedented freedom to manage their own affairs, including giving them substantial budget increases when he ordered them out of business. Second, he has made unusual concessions to the PLA, mainly in new allocations. Third, he has moved cautiously in pursuing reform policies, one reason for which is probably uncertainty about the military's response if these policies cause a crisis. Finally, on sensitive external issues such as Taiwan, Jiang has adopted positions that conform to PLA views. Neither Mao nor Deng had felt compelled to act in a similar fashion in any of these areas.

The second reason given for the military's political decline is the absence of a PLA leader superior in personal stature to Jiang after the retirement at the 15th Party Congress of the two top commanders, Liu Huaqing and Zhang Zhen. As leaders who, unlike Jiang, belonged to the revolutionary generation and enjoyed great prestige in the PLA, they towered over Jiang in military stature. Although publicly they always treated him with respect, as long as they remained in office these veterans cast a shadow over Jiang's standing in the PLA. Their replacements as the two senior officers on the Central Military Commission, Chi Haotian and Zhang Wannian, belong to Jiang's generation and cannot outshine him as revolutionary heroes. They also owe their promotions to Jiang.

How important is this fact? In the Chinese political scheme of things, the personal stature of the paramount leader is a central pillar of his authority in the bureaucracies and the PLA. The personal stature of the PLA commander is less important. The possibility that he will become a challenger for the top position can confidently be set aside, except in the most unlikely circumstances.

Short of this possibility, it may be argued that the stature of the commander is significant in determining how much influence the PLA can exert on the paramount leader. To some extent this must be so, as in any political system, but the influence is limited by the formal hierarchical relationship of the two within the Communist Party and government. This was demonstrated by the behavior of Liu Huaqing and Zhang Zhen, who did not defy Jiang despite their prestige. In any case, the stature of the leader is less important than the strength of the organization behind him, and this is a function of its professionalism.

The importance of military professionalism derives from its nature as a two-edged sword: it can be a barrier against political intervention or an impetus to it. One thing is not in doubt: the professionalism of the Chinese military has been greatly strengthened in the past 2 decades. At the top, PLA commanders have undergone a basic transition from a generation of revolutionary military-politicians to a generation of commanders whose background is strictly military. At the lower ranks, officers are younger, better educated, and more specialized. The professionalization of the Chinese officer corps has gone hand-in-hand with the accelerated modernization of the PLA in a mutually reinforcing process. The new officers have been strong advocates of a more modern PLA, while the advances made by the PLA have raised their professionalism.

What are the implications for the military's political position? On the one hand, professionalization has increased the inner strength of the PLA by fostering its corporateness, cohesion, and discipline. It has also sharpened the institutional separation of the PLA, focused it on military pursuits, reduced political controls over it, and facilitated its disengagement from politics. From this vantage point, the growth of professionalism has reduced the PLA's political presence and influence. At the same time, it has assured the subordination of the PLA to the political leadership.

However, there is another side to professionalism. A unified PLA, animated by a distinct institutional standpoint and responsive to orders from its commanders, gives the military a potent power base in dealings with other elites, including the paramount leader. A PLA that is increasingly separated from the party will find it easier to defy it if circumstances are appropriate. And a PLA less constrained by political controls will make it easier to move into politics against the leadership's will. In short, in ordinary times if the state of national and military affairs is satisfactory to the military, professionalism will work against the possibility of political intervention. But if times become extraordinary, and given the absence of constraints that had existed under Mao and Deng, professionalism might have the opposite effect.

What about the growing power of economic organizations and their leaders in policymaking councils? This is not necessarily a zero-sum situation which has to cause a decline in the military's influence. The relationship between the military and economic organizations could well be based on mutual interests rather than on rivalry. Both want the economic reforms to succeed. The military is neither qualified nor inclined to interfere in economic affairs, and its interests are limited to results and to the armed forces' receiving appropriate allocations. The relative ease with which the military agreed to withdraw from economic activities, an agreement that according to reports is being effectively implemented, indicates persuasively where the real interests of the military lie.

The result of these factors is that party-army relations under Jiang are characterized by two trends. First, given Jiang's weaknesses and the military's strengths, the military has gained a capacity for political intervention and influence which it never had before. Second, this capacity has been held in check by the common interest of the political and military leaderships to keep the army out of politics.

A striking example of this common interest has been the order to the army to give up its economic activities. Jiang could not have given the order to do so against the wishes of the PLA's top commanders. He did give it, and the order is apparently being carried out, because, for different reasons, both sides find it beneficial.

The convergence of these trends has produced a tacit arrangement: the military supports the political leadership and does not intervene in politics or policymaking—except in areas of special concern to it. In return, the political leadership does not interfere in the management of the armed forces and pursues policies that meet the preferences of the military: economic development that provides social stability sufficient to avoid a major social crisis and a firmly nationalistic policy on Taiwan.

The result of this arrangement is that the military has withdrawn from politics as never before, but it also has the potential to intervene as never before. If this arrangement breaks down, a military-initiated intervention in politics is possible, even likely. At the same time, because of the military's new clout, intervention not initiated by the military is unlikely.

This constitutes a reversal of the situation that had prevailed under Mao and Deng: military intervention on its own accord was unthinkable; on the other hand, nonintervention in response to the leader's order was also unthinkable. These are new phenomena in Chinese party-army relations.

ABOUT THE AUTHORS

BERNARD D. COLE is Professor of International History at the National War College in Washington, DC. He received his A.B. at the University of North Carolina, his M.P.A. at the University of Washington, and his Ph.D. at Auburn University. Professor Cole served 30 years in the U.S. Navy. His published works include *Gunboats and Marines: The U.S. Navy in China* (University of Delaware Press, 1982) and articles in several journals.

ARTHUR SHU-FAN DING is a Research Fellow at the Institute of International Relations, National Chengchi University, Taiwan. He received his B.A. at the National Taiwan University and his Ph.D. in Political Science at the University of Notre Dame. Dr. Ding's published works include *China's Changing Military Theory, 1979-1991* (Tangshan Publishing House, 1996) and articles in numerous journals.

JUNE TEUFEL DREYER is Professor of Political Science at the University of Miami, Florida. She served as Senior Far East Specialist at the Library of Congress and Asia adviser to the Chief of Naval Operations. Professor Dreyer has a B.A. from Wellesley College and a M.A. and Ph.D. in Government and Far Eastern Languages from Harvard University. Among her published works are *China's Forty Millions* (Harvard University Press, 1976), *China's Political System* (3d edition, Addison Wesley Longman, forthcoming), and articles on the Chinese military in numerous journals.

PAUL H. B. GODWIN is Professor of International Affairs at the National War College in Washington, DC, specializing in Chinese defense and security policy. He was Visiting Professor at the Chinese People's Liberation Army National Defense University in September-October 1987.

ELLIS JOFFE is Professor of Chinese Studies at the Hebrew University of Jerusalem and a Senior Fellow at the Truman Research Institute at that university. He was educated in Jerusalem, Hong Kong, and at Harvard University. Among Dr. Joffe's works are *Party and Army: Professionalism and Political Control in the Chinese Officer Corps, 1949-1964* (Harvard University, 1965), *The Chinese Army After Mao* (Harvard University Press, 1987), and many articles in journals and books.

ALEXANDER CHIEH-CHENG HUANG is a Senior Fellow in International Security Affairs at the Center for Strategic and International Studies in Washington, DC. He is also a Visiting Research Professor at the Institute for Global Chinese Affairs, University of Maryland, College Park. He was a Fellow in the Center for Northeast Asian Policy Studies at The Brookings Institution and a consultant for the Taipei Economic and Cultural Representative Office in Washington, DC. Dr. Huang specializes in Asian and Chinese security and defense affairs. His publications include "Chinese Navy's Offshore Active Defense Strategy: Conceptualization and Implication," *U.S. Naval War College Review* (Summer 1994) and "Taiwan's View of Military Balance and the Challenge It Presents," *Crisis in the Taiwan Strait* (1997).

JAMES R. LILLEY was born in China, educated at Yale University, and served for a number of years in Southeast Asia. He was the Director of the American Institute in Taiwan and the U.S. Ambassador to the People's Republic of China from 1989-91 and to the Republic of Korea from 1986-89. He served as Assistant Secretary of Defense for International Security Affairs from 1991-93 and is presently Resident Fellow at the American Enterprise Institute. Ambassador Lilley is the co-editor of *Beyond MFN: Trade with China and American Interests* (AEI Press, 1994) and has written extensively on Asian issues.

MICHAEL MCDEVITT is a Senior Fellow at CNA Corporation, a not-for-profit Washington, DC, area research center where he directs a multi-year program, "Project Asia." This effort is focused on U.S. security policy in East Asia. Prior to retiring from the U.S. Navy in 1997, he was the Commandant of the National War College. Other Asian policy-related assignments include Director of Strategy, Plans and Policy (J-5) for U.S. CINCPAC and Director of the East Asian Policy Office for the Secretary of Defense. He had four at-sea commands, including an aircraft carrier Battle Group. He was educated at the University of Southern Califiornia and holds a Masters Degree in Amercian Diplomatic History from Georgetown University. He is a graduate of the National War College and was a CNO Strategic Fellow at the Naval War College.

ERIC A. MCVADON, retired U.S. Navy Rear Admiral, is a senior consultant on East Asian security affairs for Areté Associates, the Center for Naval Analyses, and several other organizations, and Director of Asia-Pacific Studies with National Security Planning Associates, a subsidiary of the Institute for Foreign Policy Analysis. He was defense and naval attaché at the U.S. Embassy in Beijing, 1990-92. His navy career included extensive experience in air antisubmarine warfare and politico-military affairs, including service as the NATO and U.S. Sub-Unified Commander in Iceland, 1986-89. His recent undertakings include work on the People's Liberation Army, the China-Taiwan problem, Chinese attitudes toward regional security, and diverse issues involving the Korean Peninsula. He writes and speaks widely in North America and East Asia on security and defense matters. Admiral McVadon's publicly available writings include an article on China and the PLA in the Autumn 1996 *Naval War College Review* and chapters in the 1997 National Defense University book entitled *Crisis in the Taiwan Strait* (published in English and Chinese in the 1999 RAND book, *The People's Liberation Army in the Information Age,* and in the 1999 AEI-M.E. Sharpe, Inc., book, *China's Military Faces the Future*).

MICHAEL PILLSBURY is currently an Associate Fellow at the Institute for National Strategic Studies, National Defense University, Washington, DC, and a Senior Fellow at the Atlantic Council of the United States, where he is sponsored by the Office of Net Assessment, Department of Defense. During the Reagan administration, Dr. Pillsbury was the Assistant Under Secretary of Defense for Policy Planning; during the Bush administration, he was Special Assistant for Asian Affairs, Office of the Secretary of Defense, reporting to Director of Net Assessment Andrew W. Marshall. He has also served as a defense analyst for the RAND Corporation and on the staffs of several U.S. Senate Committees. He has taught graduate courses in Chinese foreign policy at Georgetown University, University of California at Los Angeles, and University of South Carolina. Dr. Pillsbury earned his B.A. from Stanford University, studied Mandarin Chinese for 2 years at the Stanford Center in Taipei, Taiwan, under a doctoral dissertation fellowship of the National Science Foundation, and earned his Ph.D. from Columbia University.

LARRY M. WORTZEL is Director of the Asian Studies Center of The Heritage Foundation, a public policy think tank in Washington, DC. Prior to joining Heritage, he was a colonel in the U.S. Army and the Director of the Strategic Studies Institute, U.S. Army War College. During the 32 years of his military career, he lived and worked in the Asia-Pacific region for 12 years, where he focused on intelligence, policy, and security issues. He served as a military attaché at the U.S. Embassy in China twice (1988-90 and 1995-97). Dr. Wortzel received his B.A. from Columbus College, Georgia, and his M.A. and Ph.D. from the University of Hawaii. His published works include *Class in China* (Greenwood Press, 1987), *China's Military Modernization* (Greenwood Press, 1988), *The ASEAN Regional Forum: Asian Security without an American Umbrella* (Strategic Studies Institute, 1996), and *Dictionary of Contemporary Chinese Military History* (Greenwood Press, 1999).

INDEX

Academy of Military Science (AMS), 28, 89, 115, 117, 126, 141, 146, 147, 227

Academy of Social Science, 89

Aegis-class guided missile destroyers, 301–302

Air defense system, 139, 191–194

Anti-satellite missiles (ASATs), 128, 129, 205

Anti-ship cruise missiles (ASCMs), 74

Anti-submarine helicopters, 301, 307

Anti-submarine warfare (ASW), 179

Anti-tactical ballistic missile (ATBM) system, 305

Apstar-1A, 180–181

Association for Relations Across the Taiwan Strait (ARATS), 290

Association of Southeast Asian Nations (ASEAN), 4, 56–67

   Regional Forum (ARF), 16, 56, 62–63, 226

Asymmetric warfare, 201–206

Australia, 1

Beijing, investments in defense of, 132

Beijing Institute of System Engineering, 117

Burma (Myanmar), and People's Republic of China, 2, 61, 62, 236

Bush, George, 239, 292

Cambodia, 35, 36, 62

Central Asian states, 20–24, 138

Central Military Commission (CMC), 116

C^4I^2, 164, 180, 221

Cheng Kung-class frigates, 301

Chih Yang-class frigates, 300–301, 306

China Aerospace Corp., 117

China Institute of Contemporary International Relations (CICIR), 40, 108, 126

Chin Chiang coastal patrol boats, 301

Chinese military-industrial complex (CMIC), 165–169

Chung Shan Institute for Science and Technology (CSIST), 302, 303, 305

Clinton, Bill, 21, 37, 39, 239, 303, 311, 312

Coco Islands, 66

Command and control technologies, 163, 180, 181

Commission on Science, Technology and Industry for National Defense (COSTIND), 117, 166–168, 220

Comprehensive National Power (CNP), 2, 89, 107–108, 109–110

Comprehensive Test Ban Treaty (CTBT), 67, 68

C-101 anti-ship missile, 197

Confidence-building measures (CBMs), 14–17, 226

Cruise missiles, 195–198

C^3I nodes, 133, 139

Defense Electronics Exhibition (1998), 220–221

Democratic People's Republic of Korea (DPRK). See North Korea

Democratic Progressive Party (DPP) (Taiwan), 235, 255, 309–310

Deng Xiaoping, 21, 90, 103, 112, 119, 239, 292–293

DF-15/M-9 tactical ballistic missiles, 198

DFH-3, 180

Digital Scene Matching Area Correlation (DSMAC) guidance, 198

Digitized combat forces, 146–147

Dong Feng missile systems, 198

East Turkestan, 20

Economic issues

    15-year economic program between Kazakhstan and China, 23

    military versus, in Korean Peninsula 49–50

    role of, 326–327

    Sino-Russian relations and, 26

    versus security development, 9–14

E-2 surveillance planes, 303

    Grumman E-2T Hawkeye, 304

Executive Yuan (Taiwan), 258, 259, 267

Five Principles of Peaceful Coexistence, 103, 231

Four Modernizations, 166

Four-Party Talks, 53

France, 292, 295, 300

F-16 fighter planes, 29, 292, 303, 304

Fu Quanyu/Quanyou, 64, 69, 207–208, 241

General Armaments Department (GAD), 120, 166, 168, 206, 295

General Political Department, 118, 218

General Staff Department (GSD), 168, 218, 220

Geography

  importance of, 1–6

  limitations of, 3

Global Navigation Satellite System (GLONASS), 187, 198, 199

Global positioning system (GPS) satellites, 187, 198, 199

Gorbachev, Mikhail, 25

Grumman E-2T Hawkeye early warning planes, 304

Guidance, navigation, and vehicle control technology, 174, 176, 177, 179–180, 187

Hai Ying cruise missiles, 196

Han class submarines, 188

Han Kuang 14 exercises, 307–308

Hans, 20, 21

Harpoon air-to-ship missiles, 304

Hashimoto, Ryutaro, 35, 37, 38, 43–44

Hegemony, 222–223, 231–232

High-energy lasers (HELs), 182

Himalayas, 2, 69

Hsiung Feng I anti-ship missiles, 300, 301

Hsiung Feng II anti-ship missiles, 304

Hsiung Feng III anti-ship missiles, 305

HY-3/C-301 anti-ship missile, 197

India, 2, 23, 60, 65–66, 67–71, 138, 236

Indigenous Defense Fighter (IDF or *Ching-kuo*) fighters, 302

Indonesia, 1, 64–65

Information systems (IS) technology, 183–184, 205

Information warfare (IW), 163–164, 177, 182–183, 205–206

Internal stability, 134–135

International Monetary Fund (IMF), 25

Iran, 71, 74–75

Iraq, 71–74, 75

Islamic fundamentalism, 20

Israel, 168, 194

Jakarta, 64–65

Japan
   China's assessment of the military power of, 141–143
   geography and, 1
   relations with China, 33–47, 233–234
   trilateral Track II talks between U.S., China and, 44–45
   -U.S. alliance, 36–39, 298

Japanese Defense Agency (JDA), 42, 43, 44

Japanese Self-Defense Force (JSDF), 35, 38

J-8 interceptor, 193–194

Jianghu guided missile frigate, 196

Jiangwei guided missile frigate, 191, 295

Jiang Zemin, 101–102, 239, 292

   ASEAN and, 61–62
   India and, 69
   Kazakhstan and, 21, 23
   Japanese and, 45
   political skills of, 322–323
   South Asian nuclear tests and, 67
   vulnerability of, 323–325

Yeltsin and, 24, 25

Jing Shi program, 271–277

Kang Ting-class frigates, 300

Kazakhstan/Kazakh activists, 2, 20, 21–23

Kilo-class submarines, 168, 188, 294–295

Kiriyenko, Sergei, 26

Kissinger, Henry, 92–93

Knox *(Chih Yang)*-class frigates 300–301, 306

Korean Peninsula, 28, 34

   Four-Party Talks, 53
   importance of, 219
   military versus economic issues, 49–50
   nuclear-free zone in, 48
   reunification issues, 48–49
   U.S. presence in, reactions to 53–55, 219, 233–235

Kui Fulin, 241

Kuomintang (KMT) (Guomindang), 235, 255, 257, 309

Kwang Hua Six project, 302

Kyrgyzstan, 2, 20, 21–22

Kyuma, JDA Director General 42, 44

Lafayette-class frigates, 292, 295, 300

Laos, 2, 61

Lee Teng-hui, 37, 254, 259, 290–291, 293

Legislative Yuan (Taiwan), 258, 261–262, 267–268

Li Jijun, 143, 242

Li Peng, 25, 27, 38, 61, 64

Local War doctrine, 112–113, 115–116

  assessment of Japan's military power, 142

  conflict scenarios, 121–122, 123

  institutional affiliations of, 117

  military investment allocation priorities of, 130

  relationship to other schools, 119–120

Lop Nur nuclear testing area, 72

Luda DDG, 191, 196

Luhu-class guided missile destroyers, 189–190, 295

Magic II short-range air-to-air missiles, 303

Mahathir, Malaysian Prime Minister, 58, 63

Malaysia

  geography and, 1

  relations with China, 18, 58

Mao Zedong, 104, 118, 133, 160

  See also People's War doctrine

Maritime Consultative Agreement, 241

Maritime natural resources, protection of, 135–136

Maritime Self-Defense Force (MSDF), 35, 38

Matsu, 255

Mica intermediate-range air-to-air missiles, 303

Militarily Critical Technologies List (MCTL), 159, 169–175

Military alliances, opposition to, 16–17

Military installations, concealment of, 132–134

Military investment allocation priorities of, 129–140

Military professionalism, 325–326

Military technology

  See also Taiwan military

  air force, 191–194

  assessing China's capabilities, 169–175

  Chinese military-industrial complex (CMIC), 165–169

  command and control, 163, 180, 181

  conduct of war and advanced, 163–165

cruise missiles, 195–198
future for, 199–206
guidance, navigation, and vehicle control, 174, 176, 177, 179–180
information systems (IS) technology, 183–184
information warfare (IW), 163–164, 177, 182–183
Militarily Critical Technologies List (MCTL), 159, 169–175
naval, 185–189
operational implications, 184–191
PLA's changing strategy, 160–165
post-Gulf War self-assessment, 161–163
sensors and laser, 174, 176, 177, 179
space systems, 174, 176, 177–178
strengths, areas of, 173
surface combatant, 189–191
tactical ballistic missiles, 198–199
weaknesses, areas of, 174–175

Military technology transfers, 237–238
with Britain, 168
with Iran, 74–75
with Israel, 168, 194
with Italy, 168
with Russia, 29–31, 168, 194
to Taiwan, 292, 299–310, 312

Military-to-military contacts, 18 between China and Japan, 43–44

Mirage 2000-5, 29, 292, 303

Mischief Reef, 57, 59, 237

Missiles, 195–199
Taiwan's, 304–305

Mi Zhenyu, 93, 113

M-109 self-propelled artillery, 303

Mongolia, 2, 19

Mozambique, 35, 36

Mo Zi, 106, 107

M-60-A-3 tanks, 303

Multilateral contacts/agreements, 14–15, 21–22, 227–228

Multipolarity tendencies, 14–17, 101–106

Myanmar (Burma), 2, 61, 62, 236

National Capital Area. *See* Beijing

National Defense Council (Taiwan), 257

National Defense Law (Taiwan), 259–263

National Defense Organization Law (Taiwan), 258, 259

National Defense Science and Technology Commission, 166

National Defense University (NDU), 115, 117

National Military Council (NMC) (Taiwan), 260–261

National Military Strategy, 223–225

National Security Council (NSC) (Taiwan), 257, 260, 264–265

National Security Strategy, 223–225

NATO (North Atlantic Treaty Organization), 27

Natuna gas fields, 65

Naval system technology, 185–189

Nepal, 2

Net/strategic assessment, 95–99

    China's assessment of China-Taiwan-U.S. balance, 149–150

    China's assessment of Japan's military power, 141–143

    China's assessment of future U.S. military power, 143–149

New Party (Taiwan), 235, 268

New Zealand, 1

North Korea (Democratic People's Republic of Korea-DPRK)

    crisis/collapse in, China's reactions to, 50–53

    Four-Party Talks, 53

    military versus economic issues, 49–50

    relations with China, 2, 47–48, 122

    reunification issues, 48–49

    U.S. presence in, reactions to, 53–55, 144–145, 234–235

Nuclear Non-Proliferation Treaty (NPT), 67–68

Nuclear testing, 67–69, 161

Nuclear war, threat of, 104

Obuchi, Keizo, 234

Oil/pipelines

    deal with Kazakhstan, 22–23

    imports from Iran/Iraq, 71–72, 74, 75

Operation DESERT STORM, 161–162, 206

Pakistan, 2, 67–71, 239

Papua New Guinea, 1

Paracel Islands, 59, 236

Patriot II anti-missile batteries, 305

People's Armed Police (PAP), 21, 24, 118, 135

People's Army of Vietnam (PAVN), 2

People's Liberation Army (PLA)

See also Military technology
assessment of Japan's military power, 141–143
capabilities of, beyond immediate neighbors, 3
Comprehensive National Power (CNP), 89, 107–108, 109–110
current assessment, 100–109
economic factors and development of, 11
estimating the capabilities of, 90–95
long-term modernization goals, 111–129
military investment allocation priorities, 129–140
recent acts toward Taiwan, 294–299
strategic/net assessment of, 95–99
theater ballistic missile defense, 42–43

People's Liberation Army Air Force (PLAAF), 161, 191–194

People's Liberation Army Navy (PLAN), 116–117, 161, 185–189

People's Republic of China (PRC)

Geography, importance of, 1–6
internal stability, 134–135
relations with neighbors, 2

People's War doctrine, 94, 111–112, 115, 128

assessment of future U.S. military power, 143–149
assessment of Japan's military power, 142
conflict scenarios, 120–121
institutional affiliations of, 117–118
military investment allocation priorities of, 130–132
relationship to other schools, 118–119

Perry (*Cheng Kung*)-class frigates, 301

Persian Gulf, Japanese in, 35

Persian Gulf War, 115, 120, 143, 161–162, 206

Phalanx air-defense systems, 300

Philippine Islands

conference on CBMs (1996) with China, 15–16
geography and, 1
Mischief Reef, 57
relations with China, 18

Political separatism, 23

Politics, role of, 321–328

Primakov, Yevgeny, 26

P-3 Orion anti-submarine planes, 307

Quadrennial Defense Review (QDR), 148

Quemoy, 255

Rail lines, protection of, 139

Rangoon (Yangon), 61

Republic of China (ROC). See Taiwan- Republic of China (ROC)

Republic of Korea (ROK). See South Korea -Republic of Korea (ROK)

Revolution in Military Affairs (RMA), 90, 104, 113–114, 161, 282, 296

   assessment of Japan's military power, 142–143
   conflict scenarios, 122–125
   institutional affiliations of, 117
   military investment allocation priorities of, 129
   relationship to other schools, 120

RF-104 Starfighter reconnaissance planes, 304

Russia, relations with People's Republic of China, 2, 3, 21–22, 24–32, 137

Satellite systems

   communication, 180–181
   surveillance, 178, 187

Sea Chaparral surface-to-air missiles, 300

Second Working Conference on Taiwan Affairs, 311

Security policy, Beijing's regional, 8–9

   economic factors versus, 9–14
   summary of, 18–19

Senkaku Islands, 36, 44

Sensors and laser technology, 174, 176, 177, 179

Short-range ballistic missiles (SRBMs), 309

Singapore, geography and, 1

Sky Bow II missiles, 304

South China Sea, 4, 17, 23, 56–67

South Korea (Republic of Korea- ROK)

   Four-Party Talks, 53
   military versus economic issues, 49–50
   relations with China, 3, 47–48, 122
   reunification issues, 48–49
   U.S. presence in, reactions to, 53–55

Sovremenny destroyers, 30, 168, 190–191, 295

Space systems technology, 174, 176, 177–178

Space warfare, 128–129

Spratly Islands, 57, 236

S-70 C anti-submarine helicopters, 301, 307

SS-N-22 (SUNBURN) missile, 191, 197

State COSTIND (SCOSTIND), 166

Strait Exchange Foundation (SEF), 290

Strategic/net assessment, 95–99

Strategic partnership (Sino-Russian relations), 24–32

Stinger missiles, 312

Submarine technology, 185–189

Sun Yat-sen, 253

Sun Zi, 106, 107, 107, 108

Supreme Defense Council (Taiwan), 257

Surface combatant technology, 189–191

Su-27 fighters, 29, 30, 168, 194, 294

Su-27SK, 194

Tactical ballistic missiles, 198–199

Taiwan (Republic of China-ROC)

China's assessment of China-Taiwan-U.S. balance, 149–150, 235–236

command structure of, 258, 260

constitutional reform, 254

geography and, 1

invasion of, forms for, 296–297

National Defense Law, 259–263

national security organizations, evolution of, 257–260

relations with China, 14, 19, 137–138, 280–281, 290–294

rise of political opposition, 255

Taiwan Affairs Leading Small Group (TALSG), 292

Taiwan military

challenges facing, 280–283

changes in technology, 299–310

civilian control and national defense law, 257–268

democratization, effects of, 254–255

Jing Shi program, 271–277

military technology, effects of, 255–256

problems and debates, 277–279

procurement scandals, 306–307

recruiting problems, 305–306

strategic reorientation, effects of, 255–257

Zhong Yuan program, 268–271

Taiwan Relations Act (TRA) (1979), 292, 312

Taiwan Strait/Taiwan problem

exercises, 218, 293
future and concerns over, 46–47, 310–312
Korean peninsula and, 55–56
missile tests/training exercises, 218, 293–294
recent PLA acts of, 294–299
response of Taiwan to PLA acts, 299–310
U.S.-Japanese alliance and, 37–39, 298

Tajikistan, 2, 20, 21–22

Tang Fei, 256, 262, 266–267, 281

Technology

See also Military technology; *under type of*
working groups (TWGs), 169

Thailand, 18, 236

Theater ballistic missile defense (TBMD), 42–43

Theater high-altitude air defense (THAAD), 309

Theater missile defense (TMD), 302, 308–309

Three Gorges Dam, protection of, 136

"Three no's" policy, 45, 311, 312

Tiananmen Square, 229, 291

Tibet, 19, 20

Tien Kan (Sky Interference) electronic warfare aircraft, 304

Tien Kung II air defense radar system, 305

Tonkin Gulf, 4

Turkic Central Asian nations, 20

Uighurs, 20–23

Under Sea Warfare (USW), 179

United National Revolutionary Front, 21

United States, and People's Republic of China

China's assessment of future U.S. military power, 143–149
China's views of, 103
Four-Party Talks, 53
-Japanese alliance, 36–39, 298
relations with China, 217–243
Russian and Chinese bashing of, 26–28
trilateral Track II talks between Japan, China and, 44–45

United States, and Republic of China

China-Taiwan balance, 149-150
Effect of U.S.-Japanese security alliance, 37–39, 46, 298
Sale/transfer of military equipment/technology, 236-237, 292, 300-305
Taiwan Relations Act of 1979, 292, 312
"Three No's", 45, 311-312

Unmanned aerial vehicles (UAVs), 303

Vacation diplomacy, 291

Vietnam, and People's Republic of China, 2, 3, 23, 63–64, 122, 138, 236

Warring-States era
  avoiding war with use of other strategies, 108–109
  lessons from, 106–107

Weapons of mass destruction (WMD), 48

West Turkestan, 19–24

White Paper (1995), 7, 9, 226

White Paper on *China's National Defense* (1998), 7–9, 11–19, 225–228

Woody Island, 59

Xia class submarines, 188

Xinjiang Uighur Autonomous Region, relations with China, 19, 20–24

Yangon (Rangoon), 61

Yeltsin, Boris, 24, 25, 27, 31–32

Ying Ji cruise missiles, 196

YJ-8A missile, 197, 198

Yulin, submarine base at, 66

Zhong Yuan program (Taiwan) 268–271

www.ingramcontent.com/pod-product-compliance
Lightning Source LLC
Chambersburg PA
CBHW021134230426
43667CB00005B/111